WOMEN
AND ANXIETY

Helen A. De Rosis, M.D.

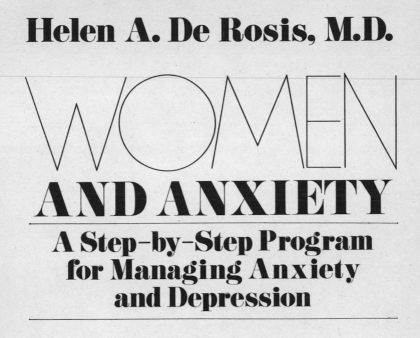

WOMEN
AND ANXIETY

A Step-by-Step Program for Managing Anxiety and Depression

A DELTA BOOK

A DELTA BOOK

Published by
Delacorte Press
1 Dag Hammarskjold Plaza
New York, N.Y. 10017

Portions of this book first appeared in *Ladies' Home Journal.*

Delta ® TM 755118, Dell Publishing Co., Inc.

ISBN: 0-440-59398-0

Reprinted by arrangement with Delacorte Press
Printed in the United States of America

First Delta printing—August 1981

*THIS BOOK IS DEDICATED TO
THE MEMORY OF MY PARENTS, WHO
TAUGHT ME HOW TO LIVE.*

ACKNOWLEDGMENTS

My thanks go to many people for their part in furthering my work: to the many people in the groups I've conducted since the early sixties; women and men who have shared their feelings of anxiety and depression with me and with each other; to those in my *Recovery From Depression* and *Anxiety Management* classes, who have repeatedly demonstrated that they are helped by following a structured program; to the professionals in health service facilities in the New York area and in other states, who have organized training programs for mental health workers; to Ruth Van Doren and students at the New School for Social Research; to trainees in psychiatry who constantly require me to clarify my thinking and expression into more applicable terms; to my patients who continue to teach me every day the language of anxiety and depression and finally reveal how the beginnings of optimism can replace despair; to Betty Kelly, loyal, patient, understanding editor, whose very high level of competence helped to shape and organize the material in this book; to Rhoda Weyr, my agent, whose suggestions, consistent expertise, and warm support I value deeply.

Plucked, at its zenith,
One perfect rose—

Providing memory
A treasury of loveliness
All of my days.

H.D.

Contents

Contents

Contents

Contents

PART ONE

SEEING THROUGH ANXIETY AND MAKING IT WORK FOR YOU

Introduction

It may surprise you, but anxiety can be a positive force in your life. It's your body's most dynamic way of telling you that something is wrong. It's a blazing signal showing you that the same old self-defeating routines aren't working anymore, and it's a warning, forcing you to slow down and take a look at what's causing your fears. Anxiety is an indicator pointing to your longing to feel more vibrant. Using your anxiety as a beacon to light your path, you can start a process in yourself to root out old, rigid conflicts and conduct your life in more fulfilling ways.

Fear makes you lose sight of the fact that most bouts of anxiety are manageable as well as self-limited. A majority of them last from a few minutes to a few hours. For the most part, the more intense the anxiety, the shorter its duration. Complete recovery from each bout is an expected outcome in most instances. However, problem anxiety certainly does exist, and it can be identified by its ongoing, intense, incapacitating or unmanageable qualities.

The first step toward management of anxiety is learning how to put it to work for you. In that way you use it to expose your repressed anger, your inhibiting dependency, your rigid ways of defending yourself. By telling you that something is wrong, anxiety motivates and urges you to reflect upon the things that hurt and defeat you. It can provide you with a stimulus for making change. It can also deepen your understanding of human behavior—yours as well as other people's. Anxiety can help you discover your strengths; and once you know what they are, you can begin to use them productively.

If you have suffered from bouts of anxiety then chances are you're still fighting to live more fully. You haven't given up. You haven't settled for a rigid, fear-ridden existence. You don't have a feeling of hopelessness about the future. Your will is active, and you're trying to find a way to solve your problems.

In as many ways as I can, I want to tell you that you can learn to deal with and overcome certain conflicts that cause intolerable anxiety. I've tried to supply guidelines to help you understand these causes, to encourage you to work to free yourself from the emotional bonds that unrealistic fears impose. So many women, caught in those bonds, have been afraid to do what needed to be done. For example: to say something incisive to an insensitive employer; to question a self-destructive relationship; to make reasonable demands of inconsiderate friends or family; to confront a domineering partner; to accept their own ambitions. I've tried to say to them, in effect: Don't be afraid. You needn't be intimidated for the rest of your life. Here are ways you can be yourself and make responsible decisions.

Years ago I discovered that I could work directly, through community-sponsored educational programs, with groups of women and men who had problems they seemed unable to resolve by themselves. They shied away from trying to deal with conflicts, mainly because they were terrified of the anxiety they might encounter when troubled areas were exposed. They didn't realize it, but they had learned to control their fear of anxiety—by avoiding any involvement in conflict. They developed defenses, such as depression and phobias, in an attempt to relieve that fear. But, since conflict is an undeniable element of life, they were in fact avoiding a full experience of living in order to keep their anxiety at bay. (That avoidance is what makes so many people feel "dead inside" and look for artificial "highs" to counter the deadness.)

As I worked, I found that if I offered some simple procedures for them to follow, women and men could be persuaded to deal with very small units of conflict, one at a time, together with the associated small units of anxiety. They learned to recognize those units of anxiety as evidence that a conflict needed resolving. Specific procedures gave them the courage to act. As they saw themselves succeeding with these procedures, they were encouraged to help themselves overcome their initial fear of anxiety as well. And so a constructive cycle could begin to replace a nonproductive one.

In addition to my teaching, writing, and private practice, I've devoted much time to working with such groups. My goal has been to guide group members to help themselves and one another. I believed that they could do that if I could offer information in understandable and usable forms. That information repeatedly emphasizes each person's *wellness* rather than illness. In other words, wellness, or "health points" as I like to say, is linked with specific information and procedures that can lead to desired outcomes.

While you are being helped to find your own health points, you can learn to use them to feel more optimistic about dealing with your trouble points. As I've indicated, "health points" refers to your wellness—that is, your accumulated resources of experience, natural abilities, learned skills, and any other strengths you possess.

You can learn to use those health points against rigid, neurotic defense structures that *seem* to protect you from conflict and anxiety. Instead of using your energy, stamina, intelligence, and talent (all health points) to *support* such defenses, however, you can use them to find out what your conflicts are and how to work to solve them. In other words you *can* learn to take much better care of yourself than ever before.

In this book I've tried to help you understand features of anxiety so that it won't seem like such a monster to you. I've developed a twenty-step program for you to use to harness it. I've used many examples of women who have learned to use anxiety as a "handle" for identifying trouble points and then working to achieve their goals.

Women have been changing greatly in recent years, and some feel compelled to change more rapidly than they can, or in ways that confuse and upset them. Because of that, they've had a larger share of anxiety in this decade than in previous ones, for under any circumstances transition can be anxiety-provoking. Recent changes have touched their whole lives—roles, attitudes, values, expectations, behavior, goals—throwing all into conflict.

With so many sources for sharp conflict between the old and the new, I want you to know one thing that can help you feel more in command of your life: *you are the major author of your own existence.* While there is much you cannot control, you write a good part of your life script. You will feel stronger when you accept the idea that you can change your script, if the one you've written is harmful. In many ways, you *can* change negative behavioral and emotional practices into positive ones.

We can work on this together, if you will come along with me on a journey through the pages of this book. *I* can help to demystify causes and symptoms of anxiety. *You* can learn specific methods of using your anxiety to survive and to bring about the changes you want. This will be no mere marginal survival, however, but one for which you can gladly take responsibility, and one you can continuously enhance in whatever way you see fit.

You see that I cannot say "no more anxiety." I think you know that *anxiety is a condition of life.* As you read, though, you will become more aware of its positive elements. Everyone experiences anxiety at one time or another, and to greater or lesser degrees. It may not be especially troublesome for you, or it may cause you deep pain. That kind of pain is what I want to help you manage and prevent. No doubt you can deal with anxiety caused by unavoidable conflicts of ordinary life stress. But you certainly don't need the onslaughts of anxiety and depression that can ravage your heart, mind, and body.

I hope, then, that you can begin to consider anxiety not so much an enemy as it is a condition of your existence—a condition you can manage and can use to help you take your first steps toward making some needed changes in your life. I hope you will begin to use the feeling of anxiety as a barometer, a signal announcing that all is not well with your inner self. You need to recognize that signal and be able to utilize it in working with the twenty-step method presented in Part Two.

If you feel you don't have the resources or motivation to work with this program, consider this. Perhaps you have more strength than you suspect, but have not known how to deploy it constructively. Perhaps you are the kind of person who needs a partner when trying something new. In that case you might find someone who can explore this method with you by asking a friend or by forming an Anxiety Management group. (See p. 19.) Or perhaps you are not interested in following a structured program like the one discussed here.

Whether or not you decide to work with the twenty-step program, I hope that certain points I make will encourage you to confront your fears and rethink attitudes that have undermined your well-being. I hope you will decide to use what I suggest in this book as the first step toward recognizing the person you really are.

Anxiety: What It Is and How You Can Learn to Help Yourself

Mild anxiety is a condition of life. It has always been endemic in the population. But there seem to be growing numbers of events that keep producing new forms of intense anxiety. Far-reaching ignorance and misinformation add to the problem. Headlines call out "Dual Drug Dependency Seen Growing," as women's abuse of mind-altering substances becomes commonplace as a means of controlling anxiety.

Feeling totally helpless, some women join fringe political groups or so-called religious cults to recapture some sense of self-control. They may degrade themselves to any point for the sake of relief from intense anxiety, for the feeling of security a "leader" gives them.

I'd like to help you learn to approach your anxieties and depressions in a different way. This book is organized as a self-help guide for recovery of your well-being. The material here helps you to understand specific trouble points you have. It also focuses on your strengths —that is, your health points. Once you discover them, you can begin to use them to help yourself.

In talking about one such trouble point, Mary Ruth made a discovery: "It was very helpful when I learned that my anxiety over driving stemmed from my thinking that I was too clumsy to control a car. All I had known was that I was terribly afraid. But it never went any further than that, and I just couldn't deal with my nameless fear." In the same way, you'll work with a method that can help to identify and clarify problems that have bothered you for years. Once you understand what's really bothering you, it becomes much easier to do something about it.

I've developed a twenty-step method that can help you understand the basis for your troublesome feelings and help you become less guilt-ridden, less helplessly enraged, less fearful and pessimistic about your future. You'll begin to find out who and what you are and to accept what you are not and what you might be. You'll stop being so hard on yourself and start feeling less tense and more comfortable with yourself.

Here is a sampling of the steps you'll work with:

Describe how one trouble point is causing you to suffer.

Describe ways you've tried to solve it.

Decide why your efforts at solution have not been effective.

Decide how you feel about the risk of making a change regarding that point.

Choose an alternative solution in dealing with your trouble point.

List what you can lose and what you can gain by making a change.

Working through the twenty steps in a specific order, you'll begin to relate to your trouble spots in a new, hopeful way rather than in old, hurtful patterns.

NATURE OF ANXIETY

Anxiety is a feeling of dread, a nameless fear that distracts the minds and hearts of people of all ages. It is a constellation of physical symptoms, of uncomfortable, troubled feelings and thoughts, that may be relatively mild or reach the point of utter panic. It is a reaction to frustration and to unresolved anger that seems to burn a hole into your very being. It is a response to unbearable stress. It represents an inability to maintain the neurobiochemical balance essential to a sense of well-being. It is a beacon light signaling the existence of unconscious emotional conflict.

Perhaps you believe that you've been working hard to manage your disrupting anxiety, and you don't have much hope that reading a book can help you. I would agree with you in part, for reading a book is only the first step. The most important aspect of your recovery of well-being and self-confidence is *working with the suggestions that are made.* You don't have to work exactly as I suggest. But if you have no other preference, I urge you to start with the procedure as outlined in Part Two, after you've read through all the material in Part One. In general, the information in this book is limited to explanatory material and illustrations that will help you understand what your anxiety is trying to tell you and how to use the twenty-step program most profitably.

A feeling is a combination of something that happens in your mind and body. As a feeling then, anxiety is produced by a thought originating in the cerebral cortex of the brain, and in response to some internal or external stimulus. That thought eventually influences a more primitive level of the brain called the hypothalamus, a part of the brain commonly considered to be the *seat of the emotions.*

At this point, thought and emotion trigger body reactions that you may or may not be aware of. You might recognize feelings of fear, pleasure, anger, joy, hatred, love, disgust, and so forth. Whether or not you recognize them, however, these reactions derive from thought, emotion, and physical responses. Anxiety feelings also consist of these three factors.

You know that anxiety can occur in greater or lesser degrees. A behavior reaction will depend upon your anxiety's intensity and the nature of its contributing factors. It might help you to understand the concept of degree of anxiety if you use an analogy of street traffic.

A few cars (minor anxiety) in the street create no problem. You can maneuver easily and successfully among them. More cars, plus rain, may produce some tension in you as you make your way through them. Still more cars, plus rain, plus darkness, produce more tension as your visibility and autonomy on the road are significantly diminished.

Greater anxiety can be likened to your difficulty in driving when you have a combination of heavy traffic, darkness, sleet, and icy roads. Under such conditions, you can neither predict nor control just how your car will function. The greatest anxiety, like the most hazardous driving conditions, may keep you indoors, sequestered from places, people, and events which you believe will only intensify an already immobilizing condition.

Feelings and behavior seem extraordinarily complex when you have no idea what motivates them. While they can become much more manageable, they are no less complex when you understand their motivation. Nevertheless, certain features of human behavior can be explained in an uncomplicated manner, and these explanations can then be used to help you perceive and deal with the physical and emotional insults caused by undue anxiety.

While I want you to take seriously your efforts to restore your feelings of self-confidence and self-worth, I don't want you to become more anxious if you feel you can't go along with some of the suggestions. Please—no more shoulds! Enjoy your work as much as you can, because there's no law that says you can't enjoy something you feel you want to do to help yourself. The pill doesn't have to be bitter. So while you're being serious about your recovery, try not to be grim about it.

INCIDENCE OF ANXIETY

How many people suffer from anxiety? My answer to that question would have to be 100 percent. Asking that is like asking how many people sneeze or catch cold. I suppose there must be a few people who don't. But we can assume that practically everyone does, and it's nothing to be concerned about, unless your health is seriously impaired. You would be concerned, for example, if you had a cold every few days, or if your colds placed you out of commission for weeks at a time, or if you couldn't stop sneezing.

In the same way, anxiety is a *condition of life*. It's something that nearly everyone has experienced in one form or another, in lesser or greater quantities, and at one time or another. Common forms of lesser anxiety are not usually very troublesome. They can be aroused any time you feel unprepared to meet some new or unusual experience. What concerns me, however, is the suffering and/or incapacitation caused by excessive anxiety. Since nonfunctioning can erode your self-esteem, you need to give your attention to such extremes of anxiety. That way you can learn to heal yourself of the hurts you receive.

—12—

Since anxiety is something just about everyone has at some time, it can apparently be well tolerated by indefinite numbers of people. Most bouts of anxiety are of a low-grade variety and are self-limited. Even severe anxiety can subside without intervention. A large number of persons learn to ignore their anxiety, defend against it, deal with it, or wait for it to dissipate. They manage to keep it from interfering substantially with their activities or with the state of their physical and emotional health.

Despite that, however, there are large numbers of persons who are sufficiently unsettled, so that they are critically hampered in their work, play, study, sex, and relationships. The Commission on Mental Health has found that 10 to 15 percent of the population needs mental health services. The commission also states that one person in four, or 25 percent of the population, suffers from consequential anxiety, depression, and emotional disorders. In other words, while only one in ten persons actively needs treatment, one out of four persons is actually suffering from these conditions.

Using the lower number of cases requiring treatment, you can roughly calculate that 10 to 15 percent of the population gives you between 20 and 30 million persons in need of mental health services. To say that those persons *need* mental health services, means that they have already reached the point where they cannot manage for themselves. It means that the depth of their anxiety, depression, or other symptomatology has already impaired their functioning to a considerable degree.

If you use the higher figure of one in four, you can also easily estimate that over 50 million people are suffering from significant emotional distress. Since anxiety is a component of nearly every instance of emotional distress, whether or not an individual complains of it, it follows that roughly 50 million people suffer from profuse and personally disrupting amounts of anxiety.

What can I say about the incidence of anxiety beyond this point? The numbers become so large that they boggle the mind, and we tend to retreat from such horrendous statistics. That retreat is unimaginable, however, for we must not overlook or ignore those people who are in despair about themselves. We need to find out what we can do to serve them.

After all, something is being done about smokers, of whom there might be just as many. Something is being done about alcoholics. Something is being done about teaching tens of millions of children to read every year. Let's pause to consider that if so many children can be taught to read every year—and this *was* being accomplished until a very few years ago!—then perhaps people could be taught to deal with troublesome anxieties so that they do not become so overwhelmed by them. Obviously, there is much work to be done to start a process of self-healing and recovery of some of your advantages.

ANXIETY AS A SIGNAL

I certainly cannot promise you an end to your anxiety. I can only promise you less incapacitating anxiety, if you can begin to work on behalf of your healthy strivings. You know that anxiety is a condition of your existence. But that condition can be managed so that it doesn't terrify or disable you, so that it doesn't interfere with and damage your relationships. One way you can learn to manage anxiety is by putting it to work for you. You can do that in two ways: first, by using it as a signal of inner trouble that you can do something about; and second, by harnessing the energy of your restlessness.

As you are aware, a cardinal sign of anxiety is restlessness, which is often reacted to with useless, agitated, and repetitious movements. You can become exhausted if the restlessness is severe and you are expending tremendous quantities of energy to keep your body in perpetual motion. You can make that energy work for you by deliberately harnessing it to useful work or to games of a physical nature. You might harness it by washing your car, working in your garden, cleaning closets or drawers, painting, waxing, vacuuming, sweeping sidewalks, weeding, etc. Most people have lists of chores that require physical work. If you have such a list, a restless period might be a good time to put your *anxiety energy* to work for you. You can also put your anxiety to work for you by using it as a signal to stop, look at, and listen to what you are experiencing. In that way you can begin to grapple with the feelings and events that unsettle you.

Even though just thinking about it may make you more perturbed, anxiety has a very important function in serving as a sign of trouble. You can actually learn to regard your anxiety as an opportunity to ask yourself what is bothering you. That question enables you to start a new process of finding out what you need and want for yourself and how you can go about achieving it.

As a reaction to the stress of emotional conflict, anxiety acts like an alarm pointing to the presence of that conflict. In the signal process, however, such intense physical symptoms can be produced that you can become terrified and feel that you're being pulled apart. The signal purpose of anxiety can be overlooked then, as you become distracted by the feeling that you are flying apart.

Your recognition of anxiety as a signal helps you deal with the symptoms when they assault you. That recognition can help you to raise important questions: What is my anxiety telling me? What message is it trying to give me? Is it important for me to pay close attention to it so that I can find out what is causing it?

In a sense, anxiety serves as a stoplight that says, Stop, Look, and Listen. *Stop* your aimless rushing about trying to keep one step ahead of a fearfulness you can't control. Try to find quiet places and things that relax you so you can get hold of yourself. Try to redirect your movements. Try to recall some of the things that comforted you as a youngster and see if it's reasonable to do them now. *Look* at where you are now and in what relation to others, to events, to your past. See if what you're doing makes sense to you, if it's what you really want to do. Can you effect a change that suits you better? *Listen* to your inner voices, your thoughts, needs, feelings. Are they kind words you hear? Or are they harsh and judgmental? Ask yourself: What is it I'm trying to accomplish? Is it realistic? What conflict is represented here? Am I blocking myself by making two conflicting, simultaneous demands of myself?

This is a time to be reminded that any person, thing, or event is only one item in a total life process of experience. That process is far greater than any single element that has a place in the whole. As a whole person, you are not, for example, the outcome of any *one* item in your development: neither a college graduate nor a high school dropout; neither a winning athlete nor a loser; neither a housewife nor an executive; neither a gossip nor a concerned citizen. You are very much more than any one of these.

If your uneasiness is masked by depression, you may not experience the acute discomfort of anxiety, and you may remain unaware of the existence of conflict. However, if you can succeed in using anxiety as a signpost of conflict, you are at least in a position to resolve that conflict and thereby lessen your anxiety. You can also rid yourself, to some extent, of conflicts that impair your functioning and sense of wholeness. But as you already know, that's easier said than done.

PRIMARY AND SECONDARY ANXIETY

People who have the misfortune to be born into the most unwelcoming and abusive families, run the risk of experiencing ongoing undercurrents of threat and insecurity. They are then compelled to develop ways of coping with these early feelings, which I call *primary anxiety.*

Children born into warm, accepting families may also develop primary anxiety if they suffer from illness very soon after birth. Children whose internal environment includes pain, tension, and distress cannot fully appreciate a tranquil outer atmosphere when they are suffering from physical discomfort. Such children may also develop attitudes of distrust and fearfulness early in life. Needless to say, however, when an illness has been successfully treated, a positive environment does much to restore a large measure of a child's confidence and trust.

Secondary anxiety refers to that unavoidable condition of life I have mentioned several times. I call it secondary anxiety because it evolves later in a person's life, in the context of personal, interpersonal, and social development as a growing, learning, functioning human being. I have indicated that if you want to live as fully as possible under your circumstances, and are willing to run risks, you will undoubtedly encounter different forms of secondary anxiety along the way, for it is an inevitable feature of life anywhere. This form of anxiety is being experienced in very intense ways these days, because many persons feel doubtful about their ability to meet the unusual and rapid changes of the century. And yet they feel they should be able to handle anything that comes their way. Wanting to run, and wanting to confront at the same time, creates a conflict that generates secondary anxiety. But it is manageable if you are motivated to take the steps to help yourself.

PREVENTION

Throughout this book you will notice that I emphasize the principle of *prevention*. You see now why I am so devoted to that principle. You see that emotional problems and severe anxiety are epidemic in this country. What's more, there's no way that all those who need services can be helped by the usual methods. But there are *unusual* methods that might begin to undermine the terrible mental health statistics that confront us. One of those methods incorporates the practice of preventive moves.

Both primary and secondary anxiety can be prevented. But, you might ask, how can you prevent something that has already happened and is here harassing you much of the time? In that case you need to know that the concept of prevention can be regarded in more than one way. In fact there are several facets of prevention. Consider the following: (1) *Prevention* of the more severe aspects of your anxiety by making efforts to diminish its intensity and duration, so that you actually *feel* better. (2) *Prevention* of the incapacitating and immobilizing features of your anxiety, so that you can *function* better. (3) *Prevention* of some part of future severe anxieties, to avoid being plagued by the anticipation of feeling dreadful and miserable, so that you can be more *optimistic* about the future.

It's true that you are strongly influenced in your development by your early environment. And there is nothing you could have done about a condition that did not stimulate and encourage your healthy growth. Are you aware, however, that as an adult you are the *primary determiner* (agent) of what you do, how you feel, and what happens to you? This is a thought that can both frighten and relieve you, in that order. The fear relates to a sudden new sense of responsibility you might feel for your own welfare. The relief has to do with the sense that you are no longer totally dependent on other people and circumstances to determine how you will feel and what you will do with each period in your life. I am not implying that you are *totally* responsible for what happens to you, because there are conditions you cannot control in any way. You have to accept that; but you can certainly take more of a part than you may have supposed. That's the message I want you to consider.

If you can accept what I've just said, then you might acknowledge that certain anxiety-ridden, neurotic practices—that is, poor mental health practices that have disturbed you for some time—can be turned about into practices that are more beneficial to your health. I'm intimating that you can take a *negative* mental health habit, tease apart the features that make it disquieting for you, find health points in it, strengthen them, and finally subject the habit to a deliberate turnabout process, thus converting it into *positive* behavior.

Consider this example. Suppose you keep your music on so long and loud that it distracts you from your work and disturbs your neighbors. You are obviously hurt by the distraction. You may also find frightening and angering the prospect of your neighbors' displeasure and retaliation. Yet you don't want to deprive yourself of the pleasure and beneficial effects of the music. You might then try turning your listening habits around by doing the following: (1) Place yourself on a schedule of listening time. (2) Find some less distracting music you might enjoy. (3) Learn to play an instrument, also with a schedule. And so on.

The benefits of your new positive behavior might then include: continuing enjoyment with music; enriched scope for listening pleasure; reduction of distraction and improved work output; increased possibility of socializing with neighbors who are relieved and delighted with the change (unless you've decided to take up the trumpet or drums!); involvement with a new and stimulating learning process.

Occasionally there may be no redeemable elements whatsoever in a negative mental health habit. In that case it would be wiser to discard the habit outright. By so doing you rid yourself of a pattern that causes you repeated distress. In the process of learning to discard harmful habits you can develop a simple three-level reminder that you can put to good use: (1) It's within your scope to change something if you want to. (2) You can find out how to go about making a change. (3) You need to put in the time and effort it takes. This handy reminder applies to almost any activity, work, or game.

In working with many persons, I've found that the same principles apply in learning how to deal with disconcerting anxieties. In this context, you use resources to move past blocks that anxiety sets before you by gathering and reinforcing assets acquired in your past. These are your health points, which refer to the many elements of your *wellness*—that is, your accumulated wealth of experience, ethnic roots, natural abilities, learned skills, talents, energy, stamina, and any other physical and intellectual asset. Anything that has furthered your total development in a beneficial way can be considered a health point.

But a distracting anxiety or a deadening depression can make health points unavailable to you. In ,that case you need to work to uncover them to restore your self-possession. The use of the three-level reminder is one way of practicing positive mental health and of overturning oppressive, negative habits. The twenty-step method is a more detailed procedure for recouping your health points and affording you relief from anxiety and guilt. It also helps you to understand why you have suffered and how you can prevent pain in the future.

I'll discuss all these points further throughout the remainder of Part One. I'll discuss how anxiety relates to conflict and compulsive behavior, and how continuing stress can lead to symptoms and illness. There will be explanations of the process by which you belittle and discredit yourself, of how you generate dislike and contempt for yourself. Some of the points may help to change that process, so that you can begin to feel more worthwhile. There are checklists to help you identify particular features of your personality. There are suggestions for you to work with if you want to explore some of your hang-ups before you start with the twenty steps. Throughout, the basic issue is to uncover conflict in order to reduce anxiety and relieve your self-hatred.

In Part Two, you'll read about a self-help program to help you manage your anxiety and depression, overcome your fear of change, and use small units of time and effort to accomplish your purpose. You'll see how the twenty-step program is used by some individuals. When you see how others have used the twenty steps, you'll be prepared to use them yourself.

You'll also read about an Anxiety Management Circle (p. 268), and how to form this self-help group by using the book as your guide. The Circle is for those of you who cannot use the twenty-step program without support from peers. It is based on a mutually supporting, people-helping-people principle.

Symptoms and Behavior: Do You Recognize Yourself?

Anxiety is an unavoidable reaction to certain life events. It requires no special management unless it produces serious symptoms, psychic pain, and interference with functioning and internal harmony. Disruptive anxiety is a self-made message telling you that all is not well. To feel intense anxiety is not to be "crazy." It is only to be in painful touch with the fact that an inner conflict has become intensified. Symptoms are *message units* announcing the state of your inner emotional world. They trigger your awareness of the need for investigation.

Whether or not resolution of conflict takes place, anxiety states are usually self-limited. Anxiety must be seen as a condition that comes and goes, as something with a beginning, a middle, and an end. Successful resolution doesn't prevent new anxiety, however. New anxiety comes into being constantly as a consequence of the nature of human consciousness, environmental factors, and ordinary and extraordinary life events.

SYMPTOMS

Anxiety is not an exclusive feeling. Anyone can feel anxious. It can be associated with many of the experiences you have, and it has numerous manifestations. You may feel anxious when you want to do something or when you don't want to. You may perceive anxiety as anger, bad humor, fretfulness, or hypersensitivity. It can be expressed as negligence, rudeness, uncharitability, or carelessness. Fickleness, dishonesty, or ambivalence may also be evidence of anxiety. Common to all anxiety states, however—mild, moderate, or severe—is a condition of irrational fearfulness, uneasiness, physical tension, and mental confusion, related in degree to the depth of the anxiety.

Needing to be liked by everyone is a sop for anxiety. Needing to withdraw, to isolate oneself, or to insist upon total independence and self-sufficiency might be indicators of and ploys to control anxiety. Inappropriate aggressiveness, hostility, competitiveness, lust for power and control, can all be ways of dealing with anxiety. Anxiety can underlie physical illness, sexual impotence, loneliness, overwork, overeating, alcoholism, drug addiction, preoccupation with sex, or depression. It is found as an element of all emotional hang-ups. It is the substratum upon which all neurotic defenses rest.

Emotional or physical signs and symptoms can be more or less troublesome depending upon their scope. Exhausted, yet agitated, you may keep driving yourself to do more. Any pain, ache, weakness, or other evidence of physical illness may be present, including fever, dizziness, cramps, nausea, diarrhea, constipation, insomnia, fainting, numbness, migraine, hypertension, or chest pressure. Due to such symptoms, your work can suffer slightly, moderately, or to the point where you may be asked to take a leave or resign.

If you are a student, you may be suffering because of a high level of distractability, which discourages study, concentration, and learning. Memory fails you. Fidgety and tense, you find it very difficult to stick to your work, to take responsibility, or to make decisions. On the other hand, you may rush into making rash judgments.

Sometimes you find yourself giving some matters much time, but the quality of your attention and concentration is an obsessive one and you review the same items over and over. Impatient with yourself for your inability to attend to details or follow through on matters of importance, you are unable to improve your performance, and you become more fearful over loss of control. Appointments are forgotten. Essential work is neglected. Sudden awareness of your behavior results in tormented guilt feelings. Your agitation increases as you try to mask your errors and omissions. You feel that you've been permanently damaged and that you'll be unable to function at your former level.

Symptomatology among all groups of workers has also reached new heights. For example, classroom work has always been demanding, under the best of circumstances. Now, new factors have been added that make one wonder how long teachers can tolerate the daily tensions to which they are subjected. Unruly, restless students of all ages (including elementary school children), trying to cope with their own pressures and anxieties, have become more demanding and more difficult to teach. Anxiety in both teacher and pupil makes classroom decorum a thing of the past, with rude, disruptive, and threatening individuals all too common.

Too many options placed in the hands of students breeds anxiety, for students often have neither the wisdom nor the volition to exercise an authority they do not seek. Out of their depth, they nevertheless feel obligated to respond to urgent—but vague and conflicting—imperatives that goad them to demand their "rights." Divisive antagonistic lines of force are established: between pupils and teachers on the one hand, and among administrators, parents, and community on the other—each group jousting for control. Children become misbegotten pawns in the ensuing scuffles.

A frustrated need to win engenders feelings of helplessness that further feed anxiety. The generation of anger, which has no place in the classroom, feeds both teachers' and students' anxieties. Absenteeism has become a prominent symptom of anxiety among teachers as a relief from mounting anger and a general sense of impotence.

No group seems to be spared the anxieties of varying life events. Chronically anxious persons can become terrified at signs of aging, something no one enjoys. Weight gain or loss, thinning hair, wrinkles, and loss of color, vigor, or sex drive intensify their fear. Unusual fussiness with clothing and other possessions may develop, as well as a growing sense of general dissatisfaction with appearance. Shopping becomes more of a chore as each item purchased assumes a greater importance than it merits. Irritability may be etched on a tense and frightened-looking face, accompanied by hasty, impatient movements, a strained voice, and complaints of a "tight head."

As anxiety levels increase, you may become intimidated by matters easily attended to formerly. There's a sense of danger and perpetual dread hanging over just about everything you contemplate. Fears can center about going to work, being at home, high places, closed or open or crowded areas. You become more timid, unassertive, or withdrawn to avoid the dangers that you believe surround you. You lose confidence and fear that you will make a mistake in something at which you are expert. When you cannot avoid what you see as harm, you may confront it with inappropriate anger and hostility. You come to restrict your activities and your motivation to perform as you have in the past. Avoidance is often considered one way to sidestep personal collapse.

In extreme anxiety or panic states (which are not common) there may be any of the symptoms above, together with dilated pupils, labored breathing, excessive sweating, bursts of aggressive behavior, rushing about, bewilderment, and even disorientation. Vigilance turns into suspiciousness and finally into paranoia or a sense of imminent disintegration, as no sense can be made of the fearful feelings, rush of thoughts, and bizarre perceptions that may have invaded consciousness.

Such states of extreme anxiety seem to confirm a self-fulfilling prophecy of doom. But just as success often produces more success, so can fear produce more fear. At such times, then, you need to cling to the knowledge that even the greatest anguish can subside. Remember that one of your greatest talents as a human being lies in your ingenuity for survival. Most anxiety attacks cannot permanently "wipe you out"; but bear in mind that an emergency center in a hospital can always treat anxiety that you really cannot tolerate.

At the other end of the spectrum—and very much more frequent —is anxiety that is fleeting and scarcely felt. Between these two extremes the language of anxiety is eloquent and the range of reactions is wide. Some persons' anxiety surfaces through physical tension. One woman, Genny, describes hers. "My throat gets so tight, and I can't breathe when I become anxious." Genny cannot deal with a volcanic anger, always poised and ready to erupt. Therefore she has frequent episodes of tension. When she is angry/anxious, Genny gasps, sobs, and chokes. She squeezes her words out through constricted throat muscles.

Genny does not have the same problem as Fanette, who says, "I'm always scared." Living alone in a city apartment, she has good reason, you might think. But this woman is also frightened when she is at work, shopping, visiting, and at places where the probability of danger is considerably less than it might be when she is alone. Yet a sense of dread remains at the core of her being.

Fanette also complains of "a kind of motor running inside of me all the time." Her "motor" is described also as a "humming noise." That feeling can have many different elements to it, depending upon your involvements. Some women's motors hum because of guilt over procrastination or because of poor work habits. Others relate it to more generalized feelings of timidity, inferiority, helplessness, loneliness, and isolation.

Feelings of anxiety usually give rise to recognizable forms of behavior. In the next section are the more commonly found patterns.

ANXIETY AND BEHAVIOR

Behavioral expressions of anxiety can be classified into various groups.

1. *Erratic impairment of functioning,* as in persons who can work or socialize well most of the time.
2. *Consistent impairment of functioning* (greater or lesser), at home, work, school, or play.
3. *Hostile physical outbreaks,* seen in parents who feel overwhelmed and totally incompetent. They occur also among anxious (and angry) young men with poor control, whose backgrounds permit them this kind of physical discharge of anxiety. Provocation for those outbursts may be slight. No doubt this category accounts for some of the impulsive random crimes that have become an astonishing part of our daily lives.
4. *Verbal and emotional attacks,* usually directed at weaker or

smaller victims. Anxious employers will unjustifiably rail at employees, teachers at pupils, parents at children, strangers at other strangers. Except where alcohol or other drugs can be indicted, episodes of wife or child abuse can frequently be traced to a rise in anxiety level in poorly controlled individuals.

5. *Withdrawal* in those persons who cannot share their feelings comfortably. When anxious, they may feel an even greater need to keep away from others. Because they tend to isolate themselves as anxiety levels rise, and still may find no relief, some of the members of this group may turn to the abuse of drugs as a cure for their anxiety and depression.

6. *Dependent, clinging behavior* becomes intensified with a rise in anxiety level. You've probably observed this in a few adults of your acquaintance. But it's almost universal in children who become frightened or anxious. Overprotective or overindulgent parents also fall into this group. Their anxiety may center on their inadmissible resentment over the demands of parent-hood. It centers also on their doubts regarding their ability to be good parents. Those doubts can drive them to absurd paren-tal excesses, leading to a backlash of disappointed expectations, dislike, and anger directed at the children. How does one love and hate a child at the same time? Only with anxiety.

7. *Common compulsions* may develop in anxiety ridden persons who tend to be perfectionistic. In this group are found the compulsive housewives and husbands who tyrannize their fami-lies with demands for order, cleanliness, or other requirements. Into this group, too, fall those persons who are incessant talkers or swearers; grunters, sniffers, or snorters; finger, ear, nose, or body pickers. The list of common compulsions is a very long one.

8. *Phobic behavior* also is an unconscious attempt to encapsulate anxiety which is experienced as a threat to acceptable function-ing or psychic integration. Fear of high, open, or closed areas belongs in this category. In a sense, the phobia binds much of the anxiety into a single unit so that functioning outside the phobic situation can be maintained without incessant dread.

Some persons display incapacitating or excessively repetitious and ritualistic behavior like hand washing, clothes clean-ing, doorknob wiping. Here, the particular ritual is like a baro-metric indicator. It becomes more florid with a rise in anxiety level, less so when the person becomes less anxiety ridden. Not all phobias are of the severe kind that become so apparent. Like any other neurotic defense, they come in all forms and cover a wide range of intensity from mild to severe.

9. *Seemingly stupid, or silly, or mildly irrational behavior* is not an unusual expression of anxiety. Placing themselves in the posi-tion of being uniquely uninformed, unreliable, or undependa-ble spares such persons the burden of a responsibility they feel they cannot or will not assume. Some form of this behavior is fairly common among women who feel they must avoid any semblance of competition or superiority with a partner who might feel thusly threatened.

When this defense is totally unconscious, the person may feel herself to be truly inferior. When it is conscious, she uses it as a ploy for the maintenance of a comfortable state (i.e., relief of anxiety). But she must be willing to accept society's view that she is more intellectually limited than she actually is.

10. *Overtly self-destructive behavior* is directly related to anxiety and to an excruciating sense of unworthiness and hopelessness. The most common means are overindulgence in alcohol or other mind-altering substances; risking death or injury in dan-gerous sports or in fast cars, boats, or airplanes; associating with violent companions or engaging in violent acts; gambling or spending beyond one's means; neglecting nutrition and general health; and depriving oneself of the comfort and support of friends and family.

Anger is a strong component of all these behaviors. It originates from the sense of helplessness inherent in anxious states. Depending on your personality, the anger is more or less apparent. Men and women who are hostile are more obvious in their expressions of anger. Violence-prone persons become easily incensed, because control of their environment is so important to them, and any sense of loss of power is intolerable.

Those who tend to withdraw, or who cling and try to please, do not behave in directly angry ways. But they may appear very frightened. That fearful look is partially related to a secondary anxiety that their buried, accumulated anger may be inadvertently exposed and will alienate those on whom they depend for a sense of security.

Consistent changes in functional levels are more easily discernible than erratic ones. For example: Eleene, a businesswoman, had to be told that her usual productivity had diminished markedly over a period of some months. She had been feeling "hyped up" during that period and was shocked by this information, for she had not been aware of a change in her performance level. But her colleagues had noted it.

When self-destructive behavior is practiced over a period of time, it becomes a means to keep anxiety levels within bearable limits. Even though the behavior may be destructive to self or to relationships, it serves its purpose of relieving anxiety in several ways. (1) When it entails danger, it contains the elements of excitement that provide a sense of aliveness ordinarily felt to be absent. (2) Taking charge even in a destructive way confers a sense of power and control otherwise totally lacking. It's a perverse form of winning when one says in effect, you can't do a single thing to stop me from destroying myself. (3) The details of self-destruction are often so distracting that anxiety seems completely controlled. A good example of this is seen in the drug addict, whose entire existence centers around the activities essential to the maintenance of a habit. Because of these distractions it often becomes impossible to root out such behavior. Only when there is an incentive for change will such practices be abandoned.

Aside from severe physical pain, intense, ongoing anxiety is probably the one feeling that is most impossible to tolerate. Such a human limitation accounts for the infinite numbers and elaborate designs of defenses that are constructed against the experiencing of anxiety. Thus, only when the original self-defeating behavior fails to reduce anxiety will another behavior be accepted as a substitute. If that substitute behavior happens to be constructive, then something important has been learned.

Body responses, too, need to be considered in this picture. As I've already indicated, the body can become accustomed to a "diet" of strong excitement. Once that occurs, it needs to continue feeding on that diet in order to feel in equilibrium (i.e., comfortable). A search for equilibrium can drive you in either direction, positive or negative.

ALTERNATIVE SOLUTIONS

Despite habits that interfere with positive mental health practices, there is cause for optimism. For we know that deliberately planned alternative modes of behavior can be successfully achieved with time and effort. Some of the points that may help you to develop a plan for alternative solutions include the following suggestions:

1. Simplify goals wherever possible.
2. Determine priorities, but be flexible about them.
3. Attend to only one issue, task, or problem at a time.
4. Structure your time in order to avoid anxiety-provoking, open-ended time.
5. If feasible, decrease the number of items that must be attended to in a given time interval.
6. Employ the company and interest of friends and family to help see you through difficult periods in the day.
7. Do not spend unnecessary time with persons, places, and things that add to your anxiety.
8. Substitute body activities or learning something for preoccupation with anxiety.
9. Ensure proper rest and nutrition.
10. Learn to assert your position, using any method suitable to your individual style.
     This last can be the most significant in helping you deal with many forms of behavior that are inhibiting your growth and well-being.

Anxiety: Its Different Forms

Peak anxiety experiences are not suffered frequently by most persons. That's why I want to address myself now to those more common varieties felt by an indefinite number of women and men. One of those varieties goes by the name of "nervousness." No doubt you've heard these comments:

"I get so nervous when I see that."

"I feel so nervous when you say that."

"I can't stand that noise. It makes me nervous."

"When I'm out at night, I always feel nervous."

These are women speaking. *Nervous* is a word they use when they feel anxious. It's also a word that you might use when you're angry. That substitution can be made when (1) you don't know you're angry, (2) you're angry but you don't want anyone to know it, or (3) you just don't know what to do with your angry feelings.

LOW-GRADE ANXIETY

Nervousness always refers to an uncomfortable, edgy feeling. The very widespread nervousness that women describe is one form of what I call *low-grade anxiety*. "I'm always a little nervous" is a statement commonly heard by examining physicians when they ask at the annual checkup, "How have you been feeling?"

Women with low-grade anxiety function well as a rule. They go about their social, business, or family life without serious interference. They can feel content, enjoy, perform at top level, be satisfied with their families and the general outlines of their lives. But there are times when there is a vague undercurrent of dissatisfaction regarding their personal lives, as unrelated to anyone else. Something seems to be missing, something elusive they cannot identify but feel is always just beyond reach. Most of the time they ignore it, feeling that they have "a good life . . . everything to be thankful for . . . a loving husband . . . stable financial status . . . good health."

Yet small, gnawing, searching feelings occasionally overcome them, making them restless. That restlessness drives them into activities that can be advantageous or not. You will hear: "I have such a lot of nervous energy. I have to use it up somehow." They've learned that activity relieves their "nervousness."

At such times housewives find it nearly impossible to remain at home when it's quiet and they have nothing in particular to keep them busy. In years gone by, these were among the women who found themselves longing to have another baby every five years or so. Nervousness would begin to mount when the previous baby went to school and left an *occupational gap* for women who built their satisfactions mainly around the care of a young child.

Restlessness can be added to the feelings of apprehension, feelings that can drive them to the point where they must "run" to get away from those "quivery feelings right in the pit of my stomach." Of course, activity is a good means of discharging any anxiety. But I want to suggest that in understanding and working with the elements of your conflicts you can do more than discharge your restlessness. As you are able to resolve conflicts, even to a small degree, your energy will not remain the nervous energy that you are driven to discharge. It can become a natural flow of energy that is always available to you, always there to draw upon and put to work *as you see fit*—and not only when you have to "run" to keep it from eating you up.

When mild anxiety (low-grade) becomes more intense, women say they are "very nervous." More severe anxiety is commonly referred to as "high-strung," "climbing the walls," etc. See how many of these words used in descriptions of nervousness apply to you. Give them one (occasionally) to three (frequently) checks if they describe your feelings at any time.

excitable	impatient
jumpy	frightened
jittery	apprehensive
shaky	timid
upset	alarmed
high-strung	helpless
sensitive	up the wall
touchy	peevish
hassled	inhibited
distraught	unstable
neurotic	agitated
unsettled	fidgety
trembly	restless
unstrung	wild
worried	manic
tense	terrified
uptight	hysterical

Don't be surprised if you've given one check to all of these items. Unfortunately we live in an anxiety-producing environment, and you would have to be a rock not to feel somewhat unsettled or hysterical now and then.

Such environmentally induced anxiety could be called *situational* anxiety. Related to a specific event, it can be aroused when you cannot predict the outcome of your involvement. It may be an untested situation or one you've already experienced in the past. Any doubt about your performance may lead to slight or great anxiety. But as soon as the outcome becomes clear to you, situational anxiety can subside in a very short time, even minutes.

So very many feelings are subsumed under the heading of nervousness or anxiety. You'll find some of them in the following statements. See how many of these expressions of nervousness or anxiety apply to you. Please check them *occasionally* or *frequently*.

1. I'm tense when I work.
2. I'm uneasy when I socialize.
3. I'm disquieted by my in-laws.
4. I get bored and restless very easily.
5. I'm easily troubled by my partner, children, parents, etc.
6. I feel worried about my children.
7. I'm fearful when I drive.
8. I get furious very easily.
9. I'm frightened when I travel.
10. I feel apprehensive about many things.
11. I get overwrought when pressures mount.
12. I'm alarmed when things don't go the way I expect them to.
13. I get nasty when I'm upset.
14. I become fearful when I feel pressured.
15. I feel fretful if I don't have a schedule to follow.
16. I get angry when I'm not "top dog."
17. I feel neglected if someone isn't giving me special attention.
18. I'm anguished when I find I can't do something I want to do.
19. I get very impatient when people intrude on my privacy.
20. I have a sense of foreboding about the future.
21. I feel dissatisfied with my work.
22. I become distraught over little things.
23. I have misgivings about new ventures.
24. I dread interviews.
25. I get hysterical if I feel rejected.
26. I tremble easily when I get angry.
27. I get rude and peevish about poor service.
28. I can't laugh at some of the foolish things I say or do.
29. I perspire excessively on certain occasions.
30. I don't enjoy many things.

If you've marked all these items *occasionally,* you can take your place alongside almost anyone. With this list I've only described common human reactions to different *pressure points* that can feel quite stressful at times.

If you've marked *any* of the thirty items *frequently,* you are being subjected to the ongoing distress of excess anxiety. But don't think you're destined to continue suffering that distress. You can do something about it. First you owe it to yourself to take notice of a state of affairs that makes you feel "so nervous." Then you can begin to take steps to care for yourself in a new way.

Probably no one is totally free from some form of low-grade anxiety, which is transient in nature. Marsha is a case in point. She is ready and waiting for her date. She's feeling slightly anxious. Marsha prefers casual dates—people dropping in or meeting her someplace. Now she's thinking: Why did I make this date? How will it turn out? Will I have something to say? Will he? Will he be a bore? Suppose he gives me a hard time about coming up later? Should I tell him I'm menstruating? What business is it of his anyway!

It may surprise you to hear that Marsha is anxious about how she will deal with any suggestions of intimacy that her date might make. But she has not learned yet how to be decisive when it comes to her sexual involvements. By contrast, the autonomous woman will (1) know how she feels, (2) not be afraid to be candid about her feelings, (3) be able to refuse or accept advances without embarrassment or guilt, and (4) be considerate of her partner's feelings in any event.

Are you one of those women who are caught in the trap of *shoulds*, which deflect them from their true opinions and wishes? Do you wonder how you *should* respond? Do you overlook that you are already responding? Are you afraid you will hurt your partner with a refusal? Are you forcing yourself to be the nice person, the one who never says no to anyone? Do you know how to refuse or accept gracefully? Or are you out of touch with what makes it possible to make a decision unilaterally? There is still much confusion, misinformation, and conflict in this area, all of which makes for continuing anxiety in man/woman relationships. Anxiety message units continue to be delivered.

Confusion of this nature is especially prevalent among newly divorced women who have not yet found a position from which to express their wishes. They often delay decisions about their own behavior until they can "find out what he expects." They are exposed to their own anger and guilt when they feel "pushed" into something for which they are not ready.

Actually Marsha has little cause for apprehension. Still, she feels anxious each time she goes out with someone for the first time. "I can't seem to be able to avoid that cold knot of fear in the pit of my stomach each time." This form of transient low-grade anxiety may occur in any context, at any time, at any age. It may arise suddenly, or slowly over a period of time, becoming most intense just before the specific anxiety-provoking event. Many persons pay little attention to it, for it seldom interferes with functioning in any significant way. They have learned that as soon as they are "into" the activity, the anxiety subsides almost completely and they can attend to the matter at hand without further discomfort. Common examples include hosting a party, being in a play, going to an interview, attending a new school, giving a speech, going on a trip, or getting married.

Transient low-grade anxiety has the same generating source as more severe and incapacitating anxiety. In Marsha's case, she has conflicting feelings about her position. She's annoyed that she should care what her date thinks, and wonders why she bothers at all to go out with someone she hardly knows. Yet it *might* be fun, she muses, and the new person may be a "real find," whom she would miss if she refused the date. She resents having to take the time to prepare for the date, feeling she ought to be able to go out as she is. At the same time she feels she needs to look her best.

Such mixed feelings lead to Marsha's discomfort. She complains: "I don't feel I'm running my life completely. I don't feel on top of things. I'm angry with myself for getting into such a snit over nothing." Feelings of incompetence, loss of control, and anger feed her anxiety. She is left having to deal with that discomfort, doing little to unravel the underlying opposing features. (In Part Two you will find specific steps to take for that purpose.)

Nevertheless, Marsha is doing a great deal of thinking about herself and her frequent bouts of discomfort and uncertainty. While thoughts will not heal her, they are a first step to a process that will sharpen her awareness, help her to raise questions, and give her courage to run the necessary risks and become more certain of her reactions.

ANGER TENSION

In many circles *nervousness* and *anxiety* are words that are repeatedly used as synonyms for *anger*. No doubt you've heard something like this example: Mrs. Dale, a resident in a nursing home, was talking about another resident, Tody: "I get nervous when he says that." Translated into emotional terms, that means something like this: Sometimes he says things I don't like and it makes me feel angry. But I can't tell him I don't like it or that it makes me feel angry. It's impolite to tell people things like that. I don't like to criticize anyone or hurt anyone's feelings. So I just say it makes me nervous. I hope he'll stop it.

You see how such a person will choose the word that is more generally accepted—*nervous* instead of *angry*. Being angry with Tody is a threatening admission to make, because Mrs. Dale is afraid that Tody may turn around and retaliate in some way. But she's just as afraid of losing that unrealistic picture of herself as a superbly polite, kind person. She's doubly angry at Tody for he threatens that picture.

When she says "I'm nervous," she's trying to convey this message to Tody: What I really hope is that you will feel some responsibility for my nervousness. If you do, you might feel guilty. And if you do feel guilty, maybe you'll change something about how you talk to me, so that I can keep from getting angry and upset.

You see how circuitous some persons have to be in order to deal with their anger and avoid the disquietude of anxiety. This circuit is and has been a well-traveled one by women of all ages. Younger women are now finding it easier to say in effect: You are saying or doing something that makes me feel angry, and I want to do something to discharge my angry feelings. If anger obscures her judgment, however, an outspoken young woman may encounter a problem when, in stating her grievance to an employer, for example, she mistakenly substitutes inappropriate frankness for tactful assertiveness. This may occur in dealing with either women or men. Rather than being thanked for her frankness, she is sometimes found to be offensive and/or threatening. Unaware of the threat she poses with her anger (employers are afraid of anger, too), she is puzzled to find herself displaced, or slipping once more to the periphery of power.

Practically no one wants a total and complete revelation of your angry feelings. That's not the law of the land, for all the admonishments you hear about being open and honest. You must know that openness and honesty can also be carried to absurd extremes and cause you much grief. No doubt, you have noted this even among public figures who seem not to understand the limitations of those they confront.

The less angry individual first decides whether or not she wants to jeopardize her position. If not, she needs to realize she has to accept a change in her behavior, if not in her attitude. Should she be unable to move to that point of decision, she is going to experience anxiety repeatedly, because of her unresolved conflict about how to handle her anger.

Her conflict will revolve about (1) her "right to confront" with her anger and (2) her need not to antagonize because of possible retaliation. In other words she insists on both positions: She wants her job, and she wants her right to express her anger directly. That would be fine if she *could* have both. But under the circumstances she is overlooking one important factor. In dealing with a particular employer her two wishes are contradictory and cannot exist side by side, simultaneously. Feeling she cannot risk antagonizing and also keep her job, she still cannot relinquish her "right" to express anger in an uncompromising fashion. Conflict cannot be resolved if both poles continue to repel with equal and opposite force. She becomes blocked, and mounting anger feeds her conflict and intensifies anxiety.

But there are different methods you can use to effect change, and that's the main point after all. If you have difficulty expressing your anger because of timidity, or because it is not in your interest to express it directly, you can gradually learn to discharge it in ways that are compatible with your personal limitations or with those of the situation. As I've indicated, it may not be in your best interest to try to confront directly, or to try to go from being timid to "coming on strong." In so doing, you may produce just the kind of retaliation you've tried to avoid.

You need to find a position somewhere in between. This is a splendid opportunity for you to practice new and more productive mental health habits. In the one instance, you can try to be less timid, maintaining a manner that is in harmony with your natural way of being. In the other, you need to learn the wisdom of selection, omission, and tact in exposing others to your wrath, however justified it may be. Sometimes honesty is like medicine. It can be good for you, but too much of it can be bad. In fact, I doubt if much business or social intercourse would be possible for long if people were "brutally honest" under inappropriate conditions.

So many women have been and still are being raised to believe that they should neither get angry nor express anger when they feel it. (Nice people control their anger, don't they?) This is compatible with the self-image that countless middle-aged women have deeply embedded in their hearts and minds. I find it still quite prevalent among younger women also. Under an imaginary mandate against angry feelings, both groups of women are unable to either feel or express anger—they get "nervous" instead. There is no rule against that, as any physician can tell you.

Fearful, tradition-bound women have been compelled to maintain a benign image of themselves. They have not been able to question it because a fundamental sense of self (identity) is tied in with it. A prominent feature of that identity (an imaginary image) is a person who doesn't become obviously angry *at any time.* Such women experience a certain security in that and cannot relinquish it unless they can feel assured of a similar security elsewhere.

I doubt that women who have long lived with such a fantasy image of themselves can ever leave it completely behind, no matter how much they may strive. But change does not have to be complete in order to be effective. Actually, in the course of my work I have found that minor changes in attitude or behavior result in surprisingly effective strides toward being able to make a free choice—which is what freedom, equality, and a sense of inner unity are all about. You need to have the courage to venture, however cautiously and hesitatingly, through the opening made by any small change, and be willing to take your first few tentative steps. Courage comes not so much from a position of strength as from a willingness to move, to change something. Strength may follow courage born of weakness.

To summarize this point, then, here are two reasons why you may feel afraid to express your anger and have to fall back on the more acceptable position of being the nervous woman rather than the angry one: (1) Hostile expression of anger can cause you grief, because you run the risk of retaliation in some form of emotional, verbal, or even physical attack, especially if you are tactless and offensive. Your anxiety is aroused by a conflict between your wish to be outspoken and your need to remain safe. (2) Anger creates conflict between your established view of yourself as a nonangry woman and the less constricted, more honest one you've been striving toward but aren't yet strong enough to assume as an identity.

I need to point also to the difficulty that different personality types have in experiencing and/or expressing their anger. While countless women hold the benign "nice woman" model as their self-image, their behavior patterns may vary widely. Overbearing women can be sensitive to the problem of retaliation because they in fact do "come on too strongly" and know that they are more likely to arouse an angry or hostile reaction.

Occasionally, however, these women are entirely unaware of their impact. While they are puzzled by reactions they elicit, they nevertheless come to expect them and see them as a justification of their original suspicions and fears. They are fairly expert at rationalizing what they find unpleasant to contemplate. Such women are always on the edge of anger, for they can *be* angry and *act* angry as well. Yet they hold a tight rein on themselves for fear of possible repercussions. The tension of conflict keeps them looking and feeling tense, uncertain, and angry, and they come to identify themselves as "nervous" women.

Compliant, pleasing women have difficulty with their anger, too, but in different ways. These are the women like Clare, who says, "I never get angry, especially with the people I love." The thought of being angry can produce acute anxiety—such as the attack of hyperventilation that Clare once had. "I felt so guilty, because I caused so much trouble. They even had to take me to a hospital."

Clare is riddled with guilt much of the time, because she does get angry like anyone else but has to squelch her angry feelings long before they are clear to her. She suffers from a double dose of guilt: first, because she gets angry at all, and then, for having to "trouble" her friends with physical reactions produced by her anger-provoked anxiety.

A more candid, outspoken woman, Gerry, says she has "triple guilt." Explaining, she says, "I get very angry with my husband sometimes, and I feel guilty about that. Then I yell at him and use nasty language. I feel guilty about that, too, because it's not nice and the children can hear me and might begin using it, too. He rarely uses that kind of language but is not impatient with me. So I feel more guilty that I'm not as patient as he is. So there you have it. Triple guilt!"

As I describe these feelings of anger and guilt, perhaps you can find your own place on this *guilt range,* which a considerable number of people carry about with them. Which is yours? Single guilt? Double guilt? Or triple?

Clare has few ways of discharging her anger or of defending herself against her own anger as well as anyone else's. "I get so upset if anyone gets angry. I can't stand it," she says. "I'll do anything to smooth things over. If I think anyone is angry with me, I fall apart. I have no defense because I feel so guilty. Even when I have sex, I'm so nervous. I can't have an orgasm, so I pretend, because I'm afraid he'll be angry with me."

Clare's guilt over her repressed anger (which she vaguely senses at times) keeps her from being assertive and from making even the most reasonable demand. Feeling so undeserving, she can do little on behalf of herself. She has ideas about what she'd like to do with her abilities but doesn't feel sufficiently worthy to put them into action. In addition to her overwhelming guilt feelings, Clare is a woman who cries easily, who feels abused, ashamed, misunderstood, who becomes the family's doormat, who has little interest in sex, who has frequent attacks of depression when she's overcome with feelings she neither understands nor tolerates.

Both of these personality types (the submissive, timid woman like Clare and the more outspoken one like Gerry) are very much involved with other persons, either to dominate or to appease. In the one case, fighting and winning make them feel strong, but fearful of retaliation. In the other, appeasing makes them feel acceptable—but resentful, angry, and ashamed of their submissiveness.

Salvia belongs to another group of women, who are not so strongly driven by a need to dominate or to be approved of. She therefore seems freer to choose relationship options. "I prefer to remain unentangled," she states. "I prefer more space around myself. I like feeling sufficient unto myself. There's very little I can't do for myself. I get nervous, though, when I feel someone getting too close to me and invading my territory."

Her own feelings of anger disturb Salvia, because they point to closeness with others, to becoming "entangled." Through anger she loses the "cool" she values. That sense of calm control is where her sense of safety lies. Salvia manages to control her environment so that she can remain comfortable. In exaggerated cases, such women may withdraw excessively and become so isolated that they eventually join the league of lonely, forgotten persons.

Although I have used examples of women in this section, please be reminded that many of the same points regarding personality types can be made about men. For both men and women, however, anger that is not discharged in some fashion can become chronic and can lead to a state of ongoing anger tension and anger anxiety.

Because of varying fears in different types of persons, then, expressions of anger may be inhibited by the use of two very common defenses: (1) Anger is *suppressed,* so that no one will know for sure if you are angry because you're trying hard not to know that you are. (2) It is *repressed,* kept from your own awareness, so that you don't even know you are angry. But however you may mask anger with these two defenses of suppression and repression, your body will nevertheless react spontaneously to an arousal of anger. There can be changes in color, or in heart and respiratory rate; blood pressure can go up; there can be behavioral evidences of *anger tension* with impatient brusk movements, shouting, crying, or withdrawal.

It's quite possible that you may look, sound, or behave in an angry way and be completely unaware of it. For example, Carol is shouting, and her friend Jane says to her, "I'm sorry that you're angry about this. I hadn't meant to upset you." To which Carol replies loudly, "Who's angry? I'm not angry. What makes you think that?"

Many anger responses will dissipate as quickly as they arise. But inability to acknowledge, accept, or discharge angry feelings can sustain that tension indefinitely. Such tension soon pairs with anxiety, and I call the combination *anger anxiety.* This is one form of body-bound anxiety.

Anger anxiety is one factor that feeds the undercurrent of restlessness found in low-grade anxiety. Women with low-grade anxiety don't feel they have any good reason to be angry, so they can seldom accept that possibility. When it becomes clear that they are angry, they feel guilty and reply with the standard response of the "nervous" woman: "What do I have to feel dissatisfied and angry about? Everything is going well. I have no major problems."

Here is part of their anger—that they *are* dissatisfied when they think they should be feeling "good" about everything. The bedrock of dissatisfaction in such a woman has to do with her inner environmental factors, not those outer factors for which she is "grateful." However successful and unproblemed her family and her life in general, dissatisfaction stems from a feeling that she is not really "making it." The "it" refers to an illusory fantasy image she holds before herself and which she uses as a standard against which to measure herself. This standard differs from ordinary standards in that it is unrealistic, and therefore impossible to achieve. It is a fantasy standard that guarantees failure.

To the extent, then, that her buried wishes yearn for the fulfillment of that fantasy image, she can never feel satisfied. Her "running" to discharge nervous energy (anger tension) is related to the eternal longing and searching for an image that is a will-o'-the-wisp and will always remain out of reach. A predictable failure feeds her anger at herself. There is no escape unless she stops to investigate and uncover the roots of her anger tension.

Rather than become involved in this investigation, certain women will avoid it. They are not familiar with the liberating effect it can have. They are frightened of what they may uncover. But since irrational fear and unresolved anger are roots of anxiety, they continue to nourish it as long as nothing is done to expose them and diminish their impact. Chronic states of anger and fearfulness provide a breeding place for the growth and maintenance of hostile feelings.

TENSION AND HOSTILITY

Hostile attitudes and hostile behavior are powered by conflict and anxiety. Anger tension is constantly being produced. It's almost as if you are keeping your anger fires banked and on the alert, just in case there is something you can become immediately angry about. Unfortunately, there's always a goodly supply of situations around that can be used to spark that ready anger into a blaze.

Anger and *hostility* are sometimes used interchangeably. But hostility differs from anger in important ways. Anger can be a natural, spontaneous, unavoidable response to any number of explainable stimuli. Feelings and expressions of hostility are usually evidences of a habitually conflicted neurotic state. Two premises provide a base for hostility: a need to protect against attack and a need to avenge real or imagined hurts.

The hostile person often feels friendless, powerless, and frightened for any number of reasons. A sense of loss of power, real or imagined, makes hostile persons believe they will be attacked, emotionally or physically, if they do not defend themselves continuously. So they develop ongoing antagonistic attitudes toward those in their environment as a necessary element of that defense. They assume that others feel ill will toward them. While that may very well be so in some instances, hostile persons do not admit that their own attitudes may have been responsible for causing that ill will. They cling to their feelings of animosity and to a belief that they must be defensive at all times in order to protect themselves. Their defensive maneuvers may show themselves in a habitual need to frustrate or injure others. Hostile message units are being constantly sent out and are repeatedly rejected upon delivery.

By contrast, common, spontaneous anger can come and go quickly, and its effects are usually short-lived. When it is continually suppressed or repressed, its effects may last much longer and may produce ongoing anger tension. Anger then becomes *chronic anger.* That anger, combined with other elements just mentioned, makes for a hostile person, who is ready to speak or act in ways harmful to oneself and others. While anger may have the characteristic of a sudden on-and-off feeling, like a quick summer rain, a state of hostility is more of a lasting condition that can be insidiously corrosive to one's physical and emotional well-being.

Like any other condition, hostility varies in degree. Some persons will react with hostility only occasionally. Some react only in certain situations or with certain individuals who arouse their anxiety and stimulate a defensive response. Some persons feel hostile much of the time and are hard pressed to control themselves in order to continue in long-term personal or business relationships. Some cannot control themselves at all. They manage to hack their way through life, burdened with the poor reputation that habitually hostile people usually have.

Hostility is a blend of many conflicting feelings. Hostile people feel they have been done great and irreparable injustices. In many cases this is true—children are especially liable to such injustices. A state of hostility thus evolves from a state of chronic fear in combination with chronic anger. However, those injustices may not have persisted into the present, and often the hostile person is still defending against something that no longer exists.

As with other forms of anger and anxiety, ways of expressing hostility vary with personality and behavior. Aggressive personality types can become greatly irritable over trivial matters. They generally show more anger than fear. Appearing unconcerned over the hurts they inflict with their attacks, they harbor deeply buried guilt and a ready wish for vindication. Rarely admitting fear or remorse, they may express hostility through suave, sarcastic tones, sadistic demands, or irrational outbursts, and can exhibit glaring blind spots regarding irrational behavior. In some, an unfailing need to "get back at" others and to avenge themselves fuels an uncontrollable vindictiveness that keeps the kettle of their hostility always simmering.

More timid and nonassertive hostile types show more fear than anger. They have difficulty in expressing the simplest form of anger. When they do, they may pale, stutter, choke up, and become incoherent. This angers them further; but their fear of retaliation drives them into petty and devious ways, through which some anger can be indirectly discharged.

People who tend to keep more to themselves can control most signs of fear or anger. They present a cold, aloof facade when they are hostile. Not easily involved, they can snipe and be cutting when an opportunity exists. In extreme instances they become sadistic by withholding all affection, support, or concern from those close to them. Because such withholding can stifle warm feelings, such people often begin to feel isolated. This chronic withdrawal from others can lead to such a poverty of human stimulation that depression may develop and become a way of life.

Concerted efforts must be made to identify and understand hostile attitudes and behavior. Only then can one begin to counteract the impact of a poor emotional input in childhood that has led to the unresolved rage, fear, and anxiety from which hostility springs.

ANXIETY AND ILLNESS

An anxiety response is a physically stressful reaction, which is well tolerated in moderate amounts. Ongoing anxiety is aroused, however, as long as the underlying conflict remains unresolved. Countless persons live with conflict and anxiety all their lives, either in repeated episodes or in a continuous, chronic state. However, as an unavoidable response to certain events, new encounters, or change, anxiety is and can be manageable. It becomes unmanageable and defeating when it is ignored or denied. Denial subverts your efforts to manage your life and to refuse being tossed about by conflict like a cork bobbing to every whim of a troubled sea.

The body becomes totally involved in emotional stress, although well-controlled individuals like to think otherwise. All parts of our bodies are interdependent. Connections between mind, body, and emotions have been clinically noted for centuries. Galen, a physician of the second century, noted that he had observed a higher incidence of breast cancer in "melancholic" women. When long-range medical histories are available, some patients show an interesting correlation between environmental factors and medical illness. Here is a case in point, outlining the causes for the generation of secondary anxiety in response to stress.

A formerly strong and resourceful woman in her eighties, Mrs. Ray said she had observed the same pattern in several of her contemporaries through the years. She gave the following history:

Life-threatening episode 1: Mrs. Ray's first expansion into the business world occurred after World War I. She wanted to "get on the bandwagon" and persuaded her husband to invest his small savings in a business venture. "We were both scared," she said. "The children were very young, and we felt that we might have made a mistake. I could tolerate my own doubts. But when he began to complain that I was ruining him and that he didn't feel well, I felt terribly guilty. It was too much for me."

His complaining threw her into conflict. While she wanted to do the "best" for her family through the business, she also wanted to be a good wife to her husband. That meant stopping her efforts to make the business successful. At this point of uncertainty and anger over a choice she didn't want to make, she contracted pneumonia and almost died. Her convalescence lasted several months.

Life-threatening episode 2: Years later, also in association with uncertain financial moves, she again fell seriously ill and was obliged to remain hospitalized for several weeks. She remembers repeating over and over to her family, "This wouldn't have happened if I hadn't been so upset about the business." Once again her husband had faltered and she was thrown into conflict over her divided loyalties. Unable to resolve her needs to be the good wife and mother and a businesswoman as well, she got sick.

Life-threatening episode 3: A few years later, with the country entering the final stage of the Great Depression, Mrs. Ray made further moves to strengthen the family's resources. Once more she reinvested their capital in the business. While she ultimately succeeded as she intended, her success was initially uncertain, and again she ran into conflict with her doubting, accusing partner, who repeatedly asked her to leave him in peace. Was she a "good" person or an "awful" one? "It was my own guilt," she said, "that destroyed me. My faith in myself, my judgment, became so shaken that I just fell apart." Illness struck yet again, and her life was saved only by the excellent nursing care she received.

Mrs. Ray provided an interesting addendum to this history: "Each time I was deathly ill, I would think: I'm going to die. But what will happen to my family if I do? Who will take care of them? I can't die. I must be strong and fight this." As she said this, there seemed no doubt in her mind that it was her strong will to live that ensured her survival. She just *couldn't* die—she had too much work to do. There was no conflict about that!

There are many studies to support the thesis that conflict and anxiety can contribute to a wide range of physical illnesses. They repeatedly point to a correlation between stressful life events and the onset of physical illness. Acute family crises; the disorganization of a family unit; the death of a loved one; poor marital adjustment; a change of living arrangement, home, school, or employment; a general increase in daily stress—all can cause illness. Researchers underscore the use of caution, however, in arriving at conclusions, because of the meticulous methodology required in order to establish validity for scientific research on stress-related illness.

In studying family stress Meyer and Haggerty found that sore throats and upper respiratory infections were four times more likely in students who were subjected to acute family stress. Working with groups of college students, Jacobs and Spilken reported that the group using health services most frequently for respiratory infections and asthma had a higher incidence of disappointment, distress, life crises, and maladaptive coping behavior patterns than did the control group.

Cluff and associates found that psychologically vulnerable people with high anxiety levels differed from control groups in that their flu symptoms lasted longer. In another study, Satin noted that of all persons presenting themselves to an emergency service, 86 percent had experienced recent significant stress events.

Minter and Kimball concluded that following stressful life events, illness occurs more often than can be accounted for by chance: ". . .The issue of how life stress affects illness is so important that decisive research to discover the nature of this relationship should have priority."

DYNAMICS OF CONFLICT AND ANXIETY

The woman who has severe emotional conflicts is constantly divided and exhausted by them. In order to achieve relief, she tries to deny her conflicts by not dealing with them directly. Instead she constructs an imaginary conception of herself, one that contains only admirable and virtuous qualities and abilities. An illusion of integrity and wholeness is erected, in which all her characteristics are good, honorable, and desirable.

What I'll try to present here is a deliberately forceful picture of an unconscious human process. It is a process that is essentially the origin of what is known as "alienation." While you may find it exaggerated, please don't believe that it doesn't apply *in some way*. I think I can safely say that it applies to all women to some degree. (Men, too, are involved in the same process, but with their particular idealized qualities and abilities.)

So without being too hard on yourself, see if you can find where you fit into this framework, with *your* fantasies and *your* poor mental health practices. Do you consistently hold yourself in poor regard by comparing yourself to totally unrealistic standards of worthiness and goodness? Are you aware of this? See how far you go with my picture of what can underlie those downgrading, "icky" feelings that you wrestle with so often. Remember, the more you understand, the more you can put your womanpower to work to change the things that bother you.

For the woman, then, who has constructed this imaginary conception of herself, blatant inconsistencies and contradictions are easily swept under the rug of an illusory image of perfection. That it exists only in the imagination is no matter. It rules her attitudes, behavior, and expectations of herself and others as if it were a true and accurate representation of herself. Let me remind you of the bargain she's made: a beautiful illusion in exchange for the pain of unresolved conflict.

The theory I'm describing here was developed early in the 1930s by Dr. Karen Horney and validated by decades of her clinical work and that of her followers. An unconscious/conscious process, it applies to both women and men of various personality types, ages, and occupations. Each person uses a particular set of ideals upon which to construct this imaginary concept.

Housewives use one set of ideals. If you are a career woman, you are familiar with the set established for you. Students and blue-collar workers have theirs, as do professional men and adolescents. Please bear in mind, then, that while the comments made here refer primarily to adult women, they apply as well to all human beings who have needed to fictionalize themselves with all manner of fabrications and fragmentary images, because they have been unable to accept the real persons they are and have rejected themselves in favor of a *fantasy self.*

In the construction of this illusory self-image, whatever assets a woman does have can become distorted and exaggerated into superb gifts. So a minor talent can be blown into near genius. The image of near-perfection that is erected bears only a slight resemblance to one's reality. When real assets are abundant, the resemblance is closer, but still off the mark. No matter how comforting the illusion may feel, it's still unrealistic, and so the woman is repeatedly disappointed in her actual self.

Except for any expertise acquired by means of lifelong efforts, most of us are quite ordinary. Unaware of that fact, the woman who constructs her exalted image is puzzled. She wonders: How can *she,* a person with such supposedly extraordinary abilities, still reside in the body of an ordinary person? If the sublime image is true, then how ordinary can she be? Those questions are quickly resolved by the decision: Of course I'm sublime. That crude person isn't me. I reject her totally and irrevocably.

You see what an incredible sleight of hand that process requires. In so doing, you relinquish the things you are and accept only the paper-thin illusion of what you are not. That's why you feel so insubstantial sometimes, so vulnerable, so dependent, so "nothing." You feel you are nothing because you have in fact "sold" yourself to the devil of your conflict in return for a comforting illusion. You keep paying a price, however, with the true substantiality of your mind and body and all the things you unquestionably are.

In rejecting the common sense and the warm, intuitive responses of that ordinary woman, you are left without valuable assets and reliable defenses. You can then be victimized in many circumstances, because in discrediting your experience you know less and can do less. You have given up your natural endowments and the riches of your own experiences.

All is not lost, however. The wish for redemption provokes that real person to emerge from time to time. This is when the battle between your untrue image and your true self becomes the hottest. Your untrue image sees your emergence not as the sign of health that it is, but as a threat to disgrace you with the presence of this *real person.* A struggle is undergone to keep that "ugly, despised" self (in your imaginary image's opinion) from being revealed. You fear that it will spoil the total loveliness of a perfect false image, the one you insist is you. In this grand scheme your need for human closeness must be set aside, for such closeness would expose your reality, which you believe would be immediately rejected by another person. You assume that you'd be found to be as "small time" as you think you are.

Despite your diligent work to build and maintain a fantasy image of perfection, inner tensions rise. You fall so short of the illusion you've created that you feel there's no use at all in trying to develop whatever real abilities you have. You just aren't worth the effort.

You go even further into contradictions, however. You decide that your self-rejection is a sign of superiority, since you can so easily detect mediocrity in yourself as well as in others. You are envious of other people's accomplishments. You don't realize that they are ordinary people like you who have worked to cultivate "ordinary'" talents. You feel there's something special about them and that their productivity has a magical quality about it. You don't appreciate that what you admire is the product of all those ordinary skills and experiences.

You cannot make any effort, because in insisting on that goal of perfection *you have rejected your effort-producing self.* Anyone knows that this illusory, superior person doesn't have to make any efforts. Obviously, to the extent that you are productive and satisfied in some areas of your existence, the process I'm describing does not pertain.

All concerted efforts to make your fabrication work are unsuccessful, for you are using the foam and wind of an illusion that cannot support the task you've set for yourself. Anger, shame, and guilt are unrelievable as long as an illusory image of perfection is worshiped. Your rage over your failure blinds you to the only possibility for recovery. It blinds you to the solution of your dilemma, which is staring you in the face all the while. You, as you are, can become the primary source of your restoration. You can own all of those ordinary assets and skills, with your intelligence, even with the limits of your experience and sensitivity. Your various health points are adequate to the task of living a decent life. You may despair over your seemingly sparse supply of aids for living. *But whatever you are is all that you have. And that's all that you will need to restore yourself.*

The principle of not insisting on the impossible is the main thing you need to accept. You need to "go with" yourself, with the current of your womanpower *as it actually exists,* and not against it. Going against that current makes the task of living many times more difficult, if not entirely fruitless. Not only is it more sensible to "go with" yourself, it's easier as well. Why make the job so hard?

Will you leave illusion behind you, though? Will you leave self-deception, self-rejection, self-contempt? Will you welcome your true self, an ordinary, limited, abundant, trembling, magnificent, strong woman, and let her save your life, your sanity, your humanity?

She can do it if you let her. That simple, straightforward, not so talented, not brilliant woman can do it because she wants to, because she is you. She has the resources to do it. She'll surprise you with her strength, her tenacity, her grit. She truly doesn't want to live scared the rest of her life. She wants to know a little joy, a little peace, a little fun. She can do it all for you, and she will, if you'll let her.

IV

Why Me?
Psychological Causes
of Anxiety

When conflicting self-images and *should* systems evolve throughout the developmental years, you unconsciously organize your life about them. For some there is a *should* (a rule, a standard) for any and every circumstance. You can identify women who are more effectively ruled by their shoulds because they are more predictable and less spontaneous. They have shoulds for the way they work, speak, dress, behave, feel, and think. Most details of their existence may be influenced by a should.

Shoulds are unconscious, perfectionistic standards that when rigidly held can control your life. Since they are unrealistically demanding, you are bound to fall short of them time and time again. Awareness of that falling short is what initiates feelings of disgust, guilt, self-hatred, and persistent anger.

CONFLICT AS EMOTIONAL POLARITY

Everyone knows that "nice" women shouldn't become angry, at least not according to an unreal image of sweetness and light. When such women do feel angry, however—which they must sometimes—an immediate polarity, or conflict, is generated. The conflict can be pictured in this way:

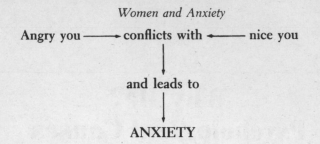

Angry you ⟶ conflicts with ⟵ nice you

and leads to

ANXIETY

The nice you should neither fail nor get angry. And here you are doing both: That's quite unsettling for one who puts such stock in the way she feels she should be. Your fear over how you might behave in your anger sets up sufficient polarity (conflict) in you to result in anxiety. (Please keep in mind that the process I'm describing is largely an unconscious one.)

You can regard unconscious conflict, then, as a condition of *emotional polarity.* Anxiety naturally follows as the outcome of that polarization, the elements of which oppose and repel each other. Since the emotional polarity of unresolved conflict is filtered through your nervous system and biochemical pathways, it is linked to your physical reactions. That's why you can *feel* anxiety in your body, much as you can feel cold, fatigue, or hunger. But since you can't always identify it as such, you may remain unaware of the original polarity that initiated the process. You may call your feeling "restlessness" or "nervousness." But whatever you call it, your body will be registering the effects of unconscious, unresolved conflicts and the anxiety that follows.

Diverse imaginary (that is, unrealistic) expectations of yourself can contrast sharply with real life events. They can also conflict with each other. Let me illustrate the latter point. Suppose you insist on seeing yourself as the most aggressive, competitive, successful businesswoman and also as the most loved person in your office. These two positions are unlikely to coexist and are in effect conflicting expectations. Beyond conflicting with each other, each conflicts with your reality. When real events expose discrepancies that can no longer be ignored, anxiety may become acute. If great or small conflicts are being fired off continuously, anxiety may be produced in an unceasing flow.

The you of reality contains your minor and major limitations and faults, as well as your minor and major strengths, your vitality, fortitude, and resourcefulness (your *health points*). Your imaginary identities contain exaggerations you *think* you must maintain to be acceptable to yourself and to others. Because the real and the fancied images are usually polarized, they are destined to clash each time fact and fiction confront each other, or when the fancy of one pole collides with a discordant fancy of another.

I think you can see the ground we must cover before you understand what drives your conflicts. So how can I beseech you to do what needs to be done to reduce the impact of these clashing poles? How can I convince you that you devalue yourself each time you set up polarities? How can I persuade you that you can learn to accept the true you, the you of reality—the one with the freckles and warts—the one who gets fat and soft—the one who doesn't always want to work, or be pleasant, or stay on a diet, or be smart and witty, or stop drinking, or be cooperative? How can I make you believe that for all the disorder of our world, you—without the impossible perfectionisms you set up—can cherish the goodnesses of the earth and the gifts we can give each other with every smile and greeting?

BASE-LINE NEEDS

One universal base-line need for human beings is for ongoing physical, psychological, and intellectual growth. Growth is a *given* of life, a natural urge. When inhibited for any reason, the resulting physical discomfort and emotional distress can contribute to an unhappy state. Base-line needs are an aid to positive, ongoing relationships. They help to nourish and encourage your given aliveness, your body power, and contribute to general comfort and serenity.

Those needs are few and not especially complex. When firmly established and kept within realistic limits, they go a long way toward preventing anxiety or containing it at tolerable levels, and toward lending some order to your life. They are essential to a person's well-being, before some of the embellishments of life can truly be enjoyed. Three of these base-line items are person, place, and thing:

(1) a *person* toward whom you feel affection; (2) a *place* that belongs to you alone; and (3) an *activity* (thing) to occupy yourself.

One or more people with whom to relate is the prerequisite for a *social network,* a primary human need. Such a person needn't be a sexual partner. I refer here to *any* person—old or young, man, woman, or child—toward whom you can direct a feeling of affection.

One example of what I'm describing is commonly experienced by teachers who enjoy their work, who like and feel affection toward their pupils, even though it may not be returned. A second example concerns a woman who, though comfortable with her work and home, knew no one who "gladdened" her heart each day. Encouraged to visit her family more often, she found that she felt an affectionate response to her small nephews—a feeling that she missed when she returned to the city. So she decided to adopt a kitten to recapture a bit of what she felt she'd left behind.

Other examples are common: parents who can feel great fondness in caring for an unresponsive handicapped child; elderly persons who feel "wonderful" when they become foster grandparents; middle-aged persons who care tenderly for difficult, invalid parents. Expecting nothing in return for their efforts, there is little to impair the warmness of their affection. To deprive them of this work is to deprive them of the opportunity to experience within themselves an ongoing, uninhibited affection.

Perhaps I can clarify this point further by making a distinction between loving (affection directed outward) and being loved (affection directed toward you). In loving, you are the originator of affectionate feelings and you can experience and direct them toward anyone, with or without that person's knowledge or consent. You can enjoy your feelings of fondness without response or participation on the other's part, although it's even more pleasant when those feelings are returned.

In being loved, you stand to receive fond feelings from someone else, but may not experience them yourself. Neither loving nor being loved depends on the other, although either may initiate or enhance the other. Theoretically, you could experience outer-directed affection indefinitely, as long as you're not hurt by the other person.

Whatever its nature, that hurt could stop the outward flow of your warm feelings, even though you might choose to delude yourself that you still felt them. Unless you recovered from the hurt, you could not feel as warmhearted as previously. In effect, you cannot be feeling the kind of affection I'm trying to describe and feel hurt at the same moment. You know this, I think, if you have read the previous chapters. In having incompatible feelings of affection and hurt (e.g., shock, disappointment, anger) toward the same person, you set up conditions for an emotional conflict. Free-flowing affection finds no place in a condition of conflict, where its flow will be temporarily blocked by incompatible feelings.

You can apply what I've just said to the love relationship in a marriage, where hurts are inevitable and cannot coexist with affection in the same moment. If the hurt can be truly overcome, affection can return unimpeded. But when hurts are continuously inflicted, or when too many hurts cannot be let go of and are assiduously filed away into one's grievance bank, the sweet wholesomeness of affection can be adulterated.

Since fond feelings and human happiness depend primarily upon people, the family can be the most reliable and most lasting provider of affection. Unfortunately, it frequently fails to fulfill that role. When the need for affection is not realized within the primary family unit, then someone else must be found to receive the warmth you need and long to experience. But often, families willing and able to love are ignored and rejected. Precious originals are overlooked and hollow facsimiles substituted.

People who cannot, for other reasons, have someone to relate to in this way, may find authentic substitutes. As our example suggested, animals can fulfill this need to some extent. But I want to reemphasize that the specific person or object selected is not so much the issue as is the human necessity to experience this outer-directed quality of caring. Although I've likened it to a necessity, anyone can live without it, but not so contentedly. George Eliot expressed this thought with her words: "Affection is the broadest basis of a good life." Together with physical fitness and laughter, feelings of affection are certainly one of the most effective and natural "medicinals" to help ward off illness and discontent.

"A place of my own" has a familiar ring for the very reason of its importance in the ordering of your life and in being a safe retreat where you can truly rest. It doesn't have to be your own house or apartment. It can be a room in anyone's home. It can be your own corner, cubicle, workshop, office, den, car, town, or special retreat. It has to be someplace, small or large, where you can feel free from the concerns that produce a sense of pressure. Those concerns may include an obligation, a person, a job—anything that requires you to be bothered, alert, on guard, worried, unwillingly involved. I'm talking about a place where you can feel a total sense of relaxation for a period of time.

This is not only rare for some, but even impossible. The time element covers a wide range. You may find a half-hour in your place adequate to recover a relaxed feeling. You might need an entire evening. While you may have to settle for less than complete relaxation, it's imperative to find that *place* where you can achieve whatever degree of relaxation is possible for you.

A case in point was a woman who kept complaining that she always felt unsettled. We both assumed that the feeling was a feature of her general anxious state. She revealed once that she was staying in the apartment of an acquaintance, a traveler who returned to the city at irregular intervals. When he arrived, he expected to have the apartment to himself. She was obliged to be prepared to leave at literally a moment's notice and to find some other accommodation.

The woman finally discovered a place of her own by renting a room in a large apartment where each of several tenants had her own private room. She was able to furnish her "home" as she chose and to come and go freely, without feeling that she might have to pack up and leave any day. She remarked, "I had no idea that a little place of my own could make such a difference in how I feel. I've always had in mind a much larger place, even though I could never afford it. But size really doesn't matter so much."

An activity of your own means something that absorbs and occupies you, something you enjoy. It may be your job, but not necessarily. It can be any kind of hand, head, or body involvement. It can be a hobby or a social or political concern. It can include almost any nondestructive activity, any form of remunerative or volunteer work, any form of play, any form of learning. Whatever it is, however, it must *occupy* your mind or your body—preferably both.

The characteristic that gives this *occupation* a special quality has to do with your response to it. To fulfill its function as a base-line item, it has to arouse your interest sufficiently for you to be more or less consistent in practicing or developing it. This kind of involvement can improve your self-esteem and help you to feel more confident. As long as it isn't destructive, the nature of the activity doesn't matter. It may be plain or outlandish, simple or complex, physical or mental, solitary or social, dull or exciting. What matters is that *you* have selected it, and it's all yours to practice as you wish.

In addition to person, place, and activity requirements, there are other elements that help to maintain an equilibrium between your feelings of emotional comfort and discomfort. They relate loosely to predictability. While predictability can be sought compulsively when anxiety drives you, it is nonetheless a necessary support for natural, social, and personal order and can be considered essential to your comfort.

Among those elements that help place you in your comfort range are *permanence, repetition, order,* and *familiarity* (PROF). You may feel content, for example, when you have bought something that you plan to keep for a time. It may be a sofa, an appliance, or a home. It gives you a sense of comfortable permanence, a feeling of rootedness. Or you may get the same feeling when you acquire a sense of history about your family or the place where you live.

Besides a sense of permanence induced by places or things, there has to be a similar feeling about a person with whom you've chosen to share your life. It's not always present in "living together" arrangements, and its absence accounts for the large number of such couples who eventually opt for the more dependable (not compulsive) permanence of marriage. Yet it cannot be promised by either partner, nor can it be demanded. But as a marital arrangement develops into a family, such permanence can evolve in a natural way.

I have labeled a sense of permanence as a base-line need. Yet some women who have tasted personal liberty balk at the idea. They feel unnecessarily restricted by it. In that case they will do without, and they feel content as long as they fulfill other base-line needs for themselves. They need to decide whether or not they can accept a personal life without a permanent partner. It is a choice many women have made. We shall know in a few years whether they consider their choice a positive or negative one in terms of long-term life satisfaction.

Repetition can also place you in your comfort range. The repeating of certain activities or rituals lends a sense of stability and familiarity to your life. Hearing the same songs, playing the same games, visiting the same places or people, all add to these feelings. Repetition is closely linked to order, another feature in this group.

Although a need for order can create contentiousness among family members, it is essential to a degree, and comforting when you can apply it appropriately and without compulsion as a regular part of your activities. Arguments against order are usually raised by rebellious people who feel emotionally coerced by requests for self-discipline. The need to habitually oppose is a conditioned, unconscious response to a feeling of being imposed upon, even by reasonable requests for cooperation.

A fourth feature essential to a basic sense of comfort is the feeling of familiarity already mentioned. Along with person, place, and activity, here then are four more elements for maintaining your comfort range: permanence, repetition, order, and familiarity. The absence of these elements can lead to discomfort—that is, to a sense of restlessness, uneasiness, and loneliness.

When you feel emotionally uncomfortable, either consciously or unconsciously, you will make efforts to reenter a comfort zone. The movement between comfort and discomfort zones establishes your emotional *comfort/discomfort equilibrium* (CDE). This is a balance between feelings of comfort and discomfort as you respond to the varied stimuli of your environment. There is a constant shifting back and forth across the comfort/discomfort line.

Newness, change, conflict, or extended absence of base-line needs almost invariably brings at least slight discomfort, which is related to the "nervousness," tension, and anxiety already discussed in previous chapters. A degree of repetition and sameness can shift the equilibrium back into the comfort range, as may permanence, reliability, order, or familiarity. Please keep in mind, though, that you need to remain flexible regarding these points, for even the most simple element for comfort may become the goal of a relentless, compulsive search.

Clearly, there is a close relationship between marriage and these base-line items for personal living: person, place, activity (PPA) and permanence, repetition, order, familiarity (PROF). The role that marriage plays in this scenario is a powerful one. Marriage holds out imaginary promises for the fulfillment of your needs for person, place, and activity, as well as PROF as outlined above.

These promises can keep you in the comfort zone of your CDE long before the marriage takes place. But when they are not kept, and they cannot all be kept, you can imagine how easily you may slide into the discomfort zone. I want to remind you that these needs are very often unconscious ones. That is, in contemplating marriage, women and men may not say to each other: You seem to be the best person to give me a comfortable sense of stability and easiness; you can provide me with a person to love, a place of my own, and something to occupy myself. Yet, such expectations may be present nevertheless. And you don't realize that you can fulfill most of these needs yourself, either alone or with a partner. You need not see yourself as a passive recipient of an imaginary promise your partner may never have made.

In other words, you can find within yourself the capacity for loving, for finding your own place and your own occupation. While the results of your efforts may be enhanced by your partner, you cannot expect to have imaginary promises fulfilled. The failure of those promises is what initiates the first disillusionments in marriage. Subsequent failures lead to angry disappointment and, finally, to persistent, sullen outrage.

In a later section of this book you will meet Dorinda, who has reached that point of sullen outrage, and Arora, who is trying to overcome her angry disappointment. They represent young women who went into marriage without thinking through the pros and cons of a long-term relationship. Because they quickly developed unreasonable expectations of their partners, conflict was created very early in their marriages.

THE CONFLICT OCTAGON

Happiness is not a continuum. Nor is suffering, even though it may sometimes seem to you that it is. What can be relentlessly continuous, though, is the intrusive impact of a *should* system on the fragile spontaneity of the personality. A *should* system has the power not only of interrupting free-flowing thoughts and feelings, but also of freezing them before they can fully emerge. From its inception, that impact requires you to be alert to endless, petty stipulations for self-acceptance.

In adulthood much of the impact of your shoulds is kept alive through your own diligent cooperation. Thus some of you need to see that it is your own agreement with prevailing prejudices that erodes your will and your spirit. That agreement strips you of the strength to propel yourself away from age-old distortions into clear, grime-free waters of accurate self-evaluation.

But you need guidelines to make your new evaluations. That's why

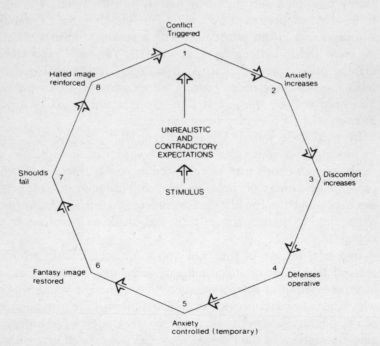

I feel I must urge you repeatedly to involve yourself seriously in the details of a sometimes tedious process of self-discovery. A graphic outline at this point may help you review the highlights of psychic conflict and get a better grip on the processes I've been describing. Think of this diagram as a free-flowing, eight-unit conflict cycle. I call it a *conflict octagon.*

You already know that equal and opposing unconscious forces will produce unresolved, unconscious conflict. These forces may include any contradictory emotional insistences (shoulds), or any shoulds at odds with reality. They can also be described as *polarized emotional reactions.* The expectations of an administrator named Eve illustrate how these forces work.

Eve believes that she is quite cooperative whenever differences arise. She goes to great pains to have others believe it also. At the same time, when there is a difference of opinion she insists upon having her own way—hardly a sign of cooperation. Unaware of the blatant contradictions of her expectations (shoulds), she is frustrated by the failure of those shoulds to place her in the winning position. Briefly outlined, her shoulds include the following points:

1. I *should* always be cooperative.
2. Since I am cooperative, they *should* cooperate with me.
3. I *should* always know best because I am bright and I try harder.
4. Since I know best, I *should* insist upon my position.
5. Because my position is the only reasonable solution, I *should* see to it that they agree with me.
6. They have to let me make the final decision, because they *should* be able to see how suitable it is.
7. There *should* be no question about my reasoning, because it is perfectly good reasoning.

Since Eve is actually not cooperating, and not succeeding in convincing her co-workers of the rightness of her position, she becomes unsettled and begins to doubt herself: *If you were really such a great convincer and so right* (as her shoulds dictate she should be), *you'd be able to get your own way. Since that's not what's happening, you are a real nogoodnik and not worth the space you take!* Eve's doubts continue to grow, because shoulds demand an either/or outcome: Either you're completely successful (in your imagination) or you're all failure. There are no in-betweens.

Because success has eluded her, Eve loathes herself for her "failures." But self-hatred is one of the most agonizing of all human feelings. It punctures an inflated pride and cannot be sustained for long periods of time. And so she falls back on an illusion of success to restore her false pride and save her face. At odds, then, are two strong adversaries: (1) the worshiped self of her perfect fantasy image, which produces the false pride just mentioned, and (2) the hated self of her totally imperfect fantasy-image, which is abandoned by even that insubstantial pride.

I must emphasize that both of these images—perfect and imperfect—are fantasy-images, entirely inconsistent with her reality. She is actually a competent, industrious worker with occasional good ideas. The existence of these illusions is maintained by her should system, which is wrapped in a vulnerable armor of unjustified and flimsy pridefulness.

Success, however unremarkable, ignites that pride and makes her believe she is extraordinary and invincible. Similarly, any failure punctures it immediately and makes her believe she truly belongs "in the pits." In a sense the "successful" should system is always declaring, "I *should* be, therefore I am." Such a sleight of mind is what feeds the pridefulness and arrogance found in such persons.

The person who constructs this system to relieve anxiety rarely lives up to the shoulds (demands) that the imaginary perfect self imposes. Nor does she ever justify the descriptions of ineptness, stupidity, laziness, or insensitivity that are hurled at her by those selfsame inner masters of her emotional destiny. Eve vacillates swiftly between self-hate (agreeing with accusing shoulds) and pridefulness, which she calls upon to combat her self-rejection. The simultaneity of two irreconcilable, opposing factors produces the dilemma of conflict, as well as the necessity to evolve anxiety-relieving measures. This point brings us to Unit 1 of the *conflict octagon*.

Unit 1: Unresolved, unconscious *conflict is triggered* each time the process I've just described is set into motion.

Unit 2: Anxiety increases as a consequence of sustained, unconscious conflict. It may be mild or severe, depending upon the force of the originating self-disgust and the conflict of opposing shoulds.

Unit 3: As anxiety intensifies or is prolonged, *discomfort increases.* It may be vague and diffuse, or may become pinpointed onto specific happenings. When it is extreme, there is great fear of psychic disintegration ("going crazy").

Unit 4: Anxiety and discomfort make *defenses operative* to achieve relief. Unconscious defenses are brought into play, as well as any conscious ones that are available. Those defenses are built around compulsive (choiceless) patterns of thought and behavior, which may or may not be self-destructive. They frequently include overuse of work, play, speech, food, or harmful mind-altering substances in order to achieve the desired relief.

Unit 5: Defenses are designed to control the worst part of your anxiety so that you can feel less uncomfortable. But *anxiety is controlled* only temporarily. Relief is transitory, because other firings of conflict and anxiety may be forming in your emotional network, ready to deliver bolts of discomfort into your system.

Unit 6: If your work to reduce anxiety succeeds (Units 4 and 5), your view of yourself improves. You believe that you are achieving goals set by perfectionistic shoulds and the *fantasy image is restored.*

Unit 7: It doesn't work in any real sense, however. A sense of unworthiness persists, because ultimately your *shoulds fail* to push you to strive for perfect accomplishment. Since you fall terribly short of the demands of your perfect image, its restoration (Unit 6) becomes short-lived. Your shoulds are predestined to fail in a contest with reality and with each other.

Unit 8: That failure of shoulds (conscious or unconscious) has the power to arouse self-disgust, and your *hated self is reinforced.* That, too, is a fantasy image. As I've just explained, you are obliged to counter a hated image with your view of a more desired one, for it is too painful to hate yourself over too long a period of time. In the seesawing back and forth between a demeaning, hated image and what you consider a restorative, desired image, you again subject yourself to the polarity of emotional conflict, where the power of your shoulds drives you to hate and honor yourself at one and the same moment—something that can only end in failure.

Perhaps my attempt to simplify what happens intrapsychically by means of this conflict octagon has made the process more confusing to you. Please don't worry though. This just illustrates how hard it is to organize the many variables of this process all at one time. When you actually get to work on your problem, it's important to work on only one very *small unit* at a time. By dealing with one issue at a time, you'll be able to work much more effectively when you start on the twenty-step program.

ILLUSIONS—IMPOSSIBLE DREAM DYING

In the previous chapter I referred to the construction of an imaginary concept of yourself, which you then try to support as if it were real. Danna, a woman in her forties, is a good case in point. Part of her construction consists of an illusory image of herself as a dependent person who needs someone to take care of her. That image is at some distance from her reality as a responsible, competent person. But in her imagination, she makes an imaginary bargain with a fantasy world of peers: I will be bright and exciting, sensitive, artistic, and creative. I will be one of the interesting, stimulating people of your circle. In exchange *you* (somebody, anybody) will take care of me. You won't let anything really bad happen to me. You won't ever abandon me. You will encourage and support me, because I will represent for you ongoing curiosity and responsiveness.

The fantasy bargain continues: *You*, not I, must be finally responsible for me. You must see to it that I am not hurt. After all, I am a special kind of person. I will do my part in providing the sunlight of emotional living. But you must protect me and see that people do not get in my way, do not hamper my efforts, do not criticize, do not give me any trouble that I have to deal with. You have to protect me from all that, because I cannot do it for myself.

All that has a certain splendiferous ring to it. But it's not real. It may be a lovely dream but it's an impossible one. And it's dying because Danna has begun to sense its lack of substance, its shallow nature. That's why she is terrified and cries, "I just don't know what to do anymore. I think I have to give it all up. Everything. I've always believed that someone would take care of me, that even if there was no one, some magical person wouldn't let me down. But if anyone is going to do it, I have to do it myself. And I'm so scared.

"And I can't. I can't do it. It will kill me first." When she is asked what will kill her, she bursts out with, "Getting well." She continues after a while. "Now that's really crazy. I can live *insane* and survive. But when I feel I might get well, I think I'm going to die.

"I know I'm not really dying. But that doesn't make any difference. It's really the disappointment of discovering that in order to go *sane*, I have to do it all myself. *I* have to make the changes. That's what's killing me. I can't trust anyone, or expect anyone to do anything for me. That's what's dying—my belief that someone else will take care of me. And it's breaking my heart."

Here is a dream that she has been clinging to and insisting on for years. Totally distracting, it's a dream that has destroyed her peace of mind and her ability to plan her life reasonably.

What she longs for is inconsistent with reality. How she sees herself is not an accurate representation of herself. She ignores many of her strengths. Yet she's as demanding, as critical, as limited, as irritable, as anyone can be. It's true that she is talented in her work with handicapped persons. But that doesn't especially set her apart. It doesn't entitle her to any kind of special treatment. She would argue that she doesn't expect anything special, because what she wants doesn't appear special to her. In terms of what she can really expect from her environment, however, those considerations she waits for fall into the realm of the impossible. It simply doesn't matter how reasonable they appear to *her*, because they are inconsistent with her reality.

Like the woman with the alcoholic husband who protests: "I'm a decent, honest, hard-working woman. I really don't deserve such a husband and I shouldn't have one." Of course you would answer, "She doesn't deserve him and shouldn't have him." But there he is, and she needs to deal with the reality of either staying with him or leaving. To expect him to be different, *on the basis that she doesn't deserve him as he is,* is totally illusory and will cause her greater pain than will dealing with the reality of the situation.

In the same way, Danna has been bitterly disappointed throughout her lifetime. A sense of "foul play," of not deserving such a fate, has plagued and distracted her from planning and working toward reasonable goals. She finds herself, then, after all those years of struggle, still without someone to take care of her, and without a clearly demarcated pathway to follow in the future. She is confused that such rightness of purpose could produce such wrongness in practice. As she comes upon these insights, she is thrown into a panic, for her base, largely an illusory one, is shaken. Disconnected from that illusory base, yet not connected with her own true substance, she feels adrift, disgraced, and abandoned.

CONTRADICTORY DEMANDS

The day of her discovery, there seems to be a different quality to her anxiety. Her voice, her words, hold the terror of finality. She feels she has cornered herself. She feels that she has no place else to go. She keeps repeating that she has to "go sane" all by herself. The indignity of it! No one is going to do it for her. She continues: "I make a big thing about everything I do. There are no halfways. If I believe I'm supposed to do something, and I don't make it, it's as if nothing I ever did or will do is of any importance. Each time, I feel as if my very existence is on the line. No matter if it's talking with my supervisor, going to a party, even buying a new dress.

"Everything is terrifying for me. I do things and people think I'm pretty well put together. They don't know what I feel all the time. I can be talking about nothing, and I can be sweating and on the verge of tears. One day I was walking in the park and the tears were flowing down my face. Can you imagine that? Bawling in the park? Have you ever heard of that?"

In talking about going sane, Danna is talking about taking responsibility for herself. There are so many contradictions, however. While she desperately demands that someone look after her, she doesn't permit anyone to do so. That would point to her "weakness," and she has only contempt for that. She will fight her family if they try to give her support, because they remind her of a hated neediness.

She wants to be strong yet doesn't believe she can. You can see what a bind she's in. She demands that *you* take care of her and at the same time that *she* take care of herself. But she's really afraid to try that. So while demanding something for herself, she can't let herself have it because she feels so weak. She feels utterly blocked. The outcome is a furious self-contempt for her fear, hesitation, and lack of control.

Danna's contradictions lead her to view everything in extremes. You remember that she says, "There are no halfways." If there were shades of gray for Danna, she would see that dependence and independence can live very comfortably side by side, for we are all dependent and independent in different ways and at different times. She would see that it's fine to be able to take care of yourself sometimes, and to be taken care of at other times.

Danna has no understanding that living is not anxiety-free, not all one or all another, but a blend of many factors, constantly sifted and selected for relevance and suitability to one's feelings and circumstances at any given time. Her tenacious clinging to contradictions produces the *sticking point* that exasperates so many therapists, patients, and their families.

Repeatedly, insight seems to have been reached. It seems clear that the demands she makes on herself must be relinquished if a bitter and constantly generated sense of self-rejection is ever to be overcome. Danna knows this; she has said it many times. Yet the insight slips away. In hundreds of ways the contradictions persist. They intrude as if they had a will to defeat her. A frustrating point, it is nevertheless one that can be approached with the thought: *I* have produced this belief; *I* have kept it alive; therefore *I* can change it.

DREAMS AND REALITY

Understanding is obviously not enough. But it can be a first step, the beginning of a process of self-healing. Comprehension in one swift flash of truth might serve to help you make that beginning. It might help you to gradually relinquish wanting something that has always been an impossibility from the very onset. Contradictory demands must go in order for you to become a whole person. You need to admit that they are not essential to your survival.

A woman came to that point when she was able to write to her husband of many years: "I had a dream in you when I married you. At first, I kept it alive through my own blindness. Then I was disillusioned when I realized you wouldn't, couldn't, fulfill that dream. I was angry with you, feeling you had let me down, fooled me, tricked me into believing you were all that great. Yes, you wanted to believe the dream too. You liked it too. But I was the one who insisted on keeping it. I was the one who kept waiting for it to come true. My glory was to come through you, not through my own efforts.

"And when I saw the dream become ashes, I felt you had killed something in me. I was angry with you for years, for killing *my* dream, for depriving me of *my* glory. But finally, I gave it up. And I wasn't angry any more. I found I could attend to my own concerns without waiting for you, without looking for your approval, even without consulting you.

"I thought: this is what independence is. It's no tremendous thing. It's just thinking for myself, deciding for myself, doing for myself in matters which don't concern you, and in which you really have little interest, if any. I can still live with you, like you, enjoy some things with you, have you for my best friend. But you aren't my shining light, against which I was compelled to batter my frail moth's wings. No. I'm no moth now. My wings are not frail, and I think that I've earned them.

"It's strange, too, how you have become stronger in my eyes, now that I feel stronger, more certain, myself. I see how easy and how hard it is to be strong, how much it takes, and sometimes how little. You don't get it for nothing. I used to think you—all men—were just strong—period! But it takes doing. Women have been strong in their own bailiwick. But when they want to move out of it, they have to learn how to be strong in other ways. That's the meaning of independence. To have the courage to move, to be able to look after yourself, to be able to make the decision to live and let live, to be more of a whole person."

Deeply embedded in nearly all women is the ultimate desire to survive freely, without the total dependence to which a newborn babe is subject. Yet that wish cannot be supported if you cling to dependence out of fear.

In general terms it can be said that Danna's insight reflects the deepest conflict anyone can have. *And that is the basic conflict between health and illness: between a will to survive as a whole person and the insistence on remaining helpless and dependent; between flexible acceptance of limitations and rigid adherence to an imaginary, controlling status quo; between realistic responsibility for self and a perpetual, hollow search for an illusory freedom.*

As long as false beliefs in fantasy and an ever-present human drive for wholeness hold equal precedence, conflict will burn fiercely. Clearly, women have to give up certain self-deceiving beliefs and learn to use available resources to strengthen that side of the conflict which holds the promise of a decent life. When they can permit the supportive elements of their womanpower to be used for their own advancement, they will have embarked upon a voyage of recovery and growth.

Why Us?
Changing Roles
and Anxiety

When we speak of women in transition, we speak of an ongoing process of change, of a passage from one place to another. Today's young woman has lived and breathed that transition for most of her life. Having lived her adolescence through the conflict-ridden sixties, even now she may not yet have succeeded in making a wholehearted transition to the new attitudes she professes to admire and follow.

WOMEN IN TRANSITION

As a "new woman," she would be hurt if someone called her traditional. Yet, for all her newness and striving for her rights, she still has strong, unconscious ties to women's traditional thinking and values. Such women, therefore, in a process of transition, have not yet found their places. Nor can they find them until they can decide where, what, and who they are at any given time. In trying to be a new woman in all respects, they are trying to actualize a new fantasy of perfection. But there are many among them who still embrace much of the old and reject much of the new. Such a combination is possible only if you know very clearly what you are doing in choosing to combine elements of old and new.

Let's say, for example, that you want to remain a "nice," traditional woman with husband and children—cooking, homemaking, and the like—yet be a new, more assertive woman with your in-laws. You may want to remain compliant or passive in certain social encounters and yet become a leader in others. You may prefer to remain in a secure, pensioned government position, yet look for independent employment when you retire. Differing and opposing goals become incompatible *only when you try to do both at once.*

That leads to inevitable failure, and finally to deep guilt that you can't perform as you think you should. Such guilt exhausts you because you tend not to recognize or dissipate your anger, one component of guilt. Undischarged anger leads to physical tension. The work your body must do to maintain that tension leads to fatigue. Thus can guilt lead to your occasional bouts of unexplained exhaustion.

Remember how women have been cushioned in a cradle of dependency? Remember how they have been molded to fulfill their special "duties"? Even well-informed college women are still dealing with the old shoulds. They despise them, but their ready guilt points to a continuing conflict with them. This is one feature that has made a transition so difficult for certain women.

While contending with old shoulds, they have new ones to contend with as well. Influenced by their peers and by other social pressures, they feel pushed in opposing directions by new images and new demands. They feel that they're expected to rush to accept any change, to go from being dependent "little girls" to responsible women overnight, with all the desires, needs, and opportunities such women might have.

Changing sexual expectations also impose added pressures on women. Some feel obliged to be "willing" under given conditions. Others have been so stimulated by new sexual practices that they are distracted by a need to seek a habitual "fix" for their new "addiction." Used for ancillary purposes, sex becomes a reliever of boredom or a tranquilizer for restlessness.

When they are ready to earn a living, many women of all ages expect their work to be interesting and challenging. Some haven't learned that little work can be described that way, for much of it is routine. They feel they shouldn't accept "boring or menial" work, even though it may be the only work at hand. They talk about their "training" but overlook the need for experience. They cannot accept that there just aren't enough "suitable" or "desirable" jobs to go around; that they are in a sense overqualified for available work; that working doesn't necessarily provide you with a stimulating few hours a day; that it means primarily what it has always meant—having an income to pay for room, board, and other necessities. One talented young woman "had" to go on welfare rather than be "forced" to work at something that didn't require her talents!

As they reap their share of failure and disappointment, women are outraged that a diploma guarantees nothing; that the promises they heard, or imagined they heard, are so flimsy in practice; that it isn't difficult to become an unemployment statistic, even in this land of plenty. They feel abused and discriminated against.

EXAGGERATIONS OF TRANSITION

Some women have been overly influenced by exaggerations made by extremists. They have been swept up by a vocabulary, by an energy, by a drama. But they have not grasped the nature of real change. They have compulsively embraced popular terms and ideas. They often find themselves confused, anxious, and at odds with others—even with their more perceptive peers, who seem to understand that compulsiveness immediately deprives an idea or deed of the element of choicefulness, which is the cornerstone of the change we are discussing here.

Another example of unsound, exaggerated response to transition occurs in certain small groupings of those who are irrationally rebellious members of varying social units. They seem to have lost the ability to differentiate between liberty and license, reason and unthinking passion. They feel maliciously coerced by anyone outside of their group, and by real needs for cooperation or accommodation to the law.

In their pursuit of what they consider their rightful liberties, they have lost touch with the elements of common civility and common sense. It seems at times that they feel righteously entitled to repetitious outbursts of indignation, poor manners, and even vicious disregard for their fellows. They no longer fulfill the basic requirements of social intercourse. Yet they expect and demand all the rights and privileges of the very society they profess to despise.

Though they wave the banner of freedom, this group is a sad one. Their failure to make themselves heard and accepted feeds their self-hatred. Hostility, tension, and anxiety levels are unusually high. At times they resort to inner- or outer-directed violence as a temporary relief from the extraordinary tensions their new life-patterns have imposed upon them.

They insist that their extreme actions are on behalf of freedom. They insist that they have chosen their course freely and with satisfaction. If that were so, it would seem that they would be more at peace with themselves, and working sincerely to better their world rather than tear it apart. Confusing their woeful personal rebellions with grander purposes, they are petulant, suspicious, erratic, undermining, hurtful, and torn by conflict. Flagrant disregard for others, boorishness, and disruptiveness divide them from their roots. Yet they are unable to fully reject those roots and cut themselves off from what they say they hate and wish to overthrow.

The new image they hold forth is not a lovable one, for there is much that is wanting in it. A compulsive, irrational, persistent rebelliousness doesn't permit this group to be selective, to choose how much they'll keep of the old and how much they'll discard. Just like the traditional perfectionistic woman driven by the compulsive shoulds of her self-image, this group, too, is driven by its parcel of shoulds: independent action no matter whom it hurts; self-sufficiency at all costs; loyalty only to group members and a leader; indifference to ordinary human needs and wants.

That self-image, too, is in its own way perfectionistic. It is no less a taskmaster than any other. It leaves no room for anything but a distorted and compulsive rebelliousness, in which goals frequently are subverted to illogical, irrational, and self-destructive behavior. Self-constructed bonds compel members of this group to act out the antithesis of the very freedom they so desperately crave.

A group that operates on the basis of all or nothing, it rebels against most social values. In so doing, its members regularly rebel against that part of themselves which still wants to live among the acceptable, still wants to be loved and taken into a supporting circle. They rail against the rejection they have heaped upon themselves. And so they are wasted on a battleground of their own making, in a conflict that will resolve nothing and finally prove their undoing.

TRADITIONAL WOMAN

Not all women seek to leave old life-patterns behind them. There are indefinite numbers of traditional "old fashioned" women who prefer to live their lives as they always have. These are the women who have been raised in the tradition of the "good, obedient girl" at home, at school, and in marriage and motherhood. Her age doesn't identify her, for she is found in all age-groups. What identifies her are her attitudes—the same attitudes that surrounded her as a youngster are the attitudes she holds today. Perhaps surprisingly, she is still among us in large numbers, even among women in their twenties or early thirties. Seemingly disinterested in change, she is nevertheless buffeted by changing roles on every side.

Although she insists upon keeping her familiar role, she cannot fully resist the changes she observes about her, and enters a transitional position willy-nilly. How different is she, then, from her mother? Is she still striving to maintain that old self-image of traditional perfection with which you are familiar? What motivates her? Has she made a choice about her style of living, or is it simply one she has drifted into?

As I describe characteristics of traditional women, you might feel that they form a stereotype, a caricature. And you will be partly right, for in their extreme forms they do. Though individually these women may not relate to all aspects of that stereotype, collectively they do uphold and live by those features, either consciously or by keeping them tucked away in a corner of their unconscious minds. In this section I shall be referring mainly to the traditional woman who is compulsively bound to her traditions, rather than the one who is free to change if she so chooses. Here are the criteria that traditional women try to fulfill *to some extent.* Check those that relate to you.

1. Depends on someone else for her primary sense of security.
2. Tries to please at all times.

3. Tries to avoid all arguments.
4. Needs external approval to maintain a sense of worth.
5. Tries to maintain harmony at all costs.
6. Cannot express anger easily, if at all.
7. Can be extremely skilled and competent, but tends to discredit herself.
8. Feelings of guilt are quickly and often aroused.
9. Is quick to assume blame.
10. Is other-centered.
11. Expresses opinions apologetically.
12. Places her own needs second to those of family and others.
13. Is nonassertive in many respects.
14. Can meet many of her own needs only covertly and deviously.
15. Hesitates to accept leadership roles, but will work behind the scenes.

If you feel that five or more of these apply to you, you have definite characteristics of the traditional woman.

Please bear in mind that some of these characteristics may be highly desirable in certain contexts and to certain degrees. But in extreme forms they can be harmful, leaving little opportunity for independent thought or action. For some women, decisions regarding behavior and life-style have been made years before and are not negotiable.

However firmly rooted they are, though, every one of these points can be shaken in a transitional period by the changed attitudes that so many women have acquired. Let's take three of them and see how a more liberated view can create divisiveness.

1. Female dependency is a thing of the past. You must learn to depend on yourself for your own sense of security. You are a namby-pamby if you still wait for some man to take care of you.

2. Never mind about trying to be so nice. Throw your weight around. You can argue if you want to. You can tell people off if they put you down. It's your right to feel angry and to say it.

3. You don't need anyone else to decide what you're worth. Only you can do that.

You can easily see how changing roles can make a woman feel guilty on many counts. For example, she still holds traditional views and thinks she shouldn't. She can't hold on to the new attitudes, yet she thinks she should. Back and forth it goes, rendering even the solidly traditional woman subject to the anxiety of transition.

One of these "solid" traditional women is Leada, who sees herself as a warm, supporting, nurturing person. She often defers to her family to the point of self-effacement. Bored by absence of peer companionship and a lack of stimulation or opportunity, she nonetheless feels that her primary duty is to her family. That sense of duty makes her more homebound than she wants or even needs to be. But she willingly suffers that deprivation, overlooking her resentment over having so little time for herself. Hard-working, she doesn't feel productive, creative, or even useful.

Another woman, Helga, talented in undermining her self-confidence, abilities, pleasures, and satisfactions, constantly humiliates and deprecates herself as a person. Deferring to parents, employer, spouse, children, and relatives, she habitually places herself in a secondary role. She doesn't even know when she's tired. While she holds most of the responsibility for the physical and emotional well-being of her family, she takes little credit for it, frequently feeling unworthy to make the decisions relating to that responsibility.

With few ways of expressing her needs, Helga feels guilty if she becomes aware that she wants something other than what she has. Feeling she has no right to make demands, she takes comfort in her pride that she makes so few of them. She can keep herself relatively anxiety free by remaining unaware of the most modest needs for rest, attention, recreation, or privacy.

Like Helga, the compulsive traditional woman feels she has neither reason nor right to feel anger or to assert herself. Unassertiveness is her style, because she has learned and accepted that only "bitchy" women are assertive. Living in this decade, she seems to be on another planet. For her the image of a "good" woman is one who is kind, undemanding, gracious, attractive, soft-spoken, poised, attentive, loving, patient, loyal, honest, faithful, obedient, and inoffensive; assertive women are offensive. "Nice" women are dependent; they let someone else take charge of their lives. They remain primarily other-centered and look after others very efficiently. They are either unaccustomed to or afraid of looking after themselves openly and proudly. It is true that they are beginning to learn to move away from their early teachings. But they are still bound by old attitudes and clichés.

You may feel that I'm exaggerating with these descriptions. You may be thinking that this woman was part of your mother's time and that she is no longer among us. I've already indicated, however, that while no one woman would practice all the patterns I've suggested, there are still those who fulfill many of the criteria and are alive and well in our midst. They live in cities, in suburbs, and in rural areas. They are single and married. They are rich and poor. In my own experience, and in widespread locations, over fifty percent of the women I've worked or talked with correspond to this picture in many of the ways I've described.

In trying to adhere to a certain image of womanliness, these women perpetuate their bondage to a myth. Physical, emotional, and intellectual development must be compatible with that myth or they feel they are not fulfilling their purpose in life. To be out of sync with that purpose is to experience anxiety.

Please understand that I am not deprecating all the qualities I've discussed. There is nothing wrong with most of them—it would be a fine world indeed if we were all patient, loving, and considerate. I am only pointing out that strict, compulsive adherence to such personal expectations leaves no room for the less perfect human characteristics with which we are all so well endowed.

In other words, no one can or does practice these virtues all the time. That would be impossible. One can't be a living saint—as even the traditional woman would admit. That's why the self-deception is a subtle one. Consciously, she accepts the fact that we're "sinners" on occasion, as well as sinless. But in her most secret fantasy (secret even from herself), perfect sinlessness is what the compulsively driven traditional woman is after. That is the image she's trying to uphold. She won't be satisfied with occasional pursuit of her fantasy. She insists on achieving it at all times. This total insistence is what forges her bonds and keeps them in good repair.

While she may be unaware of this insistence, the product of such bondage is still anxiety, for she would indeed be superhuman if she failed to resent and resist it in some way. Yet she can't admit to this resentment, since that would immediately conflict with the self-image she is trying to support. Striving to see herself only as this perfect woman, she becomes anxious when discrepancies arise. For example, if you demand of yourself strict deference, tolerance, and kindness toward those you love, what do you do when you find that you're occasionally impatient, intolerant, unkind? What can you do with feelings of anger, frustration, envy, competitiveness, ambition, aggression—with wishes for control, power, or public success?

To accept yourself only on a restricted basis forces you to reject yourself whenever you fail to measure up to your standards. You feel guilty over your failures and hate yourself for your "shortcomings." That hatred can become continuous if you're an ordinary person with equal portions of weakness and strength, goodness and badness.

PERFECTIONISTIC WOMAN

Perfectionism is often confused with a wholehearted wish to accomplish something as perfectly as possible. If you have such a goal and can succeed in it, you are in the position to enjoy your success. If you fail, you can say, "Well, I did my best!"—and turn your attentions elsewhere.

But the perfectionist, as a compulsive striver, can do no such thing. She nags herself for her failures. She is a cruel taskmaster and allows herself no relief from self-condemnation. The perfectionist has no freedom to win *or* lose; the failure to be perfect, according to individually established criteria, is an irrevocable indictment, a mark of poor character and even stupidity. Anxiety follows, an unrealistic fear that imagined inadequacies will be exposed to the world. That fear leads to much of the withdrawal, loneliness, and depression with which we are all surrounded.

I am making a distinction between the person who strives for and can enjoy a perfect or near-perfect result—when it can be achieved —and the compulsive perfectionist who *insists* on a perfect outcome with every move, even if she has to imagine that perfection. Although usually well defended against failure, she is furious with herself when it becomes clear that she is far from her mark.

Even a nonperfectionist may be sharply disappointed or angry with herself when she fails at something on which she's worked. You'll find yourself in that position from time to time. But after expressing your feelings, after trying to salvage what you've done and evaluate your errors, you can finally let go and pursue something else. The perfectionist cannot let go. She can't stop worrying about her errors and obsessing over her failures: I should have done that; I shouldn't have said that; I should have been more ready; I shouldn't have left so early.

With her uncompromising self-image, a perfectionist encloses her mind in an emotional straitjacket of impossible beliefs. She does that just as surely as she immobilized her figure in the whalebone corsets of yesteryear. Then at least she could remove herself from her bondage at the end of each day. But her mental, emotional straitjacket remains fixed, until she recognizes that *she* keeps it there with her insistent, neurotic pridefulness, and makes the wrenching decision to pry herself loose.

COMPULSIVE OR SELECTIVE SPONTANEITY

Because she is so occupied in the pursuit of her standards, there is little or no opportunity for this woman to experience any flow of spontaneous feeling or action. Predictability is the hallmark of the perfectionist, and she sees spontaneous reactions as unpredictable and therefore unacceptable.

Spontaneity is defined as something that is "done or produced *freely, naturally,* and without constraint or external force." It's seen as unstudied, uncontaminated expression. Implications of naturalness and freedom are its most appealing elements. Yet any concept can be carried to extremes, however positive and health-connoting its reputation. Even an idea that epitomizes the natural can join the ranks of the compulsive.

A woman named Jerri provides an example. "I've just got to do it because I feel it," she says, explaining her compulsive, self-defeating "spontaneous" actions. She is "hooked" onto her idea of spontaneity, which states (for her) that spontaneous action is "where the action is," and that's for her. She's made an idol out of this idea. In a sense she's extolling choicelessness. That's where she's "at" when she feels she has to be "spontaneous." The term enters her lexicon as a should: By all means—*always*—indulge your spontaneity.

If Jerri feels *compelled* to express herself freely and without constraint on any and every occasion, in her own way she's clearly become as extreme as the tradition-bound perfectionist. She, too, deprives herself of the freedom to choose her behavior. She is controlled by her supposedly spontaneous feelings, rather than controlling those feelings in cooperation with her body, mind, and social needs.

Ilene, a woman in her early twenties, has begun to consider the merits of *selective spontaneity,* of deciding for herself whether or not to act on her spontaneous feelings. She's beginning to move from thoughtless, choiceless behavior to less damaging choices. "It really isn't all that hard to give it a second or two to decide if that's what you want to do," she says with some surprise. "I've discovered that it's stupidly self-indulgent to think I should just blab everything that pops into my head."

As Ilene has discovered, the particulars of a given situation should help you decide whether or not to give your spontaneity free rein. You don't have to every time. Ilene has learned that there's no inviolable rule stating that an impromptu thought or feeling must be immediately expressed. Because spontaneous feelings and thoughts are so nourishing, they make important contributions to your pleasure. And while it's fun to express yourself easily and unhesitatingly, it's not an *absolute* prerequisite for well-being. This diagram illustrates the difference between compulsive and selective (i.e., choiceful) spontaneity.

Compulsive Spontaneity ⟶ Spontaneous feeling or thought

ACTION

Selective Spontaneity ⟶ Spontaneous feeling or thought

Selective process: Decision to act or not

ACTION OR INHIBITION

Young women often have a problem with the concept of selective spontaneity because of the simple requirement to use judgment in deciding which thoughts or desires will be broadcast "live." Having to make that decision causes them to feel emotionally coerced. And they resist the idea of selection, becoming anxious and defensive because they are actually divided within themselves as to its merits.

MIDDLE-AGE TRANSITION

Middle-aged women, more habitually inhibited, do not have the same reaction. Their sources of anxiety and depression relate to other sets of conflicting preconceptions. There is the over-forty woman who is made anxious by the feeling that she *must* change, even though she feels no real desire to do so. This is the woman, too, who never wanted to "rock the boat," never held strong opinions, always said she was content.

It was assumed that a woman could feel complete through the love of a "good man," and a secure home. It's true that this *can* be enough for countless women. But for others, it just doesn't make for an entire existence, no more than is a man's entire existence with home and family. Some women need an occupation totally unrelated to family.

Perhaps you feel that I'm suggesting that all housewives are dissatisfied and unhappy. Not at all. Those who regard their work in the home as their primary choice can certainly feel content. They've been able to find innumerable opportunities for solid productiveness and creativity in the home. They can experience their work as both duty *and* choice.

This may be difficult for you to understand. But it emphasizes what I shall be repeating many times. It is not the specific activity that determines choicefulness, but the feeling and attitude with which a course of action is taken. That's why today's woman must determine her own course of action, one dictated neither by traditional demands nor by those of her modern sisters. She runs the risk of being just as bound as previously, if she follows the crowd's lead and opts for career, or singleness, or whatever, just because it happens to be the current fad.

Choice entails knowing what it is you want for yourself, within the limits of the society in which you have chosen to live. Then you need to decide whether or not you are willing to make the necessary efforts to move toward your goal. You see once more that the content of your choice is not the determining factor for choicefulness. That factor is the freedom with which any content is selected and the thoughtfulness of your selection.

In considering new content, however, you must beware of establishing another perfectionistic image with different rules as specious in their own extremes as the old ones. That could be the case, for example, with some women who will follow any interesting leader, and who will change allegiance to ideas as easily as they change fashions. For them, the new might be just a substitution of one stereotype for another: This is what I *should* have been as an old-fashioned girl; now my peers tell me I *shouldn't* be that person any longer; they tell me that I *should* be this new woman.

Can such a replacement be superior to the old? Perhaps. But you need to learn to distinguish between fact and fantasy, between what is sound and relevant for you and what is a silly fad. To change merely the outer robes of your inner dictator doesn't free you in any way. In doing that, you can still remain choiceless and without autonomy, no matter how many "meaningful" phrases you utter, "meaningful" activities you undertake, or "meaningful" relationships you endure. Merely speaking the language of new clichés doesn't make you autonomous.

Jernine was one woman who thought this changing of roles might spare her the contempt of other women. In exasperation she said, "I really don't care to go out to earn money though. I'm needed at home and I like doing my job there. But I feel ashamed of that. Yet I'm sick and tired of people, especially certain women, looking at me in contempt when I say I'm a housewife. That 'Oh' they come out with is just awful."

Jernine feels "put down" by the "Oh" because she supports the implied derogation. She too is a product of that attitude. She too is *emotionally habituated* to putting herself down for being "just a housewife." If she were not agreeing with the subtleties of that "Oh," she would not feel it is "awful." She might think it merely a rude or dull response.

You need to accept that in years past, and still today, women have *chosen* to make a career out of marriage and homemaking, a career with numerous in-dwelling rewards. Perhaps a more pertinent title for such a career in the eighties could be that of *domestic engineer.* Certainly a great deal of time is spent on engineering personal and functional family programs. It includes the conceiving, planning, and executing of countless domestic programs in response to the needs of all family members. In some way it touches nearly all family activities and relationships.

The woman who will concede the importance and extent of her work can feel a wholesome pride in it. She need not reproach herself, nor feel embarrassed when asked "What do you do?" Her response, "Domestic engineer," may startle initially.

If pressed, she can learn to summarize her job description. And summarize she must, for she cannot go into detail about the requirements, obligations, challenges, problems, diversities, responsibilities, and accomplishments of her work. Any business or professional woman would probably have an easier time in describing work which might be far less demanding on a daily basis, and actually contribute less to the consistent well-being of any collection of people. Your own respect for whatever you do usually sets the tone for others' attitudes toward you.

With the many facets—economic, social, educational, developmental—of the homemaker's work, the question is not really one of deciding if homemaking, or domestic engineering, is a worthy career. It is rather one of deciding how you feel about that career as only one of the central foci for your life. It is deciding if and how you can alter your job description, as intrinsic and extrinsic aspects of the work change, grow, or become obsolete. It is determining that your entire self-identity does not depend upon that career alone, but upon the varied attributes of your womanhood, apart from wife and mother. Domestic engineering can be as boring or as stimulating, then, as any other career you might choose, depending upon how you choose to be and become.

Please don't think that middle age doesn't leave you time for a long transitional period of development. You have a great deal of time as long as you keep yourself physically fit. Just think, if you are forty or fifty years old, you still have some thirty years to learn something in depth, to undertake any number of leisure activities, to prepare for a new occupation, to find new companions. With a few not insignificant exceptions, you can do most of the things you've done in the first part of your life. But you can do them far better, because you have so much more experience and wisdom! Keep this in mind when you feel stiff and a little crotchety. There's still a great deal of time!

OTHER ANXIETIES OF CHANGING ROLES

The instability of marriage, home, and family has deprived many of you of an important support network. You hardly recognize that, though, since you're so busy hanging onto the life you think you should be making for yourself. Too often it isn't one that's compatible with your needs or one that you're enjoying. But you hang in there and try to juggle job, home, sex, children, and social life in ways that overtax your stamina and energy. For relief, you may resort to overeating, heavy drinking, or drugs, quickly finding that these do little to maintain your equilibrium.

And you're likely to remain anxious, because you're not resolving the conflicts you have about the transitions you've made or think you've made. You're anxious because you're losing faith in your ability to manage an unnecessarily complicated life. You're anxious because your self-esteem is being corroded, and you can't tolerate the specter of dependency, irresponsibility, poor judgment, and compulsive self-centeredness. You're anxious as you begin to realize that frenetic posturings of independence are just that—that you're as unprepared as ever to take charge.

But take heart! To feel the pain of disappointment without being devastated is to begin to approach a true understanding of what you have to do for yourself. If you're at this point, you've already taken a large step in the direction you want to go. You've learned that empty-headed acceptance, rhetoric, literature, or even legislation don't make a strong, first-class person from a dependent, second-class woman. Only your dedication and the sustained efforts of mind and body will effect that transition, a process that has no end.

You need not feel ashamed, angry, or guilty over your failure to change very much up to this point. You need only to evaluate yourself as you now stand. Evaluate your patchy, wobbly, too-quickly-accepted new attitudes and standards. See which are worth keeping and developing and which are not fit matter for your tender concern. Don't hesitate to discard the latter.

And don't waste time on too many doubts. Don't let your ambition make you anxious, for it's quite acceptable. If you think a job you want is worth a certain salary, ask for it, even though you wouldn't have dreamed of doing so at an earlier time in your life. Don't resist a reasonable expansion of goals. Don't resist a vision that you feel is all right for someone else. If someone else can, perhaps you can, too. While significant transitions move slowly as a rule, you have time now for much of what you want. You will be surprised at how well you'll move once you get started, once you decide to harness that full one womanpower to whatever task you set for yourself.

VI

Anxiety in Marriage and Other Troubles

While there has been great anxiety over the "death" of marriage and the family, there still seems to be considerable and continuing interest in these life arrangements. True, there have been tremendous turn-overs in marital partners and family units. Figures on divorce are impressive. They have reached the 50 percent mark in some communities and hover between 25 percent and 40 percent in others. Just as impressive, though, are statistics revealing that some 50 percent of divorced women remarry within two years. Divorce seems almost like a new social imperative as a solution for unhappiness. Yet marriage is still a strong factor in the *ongoing personal comfort* of millions of people.

Troubled marriages are nothing new, even though divorce rates have been lower in the past. The principal differences in attitudes toward marriage relate to the financial, psychosocial, and medical developments of the past two decades. Women now feel they have greater autonomy when it comes to employment opportunities, child-bearing decisions, and life-style choices. Greater social acceptance (although not as great as you might suppose) has given even timid and dependent women the courage to decide to keep a marriage, break it, or remain single.

Never a paradise, a marital arrangement can nonetheless fulfill countless prerequisites for comfort and security. Though unlikely in many instances, it might even provide something of what a woman writer expressed over one hundred years ago when she wrote: "Oh the comfort, the inexpressible comfort, of feeling safe with a person, having neither to weigh thoughts nor measure words, but pouring them all right out, just as they are, chaff and grain together; certain that a faithful hand will take and sift them, keeping what is worth keeping and then, with the breath of kindness, blow the rest away."

This serenity has been markedly absent in the two young women described below. But you will note how Arora, with the help of her partner, seems to have begun a climb away from almost total frustration to a growing maturity. Dorinda, on the other hand, is still wedged into a rut of insistences that her husband *should* behave in certain ways and *should* have many qualities she believes he lacks.

MARRIAGE DISSATISFACTION

Dorinda, a woman in her twenties, is the mother of two. Her daily complaints point to her expectations of her husband and her disappointment in him, as well as in herself. "He doesn't always wash the dishes when it's his turn," she complains. "He comes home and sits, says he's tired. We never have any fun anymore the way we used to. I don't think he's a good father or a good husband. I always have to tell him to play with the children, or take them out. His excuse is that he has no time because he works two jobs to give me the things I want."

Dorinda is asked if he restrains her in any way regarding her free time outside the home. Can she have a baby-sitter if she wants to go visiting without her children? Can she take a course? Get a job? "Oh, he doesn't care what I do," she replies. "Yes, I have money for baby-sitting. And I can come and go pretty much as I please. But he doesn't talk with me. He doesn't support me emotionally. We don't communicate anymore."

She is asked if they communicated any better before they were married. Her face lights up. "Yes. When we were together, we were always talking about something. I'd worry about my courses. I didn't really have to. I'd complain about the teachers, or the assignments, or the schedule, or my parents. He'd sympathize, and hold me, and tell me not to worry, that everything would be all right. He seemed so strong to me. He didn't have any trouble with his work. I was his only concern. He once said that he was happy when I was happy. But he's not interested in me anymore. I accuse him of not wanting to listen to me. He denies it, says he's tired. I can't imagine how he can be so tired and yet work so hard all the time. If he's really tired, then he shouldn't work, so we'll have more time together."

Dorinda's last remark is evidence that she expects her marital relationship to be her *occupation.* This is precisely what so many women have done, and precisely why they have been disappointed. They believe they must build their lives *only* around their families, and it doesn't occur to them that they can't use another person to provide that need for occupation I've described.

I don't want to draw an impossible picture of Dorinda. She has many abilities and likable qualities, even though they get lost in a maze of dependent poutings. Nevertheless, she represents a large number of young women whose expectancies, based on what they believe they were promised throughout their adolescence, bear little relationship to actualities.

Dorinda is angry because her self-produced, imaginary beliefs of a "good life" have not come to pass. Life has disappointed her. Her unconscious marriage bargains are far from being kept, and she is angry with her husband. (My concept of *marriage anger* is described in detail in *The Book of Hope.*) She is angry with herself also for "settling" for marriage and a family; with her children for being average, ordinary children; with conditions in general. It is a vague, diffuse dissatisfaction that she feels, and she looks for reasons to justify her discontent. Although her husband doesn't criticize her, Dorinda feels that he finds fault with her. "He doesn't like me anymore. He thinks I don't do enough. I'm not cheerful and helpful to him." Dorinda's base-line needs are being only partially met. She has permanence, repetition, order, and familiarity; but she reads all this as boredom, because she has not used them as a base line on which to build a life that satisfies her. It is her own special occupation that she is most clearly lacking.

Dorinda's belief system is scrambled about by contradictions not apparent to her. She wants certain material comforts, which requires her young husband to work at two jobs. He seems willing to do that, but his willingness may be a way of getting away from her nagging. It may also be related to his guilt that he's not doing a good job with his family. These factors propel him into the discomfort range of his comfort/discomfort equilibrium. Working, remaining silent, and watching TV may be his ways of trying to shift back into the comfort zone of the CDE.

She also wants him to give time that may not be his to give. She doesn't realize that any leisure time he keeps for himself is an emotional necessity. Furthermore, Dorinda has no awareness that she projects onto him her own feelings of disappointment in herself. He hasn't criticized her attitudes toward him, but she speaks as if he has. Unable to tolerate what she feels are her own deficiencies, she looks for relief by blaming him for his treatment of her. In fact it's *she* who has been mistreating herself. She isn't looking to her own welfare, and she's suffering for it. In hating herself, she stifles the possibility of feeling affection for anyone. True, her children could provide an outlet for her affections. But if she is angry with them as well (in the same disappointed way that she is angry with her husband) she may be blocking that pathway for loving, too.

Dorinda indicts herself for not having the kind of husband and children she thinks she *should* have—that is, very special people. If she really were the fine woman of her imagination, she reasons, then she would indeed have a special family. She thinks she should also be a "new woman," involved in "self-realization," career, and what all. Yet she makes no moves whatsoever in these directions. It's almost as if she expects words and ideas to change her into something she is not. Inert, she fumes at herself for her inertia and imaginary failures. (You can't fail if you haven't tried.) A simple point has eluded Dorinda. It hasn't occurred to her that she cannot become a "new woman," or any woman she can accept, without working on her own behalf.

Dorinda speaks of career and autonomy. But she'll consider a change in her approach to living only if she can be reassured that the change will not destroy her present status: that she will not be required to go to work if she prefers to stay at home, that she will not be required to support social changes if she chooses not to, and so forth. She needs to be convinced that she, personally, will not be deprived of choosing the way she conducts her life, the way she establishes her values and priorities. She needs to be convinced as well that she will have all the rights and privileges that anyone else has regarding pay, qualifications, and where and how she works, if and when she chooses to enter a public work force. And she has to be convinced that the larger women's movement is dedicated not to the elimination of specific grievances of specific individuals but to the broad principles of fair and humane consideration for everyone.

Dorinda's dilemma is representative of a growing number of such problems. She places herself at the center, as the primary cause of her partner's feelings and behavior. Not understanding his motivations, she feels neglected and abused, for she depends on him for *her* feeling of well-being. Her disappointment has so disturbed her CDE that she is unable to take the pleasures available to her and to make the time in which to enjoy them. She has chosen in a sense to remain unhappy, without investigating her unhappiness. She has thus far learned little about the responsibility she must take for her own satisfaction.

MARRIAGE EFFORTS

Arora, another young married woman, expected her husband to be her "therapist." "I need to talk to someone to get rid of all the tension I build up at work," she remarks. She is unaware that her "tension" is anger tension, which she builds up all day because things don't work the way she thinks they should. She continues, "He's very supportive, but sometimes he gets impatient and tells me he can't be my therapist. It's getting to the point where he refuses to hear any more complaining from me. He tells me I'm not a little girl anymore, and he's not my mother. He tells me to grow up and handle my job better without expecting so many favors there.

"I was shocked when he first said that. I didn't know I was looking for favors. So I asked him how I was. And he told me! It was very hard to accept at first. I was furious with him. We had a lot of fights. I couldn't see that I was really expecting people to be concerned about my anxieties, my frustrations, and my ambitions. I was always drawn to anyone who gave me the feeling that my grievances were justified. That was just great. But in a way it did spoil me.

"What I see now is that my parents spoiled me in this way. And I wanted my husband to continue doing it. He seemed to be willing to, but then he found that it was too much for him. I was laying my unhappiness, my anxiety, my depression on him, and he couldn't handle it. He said it made him feel anxious and depressed and worried about our future. He's had so many plans for us. But he felt depleted with worry about me, and he couldn't give the proper attention to his work.

"I knew I had to do something. But it took me a long while. I finally realized that I had a responsibility, too, in this marriage. I couldn't just feel sorry for myself and expect him to continue taking care of me as if I was a weakling. That didn't give me a chance to have to be strong."

Arora sounds like a young woman with many strengths, but who hadn't tried to develop them. She represents the most encouraging aspects of the "new woman" in that she can raise questions, listen, and be open to change. Yet see how it arouses her anxiety and resistance. Her husband met that with firm, consistent encouragement.

He seems like an unusual young man who recognizes his limitations, is not ashamed of them, and appeals to his wife to deal with hers. Not harboring resentment and anger, as so many men might under similar circumstances, he is telling her important truths, which only a best friend can do. Even in his exasperation with her he maintains a patient and optimistic attitude, feeling that she can make changes if she sees how she hurts herself by compulsively clinging to dependency.

In his kind attempts to help her fight against the qualities that retard her growth, and in encouraging her to become stronger to confront her blocks, he is probably doing her the greatest service of her life. In this instance we see how the positive features in their personalities are able to oppose compulsive features and gently pry them loose, making way for greater optimism.

One important and obvious difference in these two women is in their husbands' attitudes. Arora's husband is actively engaged in defending his position and in trying to help his wife to recognize her self-destructive attitudes. He's appropriately assertive and doesn't feel guilty that he can't be her "therapist." The secret of his success is that he is motivated not by anger but by a sincere desire to improve both their lives. Dorinda's husband seems to have given up. Circumstances may be weighing more heavily upon him. The marriage is older; there are two children; there are greater financial burdens. He may also feel guilty and thus unable to assert his needs.

PHASES OF MARRIAGE

I've repeatedly indicated that troubled marriages are not new. A percentage of women and men have always been disillusioned and disappointed in their marriage partners. In these days, however, couples are no longer as resigned as their parents were, and are less willing to remain in relationships that don't seem viable. In using the concept of viability, as if a relationship were supposed to have a life of its own, it is possible to miss the point that *relationship* is only a word. How viable it is depends entirely upon how viable the persons are and how constructive their efforts.

Common phases of a conventional modern marriage do not differ greatly in substance from those of a previous generation. They may be divided into six substance units: honeymoon, disillusionment, disappointment, decision, productive years, later years.

1. The *honeymoon phase* may last from a few weeks to one or two years. This is often the most open and pleasurable phase, a period where being an independent woman, living with someone you love, and planning a home and life together can be enjoyable and rewarding. There is frequently a good deal of playfulness, laughter, sexual enjoyment, and mutual support during this period. In good marriages, some elements of honeymoon persist, but only when both partners create opportunities for this to occur. It's during this phase that you and your partner are usually most open to each other. Much gentle groundwork can be done then in revealing likes and dislikes, strengths and weaknesses, needs, and the extent of your ability to compromise and to accommodate each other.

The honeymoon phase is a critical time to try to establish that your personal limits do not represent a rejection of your partner. But, you need to realize two points: (1) You will not be loved for what you *cannot* bring to the mutuality of the marriage, and (2) you will be expected to make some effort to change if your limits present real, ongoing disruptions. In other words, you can't expect your partner to accept habitually hurtful attitudes and behavior with the explanation, "Well, that's the way I am," without damaging the quality of your mutual affection. And what's more, to refuse to consider change is to ignore the concept of fair play in a permanent relationship.

2. The *phase of disillusionment* occurs when your fantasy expectations are dashed to the ground. This period can last one or two years, usually overlapping somewhat with the first phase. Disillusionment will occur in anyone who has sustained a long-term fantasy about what a husband or wife is supposed to be. Since reality has a way of not coinciding with fantasy, such disenchantments are bound to take place.

Reality points to the fact that no man is a husband when he marries. And no woman is a wife. There is no way they can be marital partners before they actually become involved as such. They might have read about marriage, talked with friends, or taken courses—all useful activities. But these are preparation, not the real thing. Even living together doesn't prepare you, for that is similar to *but not the same as* a marriage.

Furthermore, sad to say, innumerable couples haven't even tried to learn anything about it; and they sail into marriage unprepared for the frustrating, dull, but ever-present details of intimate living. Armed only with the glow of passion and a firm belief in the rightness of their fantasy, too many of them march into the intimacies and responsibilities of marriage as if they were going to a circus.

When they look beneath the surface glitter of a circus, and note the confusion, smells, noise, dirt, power plays—the fragility of the entire structure—they are disillusioned, long before they've given themselves a chance to see the stronger, more stable elements that have made it the lasting entertainment that it is. Glitter is part of every circus, but it is not the circus. Similarly, illusion is part of every marriage but is not the marriage itself.

Two people become marital partners as they experience marriage to each other. Willing men (but not all of them) can become kind and attentive husbands with the help of a patient and welcoming wife. Given a similar opportunity, willing women can do the same. Arora is an example of this. Another is a man in his forties who remarks, "I don't know how it's possible, but I'm always learning something new about my wife." This is a partnership that remains alive, with two welcoming and listening persons.

3. The *phase of disappointment* occurs when expectations thought to be more realistic are also found to be ungrounded. That is, you discover that your partner's life view may differ quite markedly from your own basic attitudes and goals. Or you may find that his personality includes many permanent features you had either overlooked or underestimated earlier—features you find irritating later on. No time limit can be set for this phase, for it can persist throughout the marriage if you permit it to do so. It can become chronic, a phase of hardening disappointment and of hopelessness for a better future. It can turn a marriage into a sour, bitter, and generally negative relationship.

4. The *phase of hard decisions* is perhaps the most important turning point of the many to be made in a marriage. It depends heavily on the negative or positive directions taken in the phase of disappointment. A fair assessment of your situation can be made by working with these questions:

–Will you let your disappointments continue to determine the future course of your marriage?

–Can you take a constructive approach and assess positive features of the marriage in order to build a growing relationship based on each other's assets?

–Will you try to discover what is available in terms of common interests?

–What new interests can be developed and shared?

–What interests can each of you develop separately?

–Can you accept your partner's need for autonomy as well as your own, and arrange opportunities for it to be exercised?

–To what extent are you willing to make compromises?

–Are you willing to accommodate your partner at times, even when it may be inconvenient for you?

–Can you permit a free flow of affectionate feelings?

–Can you try to limit your criticisms and bad humor?

–How much optimism, good humor, and effort can be maintained?

–How motivated are you to build a permanent, dependable, supporting, companionable, comfortable partnership, which nonetheless isn't the be-all and end-all of your existence?

Decisions made in this phase will naturally determine the character of the satisfactions to be found in the next two phases. A mutual decision to remain optimistic about a future together is what makes for the warm, supportive relationships that *do* exist, even though they may not make for dramatic statistics.

5. The *productive phase* of accomplishment, with career, family, social expansion, new skills, development of avocations, is one of continuing personal growth. While it can occur in the context of ongoing disappointment in the marriage, satisfaction will be limited. But when the phase of chronic disappointment has been left behind, the productive phase can be an exciting and rewarding time, associated with deepening feelings of love.

6. *The phase of aging* is becoming more and more an extraordinary one. It is one of mellowing, of greater wisdom, sometimes of greater mutual dependency, support, and affection. It allows time for persons previously busy with family and career commitments to investigate in-depth involvements, even new careers totally unrelated to former experiences. The phase of aging has become an extended productive phase, but without the pressures and anxieties of younger years.

Certain couples permit the inevitable stresses and conflicts of daily intimate living to control their perceptions of what a marriage can offer them. They do not view their marriage as a long-term partnership that can bring them so many of the ordinary personal satisfactions and comforts they want. Nor do they appreciate that continuing effort is required to maintain a degree of harmony and satisfaction in *any* permanent relationship, present or future.

Over and over, Dorinda and Arora refer to their disappointed expectations, to their past hurts. Some couples cannot accept a more positive present because of shared negative past experiences. They seem to have a need to contaminate their present with hurts of the past.

For Arora a turning point is evident though, when she can begin to let her hurting past go, and *remain past.* When you can consider past time units of relationship, good or bad, as in their past context, you have placed them in a more fair perspective. You will remember that they had substance at the time, that they are historically related to your present, but not a living part of your immediate present. They can become as related or unrelated as you choose to make them. That each time unit of experience may stand alone, separate from all others, does not invalidate any one of them.

Arora can now look to her present and future with her partner as to separate units of living, linked to the past but not encumbered by it, and not primarily determined by irrelevant features of the past.

In her poor opinion of herself, Dorinda has little sense of the skills she does have. Too many women have been unable to respect or enjoy their expertise and success in their own bailiwick as men have in theirs. You can see why this is so from this table comparing house-wives' attitudes with the attitudes of businessmen and women who do not have *primary* family obligations. Please remember that these are group generalities. As you go through this list, see how you would rate yourself.

Item measured	Attitude of women with primary family obligations	Attitude of men or women without primary family obligations
Competition	low	high
Ambition	low	high
Responsibility	high	high
General pressure	low to high	high
Pressure re mistakes	low to high	high
Time pressure	low	high
Total daily time investment	no regular hours; 18 to 24 hours some days	regular working hours
Total weekly time investment	7 days	5 days, more or less
Assistance	none to full-time	available
Disbursement of income	restricted	determined by income

Sense of burden	high	low to high
Interest	low	low to high
Opportunity for change	low	low to high
Satisfaction level	low to high	low to high
Sense of autonomy	low	low to high
Sense of freedom after working hours	nonexistent	high
Boredom	high	low
Enjoyment	low to high	low to high
Sense of accomplishment	low to high	low to high
Stimulation level	low	low to high
Voluntary involvement	low	low to high
Trapped feeling	high	low
Sense of oppression	high	low
Depression level	high	low to high
Anxiety level	low to high	low to high
Anger level	high	low to high
Helplessness	high	low
Guilt level	high	low
Conflict level	high	low to high

All too often, women in the home don't give themselves the credit and the respect their work deserves. They are, in fact, involved in the world's most important work as they rear their children and maintain family contentment and harmony. They have ample opportunity, however, to build self-respect, not only in other fields of endeavor, but also right where they are, as keepers of the hearth. Their time could be better organized, perhaps; that is one reason why so many women are discontented. But they need to recognize the enormous value of what they do.

Surely it's as important to place a nutritious meal before a child as it is to sell another five dozen auto parts. Surely it's as worthwhile to arrange playtime for your child and a playmate as it is to attend a luncheon with a client. How else can I say it? How can I put it so that you will accept your importance as a homemaker—as the person primarily responsible for the care of our most precious natural resource—our children?

LIBERATION: FRIEND AND FOE

In liberating themselves from the fetters of nonassertive, deferential habits, some women have gone too far in discrediting behavior and life-styles that they may honestly prefer or over which they have little choice. In striving for liberation, some women have lost a sense of the dignity of their position as homemakers. Since you can control the degree of your involvements, homemaking and liberation are not mutually exclusive states of being, as many women can tell you. You can be both housewife and liberated woman, to whatever degree is practical for you, as long as you remember that the top line is 100 percent for both together—not for each!

In feeling required to strive toward unrealistically high ideals of liberation, which can sometimes turn into new shoulds, even mature women have misread the messages of liberation. In forming new shoulds, they have turned the concept from friend into foe, in terms of their inability to freely choose their very own position on any issue. In an unexpected turn of events, many young women of the sixties also fell into the trap of substituting new shoulds for old.

Original spokeswomen for the women's movement well understood what they were saying, for they had lived and suffered it. They shared a bondage and a background from which to press their arguments. Most adult women who listened understood as well. They had been there, too. The language of the second-class woman was a common tongue. Those women were on a centuries-old battlefield, already strewn with the bodies of generations of ignored, submissive, and self-neglecting women.

Their much younger sisters, adolescents of the sixties, inflamed by their elders' passion for change, drank in the nectar of the promise of liberation. They heard admonishments to fight against dependency and nonassertiveness as prime movers of their existence. But the spokeswomen omitted something. They omitted a practicum that teenagers could use judiciously in the context of teenage experience, which differed greatly from their own. And so youngsters ran home and practiced rebellion, arrogance, and revolution on teachers and parents, who seemed at a loss to defend themselves or to help their daughters understand the meaning of the stirring words they heard.

The meanings of assertiveness were misinterpreted by many young women. They confused it with aggressiveness or frank expression of anger. Such behavior may also be asserted. But assertiveness is a broader concept than any one form of expression. It is essentially *a statement of your position* and depends upon these points:

1. Awareness of the position you want to assert
2. Evaluation of its relevance to the issue at hand
3. Selection of a time, place, and manner for asserting your view
4. Making your statement and defending it in a way that is compatible with your personality

I'm describing what I've heard and witnessed many times over. Informed, sober-minded messages were listened to by girls and young women who often did not have the experience, the wisdom, or even the interest in many instances, to receive them in the sense in which they were delivered. Wise, inspiring women missed what their younger sisters were attending to, and couldn't know how they were being interpreted and misinterpreted.

These, then, were the daughters who listened, who evolved visions of *liberation sugarplums* in their heads, with wondrous labels: *autonomy, equality, liberty.* Having thoughtlessly gorged themselves in the early days, they now suffer from *liberation indigestion,* for they never dreamed how much effort it would take to live an autonomous, responsible life.

Dorinda and Arora are among this group. They are the products of an exposure that excited but rattled them, and failed to instruct them sufficiently. They, too, learned: You deserve everything. But they didn't learn how to work with devotion for what they "deserved," whether or not it seems fair. Along with more mature women, they continue to feel the impact of the conflict between known and unknown, permanent and fleeting, familiar and unfamiliar, orderly and disorderly, sameness and difference—ideas still battling their way into women's hearts and minds. As long as conflicting insistences are held with equal firmness, anxiety is generated, for anxiety is merely the flame and smoke fed by the burning coals of unresolved conflicts.

Unintended victims of a bright promise, young women like these two believed that "all would come unto them as was spoken." From the point of view of their tender years, they could only guess at the deeply rooted prejudices against women's developing in new ways. They were unable to cope with the meanings of contradictions, injustices, cynicism, instant labels, and slogans or with their social and political implications. They had neither the time nor the opportunity to grow firmly, with trust and laughter, and with roots embedded in the substance of their own personal history.

They thought they could go forth, throwing handfuls of liberty to the ground like so much fertilizer, expecting it to bring forth freedom and equality. But no earth had been plowed; no seed sown. And so weeds of mixed messages and confusion sprang forth, nourished by "fertilizings" of so-called liberty, weeds that choked women's paths and caused them to invent new reasons for their anger and frustration. Those weeds became the distorted views of their reality and of the place in life they had made for themselves. Carrying those distorted views into a relationship—where they clashed further with another person's reality—could only lead to greater disappointment and a greater, though different, loss of freedom.

AND STILL THE YOUNG IN THESE CHANGING TIMES

Many women today are torn by conflict regarding their roles as parents. They feel guilty and anxious about their attitudes toward their children. Too many of them find no way to separate themselves even occasionally from their youngsters' dilemmas. And so they become increasingly worried, as they try to meet needs they are often ill equipped to manage. They speak of pressures "out there," but only partially comprehend the enormous impact of influences with which the young must cope.

Even apart from negative external influences, the adolescent transitional period is a troubling time for the family. In its normative state adolescent rebellion is a "cry for help," a shout for permission to grow away from childhood into adulthood. Both child and parent may be afraid to let that happen. But when it starts early and proceeds slowly, its gradual changes are barely noticeable. Unfortunately, however, the process is frequently too long resisted, and a head of rebellious "steam" builds up. The child begins to feel guilty because she wants to change; and the parent begins to feel guilty because she doesn't want to admit or encourage that change. Both are made anxious by the depth and strength of their new feelings; the one needing to grow against any odds; the other needing to remain fixed, fearing the loss of her authority and identity. In recent years, however, the familiar teenage rebelliousness has gone well beyond its former bounds. In more than a few families it is no longer the "natural" rebellion that everyone has come to expect of adolescents who need to moult their baby skins and spread their wings into adulthood. It's become a malignant rebellion of youngsters who see their parents as the enemy, and who conspire with their peers to belittle parental guidance and overthrow parental authority. Egging each other on, they acquire a certain strength; and they can exasperate and stun reasoning, but helpless and despairing, parents.

Parents find that they cannot counter, with their adult values and affections (sometimes rather tattered), an unprecedented cascade of social changes—some absurd, some liberating, some harmful, and some they neither understand nor accept. Many are changes that were never meant to be placed in the hands of youngsters. They were meant for a supposedly thinking adult population, who would be able to experiment prudently and make sound decisions regarding innovations of all kinds.

Mutual resentments of mothers and daughters have destroyed trust and replaced affection. How, then, can a mother feel about a daughter who makes her feel like such a poor parent? And how can a daughter feel about a mother who makes *her* feel like a "rotten little kid"? So they lose each other and are in perpetual pain over the loss.

What has been happening is that a large number of adolescents have not been given the opportunity to grow, to learn, to work, to play, quietly and simply, with concerns relevant to their age and experience. While they do require exposure to available incentives and encouragements, there have been far too many stimuli for both rich and poor alike, too many options, too much pushing to achieve.

Some of these youngsters, who seem so wise, have become anxiety-ridden and overly skeptical before their time. Others seem almost jaded by their experiences. Too many pressures are putting too much stress on many of today's teenagers. They even worry sometimes over future responsibilities which, from their vantage point of inexperience, can only appear overwhelming.

Young people's exodus to drug abuse, considered an easy nirvana, has been an unwittingly self-destructive attempt at self-preservation, their attempt to pull themselves together after being assaulted by too many stresses of modern existence. There are now several generations of these youngsters, bred on anxiety from so many sources, with scrambled minds and views. They have found their timeless dreams another way; and quieting their anxiety with drugs, they've missed their first chance to cope constructively with their frustrations while attempting to resolve their conflicts.

Many of them stumbled their way through adolescence, covering their anxiety in any way they could, actually believing they "knew it all." Scores of them were allowed by their elders to believe that. With their high IQs and large information banks, some of them were regarded as premature adults—almost like new toys for their elders to watch and enjoy.

While thousands upon thousands of youngsters persisted in wasting themselves, there were (and are) many who survived their bizarre goals and their suffering of mind and body. When they finally decided to move into different directions, they found new strength in a depth of understanding and compassion not commonly found in the young. Because much of their anger was spent, and because life is such a dramatic instructor, they learned to be sensitive to the limits of other mortals and to regard those limits only as different from their own—a not insignificant benefit of those lost years.

In the thirties educator-philosopher John Dewey wrote that "when youth is educated as youth, and not as premature adulthood, no nation grows old." In loading the goods, services, frustrations, privileges, goals, teachings, decisions, anxieties, aspirations, and failures of adults upon children, it may be that we have made them prematurely old; and perhaps our nation, too, has suddenly grown old, tired, and disheartened in the process.

Women can discharge their anxiety concerning their children, however, by working to arrest that process and turn it around with their collective and individual efforts. They can do that by using the restlessness of their anxiety as energy units to apply to this work. Thus they can find a productive application for anxiety in a very real sense. You will hear more about anxiety as a positive force in the next chapter.

Keeping in mind that it takes purpose, direction, time, and firm resolve to grow, learn, change, and to develop your imagination and strength, you can strive to give your children the equipment they will need. Much of the equipment flows spontaneously from the ready, unpretentious support of a reliable family structure. But much of it can come directly from you, from your own person, even without that supporting structure. You have the wisdom and experience to do that. You need not despair over something you don't have, for that can only distract you from the resources you *do* possess within yourself. Everything you need is there for you to use. Begin to trust yourself to put it all to work.

VII

Anxiety as a Positive Force

In order to finally live in harmony with your human and physical environment, you have to recognize and accept reality, at least to some extent. Whether you like it or not, certain tolerable levels of anxiety are undoubtedly part of that reality. If that is so, and anxiety is occupying space in your emotional life, it is very much to your advantage to consider anxiety as a motivating positive force and a potential source of power. Such a view may further encourage you to work to harness your anxiety for productive living.

ANXIETY ENERGY

Harnessing energy units of anxiety in a positive way confers certain constructive properties upon it and it produces a counterpoint to the unharnessed anxiety energy that leads to the wasteful restlessness so familiar to you. How, then, can you make the best of anxiety energy units that are being fired off by each bout of anxiety?

Through those energy units, anxiety produces a power that can rule your life in a negative way unless you turn it into a positive force. Anxiety energy might drive you to make decisions or to do things that are unwise or self-destructive. Just think how much more beneficial it would be if you were to use those units to help you examine your anxiety and learn to manage it for greater comfort and assurance. By viewing anxiety energy as a positive power source, you can find out how to accomplish that.

I want to emphasize that the anxious state is *not* to be regarded as a *preferred* state because of the energy units it can produce, for I do not hold with persons who believe that anxiety is essential to productivity. While I believe that anxiety and productivity can and do coexist, I also believe that less divided and less anxious individuals can be even better motivated to produce, because of the pleasure and gratification that their involvements give them. They can work and create without having to wade through fields of anxiety and its associated depression.

Anxiety energy is especially useful in providing the drive to push through the inertia of depression. I am suggesting this positive approach because it does no good to ignore anxiety that is present anyway, invading your existence with habitually irksome stumbling blocks. I am suggesting that instead of letting anxiety inhibit or harm you, you can turn it around to serve you and your needs.

WOMEN USE ANXIETY ENERGY

During the past few years you have witnessed how the anxiety of frustration, anger, and helplessness has powered women in positive ways. Breaking away from their image as dependent, secondary persons, they have become determined to reach out and make conscious and deliberate changes. This, despite the fact that change, beneficial or not, almost invariably produces new anxiety.

Nevertheless, women have finally discovered that their partners' monetary or professional success has little lasting impact on their own sense of competence and achievement. These are women who had previously believed that their "fulfillment" could come to them only through their partners'. Driven by that belief, they urged their men to produce, often in directions that created ongoing marital conflict. Such urgings thus became part of a deteriorating relationship. They also led to a never-ending promotion in terms of personal satisfaction, for the efforts made were always in someone else's behalf. That left women with a sense of inner impoverishment, for their exclusive nurturing of others left little or no nurturing time for their own self-development. Women have finally learned that careful attention to their own emotional and developmental needs is one cure for an anxiety that is related primarily to their own dissatisfaction with themselves.

ENERGY UNITS

A state of anxiety produces what I call *energy units*. They "circulate" in your body and can create the jumpy, nervous, running-motor kind of feeling you've come to recognize. Energy units may be discharged through either structured or fragmented activity. If they cannot be discharged by these means, they continue to circulate and create the physical and emotional discomfort I have described.

In speaking of the discharge of energy units, I refer to a literal *outlet* for feelings of anxiety. Undischarged anxiety can "puddle" in your body and produce the many physical symptoms you've come to associate with anxiety. Think of this puddling, if you will, in terms of an anxiety abscess filled with "gunk." Our task is to mobilize these puddles and get rid of the "gunk" through anxiety discharge.

From a physiological point of view anxiety is essentially a lingering fear reaction that affects the biochemistry of the body. Stress, or danger in the form of conflict, has its impact by triggering the production of hormones, among which are epinephrine (adrenaline) and norepinephrine. These substances stimulate organs to supply more blood flow and energy to muscles in preparation for defense against various forms of stress. When one of the stresses is anxiety generated by unresolved emotional conflict and no action is taken, primed muscles are left in a state of increased excitability.

Here, in my view, is the origin of energy units, which can give rise to a restlessness created by undischarged anxiety energy. All this preparedness has no place to go, in a physical sense, unless you're ready to thrash about to relieve those feelings of increased excitability. The restless, unfocused activity associated with anxiety is precisely that—a thrashing about in an unconscious effort to discharge unused energy units.

You can see, then, how emotional conflict can trigger a body reaction that is experienced as anxiety. It's such a frightening feeling that you will make every effort to ignore it, hide it, cover, mask, or bind it with psychological defense systems, for there is no perceptible physical danger to defend against. And I am suggesting that physical work and other activity can relieve that feeling, by discharging the effects of a biochemical buildup that has no purpose in a body supposedly at rest.

One difference between an anxiety reaction and a fear reaction, where you are obliged to defend yourself physically, is that you will necessarily be active in the latter, by either attacking your enemy or by running away to spare yourself. When you become anxious, however, you are less likely to be so active. Yet the same chemical reactions may be taking place, and you are required to deal with substances that are produced by a change in your internal biological environment. Restlessness is expressed through pacing, trembling, wringing of hands, excessive perspiration, and other repetitious and random movements. It is in the context of this reaction that much beneficial, or harmful, work can be accomplished by the energy units produced by your anxiety.

You have noted how these events can go beyond the bounds of endurance at times, and how defenses have to be devised to control effects of ongoing anxiety. Medication for anxiety (tranquilizers) works on the principle of intercepting biochemical reactions. But for ordinary anxiety levels you are obliged to use neither unconscious defenses nor tranquilizers if you can put the energy units of your body to use on your behalf.

In this context, you may be interested to know that several medical studies indicate that improved physical fitness will produce reductions in anxiety and depression. One study, conducted by Dr. H. A. De Vries, showed that there is decreased electrical activity in muscles, i.e., excitability, when a person becomes more fit. That decrease can be experienced as lessened tension and restlessness, and therefore diminished anxiety.

For a moment, think of your body as a purely physical entity that needs only to be fed, rested, and exercised. If you do this properly, it will work prodigiously for you—one way or another. It's up to you to decide which way. By a constructive use of energy units you may surprise yourself with your accomplishments. However modest your achievements, they may diminish some element of your self-hatred and place you in a better position to tackle your primary conflicts.

ANXIETY DISCHARGE

Although anxiety can sometimes be overpowering and require professional intervention, aids are available to you, mainly through mobilization of resources that you already possess but haven't yet exploited. I cannot emphasize strongly enough that those resources lie within your power to use. They can be used in cases of extreme anxiety as well as in lesser anxieties. I have referred to these resources as your health points.

In addition to those aids, I have been pointing out that you can use the power force of your anxiety as an aid also, by directing your anxiety energy units to some useful purpose. However, recognition of the existence of an anxiety state, mild or severe, is a first step. That can be accomplished by asking questions based on Steps One and Two of the twenty-step program illustrated in Part Two: First, is there something specific that is troubling you and causing you to feel tension, guilt, anger, or anxiety? If you can isolate a single trouble point, then ask yourself: How do you suppose that point is causing your suffering?

Talking over your dilemma with a person you trust may be a second move for you. Ventilation of fearful thoughts through *verbal discharge* can be more beneficial in releasing anxiety than you might suppose. Just keep in mind that you can't depend on a friend to serve as a perpetual listening ear. There is more you can do for yourself that will give you a feeling of greater autonomy.

Use of the entire twenty-step program is of course indicated at any time you are ready to work on your anxiety in this way. But at some points of intensity you may need temporary external support before you can proceed with the program as outlined. If that's the case, you can reserve that option and move directly to the use of physical discharge of anxiety, as I have just discussed.

I have also described how fear reactions, including anxiety, draw on your body's natural functioning and bring on a response of "fight or flight." When that happens, you feel a sudden surge of strong feeling through your body caused by the release of adrenaline into your bloodstream. Fighting, running, and being actively competitive or aggressive are some of the ways you can discharge the effects of adrenaline in the body. These ways may not be convenient for you, however, or match your particular style. But I would urge you to try to find some kind of game, sport, or exercise (indoors or out-) that would help in activating your muscles, or in confronting your anxiety more directly.

In recent years there have been many new methods for dealing with that confrontation. Research points to the effectiveness of some of these methods which include muscle relaxation responses, breathing exercises, biofeedback techniques, and visual imagery and behavior desensitization procedures. Other popular attempts at anxiety control are associated with transcendental meditation, Yoga, Zen Buddhism, and other belief systems.

But even without these methods, or any kind of *work discharge,* mild bouts of anxiety will gradually dissipate if the conflict that produces them assumes a less pressing central role. Anxiety will dissipate then, along with changes that resolve an underlying conflict. But one of your basic conflicts may remain persistently unresolved. In that case anxiety can be generated almost continuously. If no means of discharge are available, anxiety becomes chronic and *body bound.* You might then experience free-floating apprehension, unattached to any specific circumstance.

A woman with that kind of anxiety had a dream: "I was in some kind of battle. I was very frightened and wanted to get away from it. So I jumped on my horse and rode off in all directions." She paused, then asked: "Did you hear what I just said? I said I rode off in all directions. That's impossible. But that's what I want." It's clear that her conflict cannot be resolved until she begins to establish priorities for herself and stops insisting that everything she wants has to be accomplished "in all directions" at the same time.

Body-bound anxiety may be expressed also through a myriad of physical symptoms found in chronic anxiety states. Most common are muscle tension, persistent headaches and back pain, bad breath, skin disorders, insomnia, and unusually frequent upper respiratory infections such as colds and sore throats. While you cannot practice some of the activities you've selected for anxiety discharge when you're physically ill, try to find one that you can practice even if you are in pain or confined to your bed. It's true that muscle tension with pain is relieved with muscle-relaxant medication. But it can be relieved also with a womanpower relaxant of gentle exercise and compassionate self-care.

USING ANXIETY TO GROW

As you see results of your real efforts, whatever they are, you can feel more in charge of your body and in control of your life. This is an area that large numbers of women are still learning to confront more assertively. I know I've mentioned it several times already. But the move from dependency to being in command of yourself is probably the most difficult for some women to make.

A common trait that some of these women share is their suspiciousness. Such women have no sense of power regarding their own place in the world or their abilities to accomplish their goals. They are not proud of this characteristic, but it's used as a defensive maneuver, as we'll see in the next chapter.

They feel weak and incompetent, and their suspicions help them feel more in control, even though they often arouse anger in their families. A basic sense of insubstantiality, of having nothing, makes them become easily envious of others. Their envy makes them say unkind things and have unkind and even murderous thoughts about selected persons. Unable to accept those thoughts as their own, they project them outward, where they are imagined as coming from outside of themselves. Thus, their suspicions are grounded in their own rejected thoughts.

Considerable anxiety is usually generated in this condition. But it can be used to help you overcome your suspiciousness. In so using anxiety you might be able to shape some of your attitudes in a way more acceptable to you. In order to do this, you first need to try to be aware of an occasion when you think you *know* what another person is feeling, thinking, or going to do, without having been told. If you are aware of your anxiety reactions you'll know when this is happening, for the level of anxiety will rise perceptibly when you are having a "bout."

Should you find there are many of these occasions, please don't be troubled. You need only to deal with one at a time. Try to select just one time in a day or week when you find yourself dogged by these thoughts: Now what is she up to? What is she saying behind my back? I think she's trying to undermine my position at work by . . . You fill in what you're thinking.

Once you've isolated the thought, you are ready to go to work on this problem. Write in a record book as you try this procedure. Write the following questions one at a time. Then try to give yourself an answer of one or two sentences, or longer if you wish. Yes or no answers can be a help, too; but a little further thought on your part may yield unexpectedly pleasing results. You'll find that the anxiety which motivated you and powered you to act in the first place is becoming more manageable and less frightening.

1. What specifically do I think this person is doing to me? (Let's use the letters *XYZ* to represent this answer. Write it down as clearly and simply as you can.)
2. Am I absolutely sure that XYZ is actually so?
3. What hard evidence do I have, besides my own intuition, for that absolute sureness?
4. Is XYZ compatible with what I know of her/his personality?
5. Does XYZ seem realistic and logical in the context of the situation?
6. What features make it so?
7. What does that person stand to gain by XYZ?
8. What do I stand to lose by XYZ?
9. What does my believing XYZ do for me?
10. Does it enhance my status in any way?
11. Does it make me feel superior that I can be so sure of another person's intentions?
12. What would happen if I decided to relinquish my belief in XYZ?
13. Would I feel more anxious?
14. Would I feel relieved?
15. Would I like that?

After you've responded to these fifteen questions in your record book, read them over along with your answers. Add whatever you want, and ask other questions of your own. Remember—all the procedures in this book are suggested only to give you an idea of how you can go about helping yourself.

Defenses such as suspiciousness are widespread, because so many persons find it impossible to accept the reality of limits. Regarding the life of the emotions and the mind, certainly one of the most difficult things in the world is to recognize your own as well as others' limitations. Personal limitations are only one form of reality. You can remain angry and suspicious with someone for years just because that person is limited in ways that you cannot accept. You cannot be realistic concerning that person, and you believe that she is deliberately frustrating you out of maliciousness.

In overfocusing on the points which spell out human limits, you neglect to look across the width of the entire spectrum. There is hardly a limitation in anyone that you couldn't probably counter with some asset, were you to search for it. The existence of limitations— and they're natural occurrences—is what you repeatedly hate in both yourself and others, but only if you are unaware of the asset side of the coin. Recognizing and accepting limits as such can relieve you immeasurably and lessen your suspicions.

But that acceptance is extremely difficult. It's just as difficult to strengthen your health points. Even with all the seen and unseen limits, there is a rich supply of assets in each human being, only waiting to be mined. You can use the power force of your anxiety to uncover those assets. For no matter what your limits of ability, pleasure, or satisfaction, there are provisions for other unexplored pleasures and contentments. Believing that will permit you to find them. Believing that will permit you to leave your suspicions behind you and take steps to care for yourself in a new way.

MENTAL HEALTH DIET

The new way you select is entirely up to you. There are many pathways available these days. You hold in your hand the right to select your own way of caring for yourself. You're also the only one to decide whether to use your anxiety to power your efforts, remembering that as you use it, you dissipate it. And please don't worry that you'll run out of anxiety energy to harness to your task. That will take a while to happen. *Should* it happen, though, you can continue the work, if you wish, under the power of your enthusiasm and genuine self-interest rather than the fear and discomfort of anxiety.

Helpful information and materials available to the public are like different forms of diet suggestions—*a diet for mental health*, if you will. Everyone knows that there are weight-loss diets for every kind of person. Some are good. Some are not so good. Perhaps we can say that there are mental health diets for every kind of person, too.

Your first job in selecting a weight-loss diet is to find one that suits you in terms of *your* needs, *your* personality, *your* convenience, *your* style of living. While some may not work for you, there's bound to be one that will. For success, the best maxim to be kept in mind is the one that states: Any diet you choose will work—*if you stick to it.*

Diets that don't work are diets that aren't followed. They aren't kept. Except in cases of unusual metabolic disorders, it's reasonable to say that any conscientiously followed diet will result in some weight loss.

A plan for improved mental health might work in the same way, if it is suitable for you and if you follow it. There are many available. They range all the way from medical intervention with hospitalization and medication, to nutritional programs, to a variety of individual and group psychotherapeutic methods, and to more recent educational or self-help programs.

Regarding the latter programs, one point must be emphasized. The very term *self-help* indicates that any person using these methods has to be motivated to do what is recommended. Here the analogy to the dieter is the most obvious. After all, isn't a weight-loss diet a self-help procedure, too?

In order to succeed, a program for improved mental health must (1) suit your personality and your special needs, (2) inspire you to be motivated to try it, and (3) be followed conscientiously. That last doesn't mean you must adhere to the program rigidly—only reasonably so that it can help you. But you need to accept its basic premises and give it a fair try. The mental health program you select has to contain features that make it a *caring for yourself process.*

If you are practicing poor mental health, you are not caring for yourself very well. Maybe you think you are. But if you're miserable and tense much of the time, you're doing something that isn't in your best interest. I know that circumstances around you can contribute to your misery. But remember—you are always interacting with those circumstances. Your own input can exert a new influence, if you believe it can.

Furthermore, if you were taking care of yourself in a constructive way you wouldn't be troubled by practices that are obviously harming you and causing your distress. Can you accept the premise that you can have a more positive impact on how you feel, that you can use your anxiety as a positive force and learn to care for yourself in a different way? If so, you've established your motivation to work with the program in Part Two.

In this section I'm asking you to see if you can begin to think in terms of a mental health diet—a diet to shed not pounds, but the number of poor mental health habits that weigh you down with feelings of ongoing distress, helplessness, inferiority, pessimism, guilt, anger, depression, and anxiety. If my use of the term *mental health diet* bothers you, share with me one definition of *diet* from Webster's Dictionary: "a habitual course of living, thinking, reading, or, specifically, feeding." The phrase bothered Noreen, a woman in her thirties. She found it difficult to accept the concept of a mental health diet. She had complained of not being able to "stay put in one place," of little "tremorlike waves up and down my arms." She spoke of "butterflies" and diarrhea. She was surprised to learn she could do something about her symptoms through a deliberate effort to put her anxiety energy to work.

One key to those efforts is to keep your body as fit as possible through rest, exercise, and proper nutrition. Another is to keep it occupied in purposeful movements as opposed to erratic, useless, restless, and exhausting motions. Noreen learned to plan time for some form of body movement. She decided on dancing, for she had plenty of "nervous energy" to use.

Your activity may be exercise, sports, dance, house cleaning, running, music, gardening, walking, shopping, needlework, building, crafts, or one of a hundred other things. You need to accept that there are a variety of such activities. But they must be actively selected and utilized. And because you may resist your mental health diet at first, keep in mind the necessity to use small units of time and effort when you start.

If you feel some relief when you start on an activity, don't expect that relief to last beyond the actual involvement at first. As you continue in the activity, however, you will find that your relief begins to last longer and longer. Noreen had to find that out for herself. Relieved while she was dancing, she felt just as anxious when she returned home. It was only after she became more interested in her dancing, and was discharging more of her restlessness through it, that she found the period of relief stretching into longer intervals.

Your improved mental health may be strengthened, too, if you can learn that discontent is so often housed in disappointment—in oneself and in others. Can you imagine what it might feel like if you could magically wipe away your disappointment, say, in a partner or in a friend? What would be left? Would anything be gained? Anything lost?

Generally, troubled persons expect much more than is realistic from the people they encounter and from the many detailed events of the day. They sometimes believe that contented persons live grand, eloquent, exciting, "meaningful" lives, always moving out into wide vistas, with noble purposes. Feeling unable to achieve "nobility" on any scale, they remain discontent, bitter, sadly discouraged. They don't know that there are few "peaks," few grand purposes. They don't know that contentment comes mainly through the small encounters, the *seconds* of a relationship, and rarely through broad sweeps of remarkable interpersonal happenings.

Learning this, perhaps they learn that they, too, own the sunshine, the sea, the rain, and the air. There is fun; there is play; there is laughter for them, too. They don't necessarily deserve it. No one does. But it's all there for the taking. In their insistence upon looking for something that doesn't exist, however, they overlook the treasures they share with the rest of humanity.

ANXIETY AND DEPRESSION

In discussing anxiety as a positive force, as a potential source of power to be harnessed for your self-cure, I need to remind you that there are some forms of unrelieved anxiety that won't respond to such use. Similarly unresponsive is unexamined anxiety, which you don't permit to emerge into your consciousness, whatever its extent. Remember, I've said that you have to know you are anxious in order to decide to use your anxiety energy in a positive way.

Unrecognized and unexamined anxiety cannot be used in this way. It's like a festering abscess that's completely capped. In many cases the cap is a depression that serves its purpose of keeping intolerable anxiety feelings under some kind of control. Since this process is an unconscious one, it is difficult to identify and examine an anxiety that is not permitted to emerge except by accident, when its own inner force causes it to erupt. Then it becomes so frightening that a quick attempt is made to *de*-press it again, so that you can feel a transient relief. This is the point at which you may be able to exercise a choice if you are aware of what is going on. This is the point at which you might turn that explosive force into positive effort, instead of trying to clamp it down again.

People have told me they feel that anxiety can be "more constructive than depression, because it is more dynamic, and pushes you along." That point is most clear when anxiety is compared to a deep depression, where everything can come to a halt. It can take extraordinary effort to become mobilized again. Although I have been discussing the beneficial use of examined anxiety, the propulsion of even unexamined anxiety can be something like spinning along on the top of a wave crest at excitingly high speed and not looking around to see what will happen next—surely a more dynamic condition than depression.

The anxious person and the depressed person share many feelings in common. They both experience feelings of inferiority, helplessness, loss, guilt, poor self-esteem, and apprehensiveness. But there are considerable differences, in that anxiety is linked to activity, as I've just described, because of the inherent restlessness associated with anxious states. Depression, on the other hand, is linked to inactivity, because a basic hopelessness leads to a loss of motivation to remain active.

Central to anxiety are feelings that propel you to be alert, on the ready. No doubt those feelings account for the high incidence of insomnia noted in anxious persons. Your protective instincts are operative. Your efforts are directed toward reducing danger and securing safety. That fearfulness may or may not be related to anything in particular. It may be free-floating, a generalized morbid fear without an apparent source.

Anxiety is repeatedly described as an "active feeling, as if my motor is running." Depression is a nonactive condition and a "heavy, tired, stagnant, dead feeling." When anxiety and depression join forces, however, you can have symptoms of both conditions in what is called an agitated depression. The agitation and restlessness of anxiety keep you highly "charged up" (nervous energy) and mobilize you to keep moving, to do something to relieve yourself. They can keep you "looking forward to something else . . . a feeling of wanting to overcome, to win." In contrast, depression can immobilize and lead to feelings of pessimism, hopelessness, and wanting to be left alone.

In anxiety, multiple defenses are relied upon to reduce the strength of the discomfort and driving force of buried conflicts. The failure of those defenses, as well as the failure to utilize anxiety, can lead to a depression that might be considered the final defense reaction against anxiety feelings that are no longer bearable.

Depression, then, serves as an anesthetizing agent to relieve the impossible tension of certain anxious states. The person who tends to become depressed is hypersensitive to conflict and anxiety and develops an aversion to them. In such cases, then, depression is unconsciously selected as the lesser of two evils, the less uncomfortable condition, as evidence of a hopeless attitude toward restitution, or as a settling for base-line survival.

In some instances, however, depression also can have a salutary effect, when it can be used as a stopping-off point, as a pause for reflection, reevaluation, and for marshalling your efforts to find a way out of your misery. At times, unfortunately, only the most extreme pain will serve as a strong enough incentive for you to make moves and run risks that might change your life for the better. Kaye, a woman in her thirties, illustrates this point.

"When I went on vacation, I was so disgusted with myself," she says. "I was sick and tired of feeling sick, of making excuses, of feeling such panic, of just waiting to squeak through each day. I just sat for days. I felt I was sinking into quicksand. But I didn't feel like fighting anymore. I let a feeling of torpor sweep over me. I didn't have to do anything, so I did nothing—just slept, ate a little, sat and looked at the water. By the end of the week, I felt I had hit bottom and had no place else to go. I was crying a lot. Then I had the thought, Christ! What was I doing to myself? I'd had it with this wailing and whining. I can't go on like this. I have to kill myself or do something different to change this rotten existence.

"After that day, I began to feel I was slowly floating up through the quicksand. I began to notice other people around me. My body felt as if I had been kicked, punched, and beaten. I was sore all over. Somehow I had been beating myself for years—scared, scared! Was I doing the right thing? Was I saying the smart thing? Would they like me? Pound, pound, pound. No wonder I ached and felt sick all the time."

Kaye continues: "I returned home at the end of the second week, still feeling sore, but less hassled than I had felt in a long time. I spent the next week straightening up my apartment, shopping a little, walking around the neighborhood. I seemed to be counting the things that weren't impossible to stand. Maybe life wasn't great, but it didn't have to be the misery I had made it.

"You need time to do what I did. Before I left on vacation, I never dared stop. I kept running and filling in time so I wouldn't be idle, not be alone at home. But you need to be idle and alone some of the time. You need time to think, to decide what you want to do next.

"I felt sort of down when I returned, but quiet. Not that shaky, frightened feeling. I even thought about whether or not I should leave my job. But I knew that wasn't the problem. *I* had to do something different and I was sure ready. I wasn't going to keep on punishing myself the way I had. I felt I was finished with that!"

Kaye's words tell you that she is taking first steps away from old habits and old attitudes. They have kept her locked in a false position, trying to be a person she is not. She's insisted on it for years. In struggling to achieve it, she's ignored the truth of what she really is.

By doing that, she's undermined positive features of her personality, experience, and abilities. She's locked herself into an effort that can't succeed, because there's no fundamental validity in what she's been trying to be. As she tried, she felt herself to be "phoney." All of this has so distracted her that she hasn't been able to put her anxiety energy to work.

When Kaye stopped "fighting," she was trying to stop going *against* herself. But the change was too frightening and she became depressed. But she was able to appreciate that the depression marked the end of a struggle for falseness and the beginning of an attempt to find her own truth. She felt "quiet" and wanted to be "idle and alone" so she could think. She sounds as if she's really ready to let go of her fantasy self and find a way to her truth, her reality.

In other sections, you'll hear more about the struggle for selfhood, which requires you to give up your insistence on being someone you're not. Your work with the twenty steps will help you to find your own truths and relinquish crippling shoulds.

VII

Misguided Anxiety Defenses— You Can Overcome Them

As a condition of persistent tension, anxiety can have a total effect on the body. It influences bodily functions through certain brain centers that are part of your *emotional network* and through the autonomic nervous system. That is the system which controls nerve and blood supply to the organs of the body.

Because of these connections, anxiety can indirectly influence innumerable bodily reactions, many of which have already been mentioned. These reactions include tension, weakness, fainting, nausea, tremor, restlessness, agitation, tics, sweating, even halitosis and strained voice. Anxiety can lead to hyperacidity or spasm of the gastrointestinal tract, to diarrhea, flatulence, and constipation. It can give rise to hyperventilation, palpitation, irregular heartbeat, and flushing.

Through an emotional network anxiety can literally throw parts of the body into a spasm of tension. The term "uptight" is an apt descriptive term. Although it refers primarily to a sense of emotional tension, it necessarily encompasses the physical tension that accompanies anxiety. Anxiety tension can sometimes be best treated by vigorous physical activity. However, other less than vigorous activities have the capacity to discharge anxiety tension as well.

Although ongoing anxiety will produce varying degrees of ongoing tension, active body movement can offer at least transient relief. That is all to the good when you consider that the body can use even a small time of relief to repair any damage inflicted during a tense state. The main point here, then, is for you to know that much of your discomfort is caused by the tension of anxiety. Unless you begin with that, you may hamper your efforts to become less tense and anxious, and neglect a well-planned, deliberate strategy of recovery.

NEED FOR DEFENSE

To some extent you have seen what unrealistic shoulds are and how they collide among themselves as well as with reality. You will learn more about them in Chapter Ten. Failure of your shoulds can be deeply humiliating and emotionally painful. For example, when according to your shoulds you cannot stand to see yourself fail in your efforts to find just the right job you think you *should* have, or be the sort of parent or partner you think you *should* be, or look the way you *should.* These failures may be felt not only with major issues but also with many of the details of living.

Because you cannot tolerate these many fabricated hurts, you find that you must defend yourself against them. A terribly high price is extracted, however. In your preoccupation with what you feel is an essential defense system, you are thrown off balance and are diverted from the business of living your life in an unafraid way that is suitable in your circumstances. Furthermore, in the event of unmitigated anxiety you can become dedicated to lifelong compulsive defensiveness for the survival of your emotional integrity. Emphasis on a point of sheer survival restricts your outlook and leaves little room for joyful expansion of emotional horizons.

Consistent with a feeling of helplessness and restrictiveness, your only seemingly reasonable choice is to develop anxiety-relieving measures. You cling to them compulsively (i.e., without choice) because you believe that any alternative is incompatible with your psychic survival. Although that is seldom the case, you will not deviate if you believe it to be your only option. You will accept an alternative only if you can be convinced that you will not "self-destruct" should you try to effect a change.

Defense mechanisms are developed to protect against painful emotional assaults. They keep anxiety from interfering too greatly with your functioning and general welfare. To some extent everyone constructs defenses against emotional threats. Wherever threats are real, defenses are relevant. Where they are not related to reality, and are constructed as a result of severely conflicting psychic elements, those defenses become nonselective, indiscriminate, and compulsive, falling into the category of neurotic anxiety-reducing measures.

Sometimes they succeed in binding forms of anxiety that present a serious threat to the personality. When they don't work, however, anxiety builds. In cases where defenses fail completely and anxiety rushes to the surface of consciousness, it can impale you with its shattering force. At such a time, if you can maintain one iota of optimism or humor, you might consider it an opportunity to discover what your anxiety is trying to tell you. (See the section in Chapter One, "Anxiety as a Signal.") What's more, you may inadvertently find out that a particular defense need not have such a strong hold on you and is not as essential to your emotional soundness as you have supposed. There are questions in the next section that might help you find out something about your need for defenses. Only by identifying them, and familiarizing yourself with their features, can you begin the process of overcoming them.

NEUROTIC ANXIETY RELIEVERS

It may be useful to you to find out if you are using any of these neurotic anxiety relievers. Perhaps you can spot them in yourself and see how they overshadow your awareness. If you can identify any of them, maybe you'll be interested in deciding whether you want to continue using them. Ask yourself the following questions to make your determinations.

1. *In trying to ignore something that's troubling you, do you find that it seems to evaporate from your memory?*

"I don't remember much of my past," says Fleur. "When people

remind me of different things, it seems that they happened to someone else, a long time ago."

Certain adults "can't remember anything" about their childhood,
thus blotting out the fear, helplessness, and rage they may have felt
against a parent, for example. A woman "can't remember" her child's
birthday because she felt so inept, resentful, and guilty when her child
was newborn. A man doesn't remember an auto accident he had
because he is so ashamed of his poor driving.

If we regard such outcomes from the point of view of a should
system, it seems that these people have something in common: one
should never have certain feelings toward a parent—one should never
be an inept parent—one should always drive carefully. Rating their
shortcomings, which apparently cause them considerable emotional
discomfort, they unconsciously devise a defense that obscures the part
of their memory that reminds them of their failures. In doing so,
however, they also obscure elements that are part of a living experience, and so diminish the substantiality of their past.

Steps may be taken to disrupt the hold such shoulds have. Certain
questions are useful: Are you dealing with a should? Do you still feel
a child should never feel helpless or angry, or hate a parent? Did you
have a good reason for neglecting your newborn? How many drivers
do you know who have never had an accident? And so on. The point
in raising these questions is to present the opportunity for the
reevaluation of old attitudes. It's true that as time passes many things
change. But it's also true that attitudes may remain buried (but
potent), unless they are unearthed by raising a first question, and then
held out to the light of your experience and more mature wisdom at
this time. Very often a single question can turn your thinking around
on something troubling that you never have identified or thought
about.

2. *Have you ever caught yourself denying an event that revealed poor
judgment, unkindness, arrogance, or any other quality of which you
might be ashamed?*

Flora always complains about the way her daughter dresses. She
completely denies, however, that she never bought her any attractive
clothing, providing only "functional" things.

When reminded of this, Flora denies it flatly. "She was impossible," Flora says of her adult daughter. "I couldn't get her to wear a dress or comb her hair." Yet relatives remember how the child cried when she wanted a "party dress" and her mother insisted that the children were all going to the party in jeans. Flora thus spares herself the pain of the image of the uncaring, callous woman who didn't want to be bothered with a party dress.

Flora is better able to deal with herself if she can understand that her disinterest was valid for a good reason. Her daughter *was* careless about her appearance. Repeatedly exasperated by this, Flora decided that she would have nothing to do with the matter and did in fact become totally uninvolved.

Denial is a commonly used defense. I think you can see how anxiety-provoking it might be to try to uncover what's being denied. You may be unwilling to run that risk. But let's see what you might risk by maintaining certain denials. You must remember that the truth is always somewhere within you. You are therefore required to expend effort to maintain your denial, which is always at odds with that truth. You are having to support that struggle interminably. Is that how you wish to use your time and energy? Your answer to that question might help you to realize how useless and nonproductive some of your denials are.

3. *Can you remember being told that you were rationalizing when you were in disagreement with someone?*

Rationalization is perhaps *the* most common defense; it's used by nearly everyone at one time or another. It is essentially a process of self-deception through the use of faulty reasoning. It refers to the fabrication of sincerely delivered explanations, reasons, or excuses for an attitude or deed that does not seem to be readily accepted. For example, rudeness is frequently rationalized. In explaining her behavior, which she does not see as rude, Clarissa declares, "You just don't like anyone to be uninhibited. You like to be so genteel. You don't realize that I'm doing you a favor." Her reasoning justifies the act and keeps her guilt from overcoming her.

Another person, David, remarks righteously, "I couldn't let Jack come inside, because I knew he would get drunk and break up the party." The invited guest was an alcoholic who had been sober for a number of years. Others at the party knew David resented Jack's being able to control his drinking when he, David, could not—even though David had never reached the same degree of alcoholism.

Again, the questions: What is at issue here? What am I afraid will happen? Am I deceiving myself? Am I deceiving others? Am I afraid of appearing foolish? Do I appear more foolish by insisting on my position when it is persistently pointed out that my view may be a distorted one? Am I willing to make a tiny change and listen for once before I give my reasons for my behavior? Can I say just once, "Well, you may have a point"?

4. *Do you find yourself arguing against your abilities in a discrediting fashion?*

This defense has the function of maintaining an emotional equilibrium by disowning your experiences and talents. Millicent was unwilling to acknowledge that she could chair a committee even though she had conducted a successful campaign to make changes in office procedure. "I don't know why they are asking me to chair. They don't know I've never chaired before."

Millicent sees no cause-and-effect relationship to the request and is puzzled by this show of interest in her. She is compelled to keep certain qualities of leadership in herself separate from her idea of herself as a follower. That way she can keep her expectations of herself at a minimum. Coming closer to other facets of her personality and abilities causes her to feel anxious because of an increased sense of responsibility that she feels she can't maintain.

Millicent lives with herself as if she has little compartments for different parts of herself. She doesn't permit them to intermingle, so that she can get to know herself as a highly competent, assertive woman. Ultimately she is afraid of the changes that such a woman might be expected to make or might want to make. She feels she can maintain control better by keeping herself fragmented into the follower, the self-effacing woman, the only occasional leader.

Please bear in mind that most of these defenses evolve unconsciously in both women and men. They cannot be dealt with as long as they remain completely unconscious. Your questions can help you to recognize some of these patterns in yourself. Only then might you begin to try, *ever so slowly*, to overcome conflicting and inhibiting attitudes and actions that continuously feed your anxiety and retard your emotional and intellectual growth.

5. *Are you a woman who keeps her feelings in low gear in order to remain emotionally detached and un-anxious?*

That's what you do to try to control and predict your anxiety and keep it in check. You've established an inner control system that automatically censors an array of impulses and unwanted feelings. If such a feeling is in danger of erupting, the control system can turn it off, so you don't have to deal with any new or disturbing reactions.

Anger and fear are the feelings most commonly controlled by this system. It has succeeded when you don't even know you're angry or afraid. Seline is an extreme example of this. She has the reputation of being "cool." Nothing ever bothers her. She carries herself rather rigidly, and at times she has an expressionless face. She keeps things from getting "under her skin."

Once, when her employer made overtures to be her friend, she asked to be transferred, rather than deal with the unpredictability and closeness of a woman/man relationship. She had no confidence in her ability to handle the situation and either reject or accept his friendship. She felt no anxiety at the time that this occurred. Later she realized that she was afraid she would lose all control of her feelings and disgrace herself.

It was an unrealistic fear, for her habitual control would have supported her. Not trusting herself, she became so anxious that she had to leave the "field of action." Raising several simple questions about the actual event might have spared her the need to make a transfer at that time.

6. *Have you spent years sharpening your mind and do you feel that it is supreme over any other human resource?*

Certain women who do this often have contempt for anyone they consider less bright than themselves, all the while fearful of the competition that an equal might represent.

Sophie is one of those women, suspicious of other people's feelings and spontaneous acts. She demands that things be thought out and clearly defined. Having put in so much effort herself, she is proficient at careful consideration of issues, but she has no patience for the kind of hit-and-miss thinking and planning that is so common. She knows that clear thinking is admired and has dedicated herself to that end.

Sophie maintains a steady view of her superiority, but is careful not to surround herself with too many people like herself. Thus, her superiority remains largely unchallenged. She can keep her fear of her own possible "sloppy thinking" from making her anxious.

Highly critical of any thoughtlessness, Sophie makes much of her own thoughtfulness for fear of being thoughtless herself. She is relentless with denials and rationalizations when she is less than brilliant— which is often. There is no arguing with her when this happens. She will defend her position adamantly, even in the face of glaring contradictions. If her defense fails, she is subject to sudden depression and withdrawal, for which she passionately hates herself. "It's all right for others to get depressed," she reasons, "but not for me, because I *know* better!"

Sophie feels she must keep in top form, for she believes that her intellect is her only means to whatever glory she will achieve in her lifetime. All other pathways are strewn with rocks and snakes. *Her* chosen path is the only safe and sensible one. In working so hard on one segment of herself, she overlooks other aspects of her total personality. Because of that neglect she is underdeveloped in many respects. In immediately evaluating others on the basis of their functioning IQ, she overlooks features that might afford her companionship and other lighthearted pleasures.

7. *Do you tend to avoid acknowledging contradictory characteristics in yourself?*

Sonya is like so many people who produce blind spots when it comes to their strengths and admirable qualities. They don't see anyone but a dependent, uninformed, naive little girl, who is nevertheless doing an adult's work. So they cannot put their strengths to work in developing themselves further.

Since growth cannot be inhibited in certain people, it takes place despite such blocks. But Sonya's task would be far easier and more rewarding without the resistance of needing to see herself as incapable. Here again the issue of responsibility creates the conflict: (1) I cannot be responsible because I'm just a girl and I'm weak and helpless, and (2) I want to be responsible because I'm really an adult and sufficiently strong to function as one. These two elements, opposing each other, create such anxiety that Sonya gives up the struggle and reverts to helplessness, thus avoiding the conflict and momentarily stemming the flow of anxiety.

On the other side of the coin are the persons who produce blind spots regarding their limitations. They have to believe that they are all things to all people, invincible and all-knowing. Such a stance requires cutting off any recognition of the many limitations inherent in humanness, regardless of sex. Tremendous relief can be experienced if you permit yourself the luxury of admitting your realistic limits, while keeping and enhancing the assets (health points) you have.

8. *Have you ever heard yourself uphold certain values, despite their irrelevance to realistic goals?*

This is reassuring when you don't feel so certain, when you are afraid someone will challenge you and make you seem indecisive.

Fara is proud of her position as a supervisor in a department store. But other workers have learned not to ask her to deviate one bit from the rule book. She knows all the rules and often behaves like a tyrant, since she's always right, and since no one else bothers to study the book so assiduously. Her belief in her honor and goodness is secure, and she has contempt for those less "fortunate" than she obviously is. Since no risks are run and no changes made, the likelihood of arousing anxiety is kept to a minimum. But few people can relate to her in a friendly way.

9. *Have you been called a cynic because you are pessimistic about the future?*

Cynicism is a common defense for the person who is torn by strong conflicting values. If the cynic can feel convinced that nothing has any worth, anxiety aroused by conflict of values abates to some extent. Deeply troubled, the cynic is a passionate person whose vulnerability drives her to mount offensives to obscure her strong feelings, ones she cannot tolerate.

In this regard Meara manages to put down most things others want or enjoy. "What do you want to do that for?" is often asked in a contemptuous tone of voice. At a party she remarks, "These people don't want to be together. They're just going through the motions." Because she is so timid, she has to pretend that she doesn't want to be like everyone else. She deplores that. Furthermore, she is so fearful of rejection that she feels she is protected if she is the first to reject —which she does, indiscriminately.

Barney is another cynic who is constantly pointing to selfish motives in everyone. He is terrified as well that he will be "grabbed" by some moral principle that will divest him of his free will and his critical faculties. His cynicism sets him apart and gives him a specious sense of freedom and originality. He feels protected by the distance he creates between himself and "those people out there" whom he doesn't consider worthy of his company.

His family sees him as a disgruntled, disappointed, and rejected man. He is involved in many activities but has to belittle them all. When asked why he bothers with them, he replies with fine-sounding rationalizations: If you don't know about something, you can't very well criticize the people involved in it! His life revolves around being the necessary critic. Who knows what would happen to the world but for him?

So Barney provides himself with a purpose to his life, an otherwise forlorn existence without substance or warmth. He needs to discover that there are more rewarding purposes about which to order his life than he could begin to realize in ten lifetimes. He has lost contact with the brilliance of the most modestly lived but *wholehearted* existence. Believing that he has been deprived of something that others have, he is compelled to destroy well-being wherever he finds it. With his many strings of derision, he makes pitiful attempts to mend the broken heart found beneath the cynic's tragic mask.

10. *Are you frequently sure you know what other people are thinking and feeling?*

This can be a sign of deep insecurity, for it is a quick, magical shift into a feeling of control. Minnie is a person who needs that sense of control. She is always sure she knows just what her fellow workers are thinking about her or about anything else. She uses others to express her own fears, suspicions, or malice: *She* would never say such and such, but she's sure that Rosemary would say it, given half a chance.

Minnie is certain that there are persons who want to hurt her. That's her rationalization for striking first in order to protect herself. Here are two defenses working in concert. When too much anxiety is aroused, Minnie chooses to withdraw. She remains certain, however, of the correctness of her suspicions. When practiced excessively, this defense lays the groundwork for "paranoid thinking," a term that's come to be far too loosely used. Minor projections of everyday usage are inaccurately labeled as paranoia. It is not unusual to overhear the term used in casual conversation.

Beneath a facade of arrogance and aggressiveness, people like Minnie are terribly frightened. Attempts to reduce that fear are few, for they incur hostile reactions. Minnie's striking out is not premeditated; it's simply a reaction to her suspicious fear that she'll be attacked and emotionally crushed unless she defends herself. When it reaches this point, reassurance is of little use, and it is necessary to wait until the anxiety level drops.

Milder forms of this kind of suspicious thinking are extremely common. And because it can be so destructive to human relations, in Chapter Six I've discussed a procedure one might use in order to deal with it.

DISPLACED FEELINGS

I've already described how anxiety is generated by the clash between two conflicting demands. When you feel anxious, it's so uncomfortable that you make every effort to be rid of it. You do that by trying to keep it from your awareness. So you are often busy trying to cover, mask, dampen, or ignore your anxiety through your defense system.

You are compelled to defend yourself because no one can tolerate anxiety for too long. In so doing, you are actually attempting to distance yourself from uncomfortable feelings. In a sense you are trying to *displace* those feelings that trouble you. The greater the displacement, or the greater the distance you can place between yourself and your feeling of anxiety, the more comfortable you hope to feel. But when you do that, you are making it even harder for you to understand your anxiety and to prevent it from growing and doing you more harm. Nevertheless, you may very well continue with your displacing because you feel you have no other option and it does take the edge off your discomfort.

If you should find yourself persisting in self-injurious pursuits, you need to remember that your purpose is a logical one, even though the internal logic of a troubled person can appear irrational to an outsider. So let's inquire what the logic can be in a woman who, for example, overworks or overeats, or who is an alcoholic. Such women will not give up their self-harming ways, because they are fully convinced that these are the only ways they can control an anxiety that they feel will tear them apart. That belief keeps them rooted in compulsive detrimental conduct. Let's investigate that a little further.

While it's true that some women seem to have a perverse wish to destroy themselves, I don't feel that such a wish is the primary motivation of their persistent self-ruinous acts. I believe that self-damaging deportment is accepted, not because of its hurtful nature, but because it fulfills some purpose, some psychic need. In a way, it's chosen as the lesser of two evils: (1) I am slowly destroying my body, my self-respect, and my relationships, and (2) I am terrified of my anxiety and feel I will be torn apart by it and go crazy.

These women can obviously tolerate the first more easily than the second. By maintaining their psychic integrity, they feel they can at least survive, however marginally. And survival always leaves the door open to the hope that something might happen to make life more bearable. In the present, however, they can make it bearable only by practicing the form of behavior which, though destructive, gives them a sense of cohesion.

I know I keep offering you no easy solutions, but, instead, hard work to establish goals that are compatible with your reality and to identify priorities that are reasonable in the context of your present style of living. You can only be kind to yourself, however, if you find you cannot do something you believe might be useful. Bear in mind that anxiety can keep you from being interested in something outside of your own unhappiness, from being able to develop a relationship, from taking specific steps in your own behalf. Be easy with yourself if this is the case. Leave time for retreat, and then try again. Remember the smallest effort is important for you to experience, even when you can't achieve the goal you set.

You may hear that you are egocentric, only concerned with yourself. That's a characteristic of many anxious persons, for unreasonable fear can drive you to be very self-centered. But there is little satisfaction associated with such self-centeredness. It's really not much fun. If you find you're "doing for" yourself all the time, to the exclusion of being at all concerned about others, know that you are only trying to bind your anxiety. Try to be aware that you may not be able to do anything differently *at this time*. And then learn that your focus on yourself can change as your anxiety level drops.

Much defensive conduct is not by nature destructive or socially unacceptable. Any form of useful, acceptable activity can be subverted into a choiceless compulsion, with the same purpose of binding anxiety. So any psychological insight you achieve is all to the good. But remember that such insight is an intellectual process and cannot stand alone without the experience of *doing*, when you try to make the changes you want. People are as much *doers* as thinkers and feelers. When you are trying to manage anxiety, the achievement of insight is only one move toward resolution. It must be followed by learning that you can *act* upon your insight and *do* something for yourself. A tangible outcome of a tangible effort on your part will point to unmistakable change.

In order to get at the root of anxiety, then, first you have to identify the factors that cause it. Displacement of feelings will not help. You can begin to identify without too much discomfort by following the procedure I've suggested in the next chapter, in the section "Starting Your Reentry." Think of the need to do this in the following way:

You know that when you are physically ill, you feel weak. You can also feel discouraged and lacking in confidence. Similarly, mental and emotional states can influence your physical state. When you are anxious or depressed, you are not likely to feel physically vigorous. Your most vibrant physical feelings are likely to be associated with a contented emotional state. There's no way of separating physical, mental, and emotional states. They're all part of your body, and they interact and are interdependent whether or not you are aware of it.

Using a principle of unity, then, you can understand that what you do during a day will be related to feelings and thoughts, just as feelings and thoughts will relate to what you decide to do. Therefore, starting with your first list of activities in Chapter Nine, you can find out what your associated feelings and thoughts are. Thus you can uncover hidden (unconscious) elements that feed your anxiety.

Unconscious displacement of painful feelings goes on almost

every day. Sometimes it works and sometimes not. When it doesn't work, other means of relief have to be found. Too often those other means are even more damaging. Countless persons have discovered the mind-altering capacity of certain drugs, *including alcohol.* That capacity is what accounts for the popularity of such substances. By altering the mind drugs can mask or alter feelings. And in that process anxiety is masked as well and made to feel less disturbing.

In the final accounting, however, the drug route doesn't work. There are two principal reasons for that. One is that when misused, many drugs can damage the body in some way. The other is that anxiety levels can actually become greater through drug abuse. That's because drug-free periods may become progressively more anxiety ridden, so that it becomes impossible to remain without the drug for too long. The fix is not unique to hard-drug users. Users of any drug need their fix also, whether it's tobacco, coffee, or something stronger and more harmful.

I think you can see, then, how easy it is to acquire an addiction to a substance which is introduced as an anxiety-relieving measure. A large number of habitual abusers are unaware that they take drugs to quell anxiety. They think they do it only to feel good. But "feeling good" is merely feeling temporarily rid of anxiety tension. Youngsters are particularly susceptible to drug abuse, because they, too, feel great anxiety. In demanding immediate relief, they flock to use drugs, for they have no backlog of experience to withstand and cope with the anxiety to which they are subject.

Displacement of feelings occurs in either event—whether drugs are abused to displace intolerable feelings or whether your unconscious mind helps to defend you against them by denying or forgetting. In your setting these feelings as far from you as you can, too often you lose or displace more than you had expected. And you tend to find yourself distanced also from feelings of fun, of playfulness, of delight in small details, and of pleasure in your own abilities.

You don't notice, for example, the fresh smell in the air after a summer rain, or the sunshine reflecting from a hot sidewalk at midday. You may not notice a child's expressions or postures that are very funny. You miss opportunities to enjoy playfulness and other moments of possible pleasure. You miss feeling the power of your own developing self.

In unconsciously displacing your feelings, you are in very crowded company, you can be sure. I have described this process, however, so you can see how you displace and lose parts of yourself in order to relieve yourself of anxiety.

Being distracted, because of a need to keep anxiety at bay, interferes constantly with a sensitive emotional involvement in the small events of living. You may go through the motions of these events, but you don't experience the gratification that might be there. You are so grimly directed toward a need for relief that you overlook the little nuggets of enjoyment, humor, or beauty scattered free like pebbles throughout the day.

IX

Strip Away Anxiety— Find the Real You

Why do you suppose so many people have to "find" themselves these days? Do you think that's a natural part of your development? Has it occurred to you that in speaking of yourself, you might not have anything to find unless, of course, something has been lost in the first place? After all, you are yourself and with yourself all through life from the very first moment. How can you need to find something that's right there with you every second?

LOSING AND FINDING

Yet so many persons do lose themselves in a sense, in terms of the displacement I'm discussing. They don't realize how hard they work (unconsciously) to do that. Nor do they know why. Having lost themselves in order to achieve relief from unbearable feelings, now they must work to find themselves. Otherwise they remain in a limbolike state of nonbeing. In a way, they have thrown themselves aside in a fruitless attempt to feel more anchored, more secure. In so doing, they unwittingly separate themselves from the security of a base of genuine feelings. Throwing away and separating will not restore a sense of substance. You can do that far better by building or adding to what you already have. That way you can enjoy a continuing sense of wholeness.

To some extent nearly everyone goes through the losing process I'm describing. Where you've lost more of yourself, you have that much less to contribute to the mutuality of positive exchanges. Where you've lost less, you can participate in life with greater involvement.

In asking you to make the following lists, in persuading you to review vignettes of your life—one day or one hour—I am attempting to help you reestablish connections with those lost parts of yourself. I'm trying to get you to reconstruct the lines of memory, the lines of feeling, the lines of experience, that make you the person you are.

In denying your own emotional and experiential roots, you overlook the richness of your life up to this very moment, the richness of good and bad experiences, good and bad relationships, good and bad life-items of all kinds. Yes, I'm including the bad with the good, because while you've enjoyed and learned much from the good, you may have grown wiser and less easily discouraged through the vicissitudes of the bad.

Participation in this work is one way you can find unique lost feelings, lost thoughts, and lost deeds. Both positive and negative, all are part of what you are now. You can add to them as you choose. But please don't ever think that there's nothing to you. The most modest, the most timid, the most ineffectual person is a grand store-house of reflections, sensibilities, attitudes, opinions, and encounters. I'm asking you to go rummaging in that storehouse of your own being. You'll find there small treasures of a humanness that you have forgotten all about, one you have misplaced, displaced, and lost through the years. In losing them you've almost lost parts of yourself.

REENTRY

Emotional suffering can sometimes throw you into such abject despair that you can think of nothing but your wrenching misery. Yet you cling to a fragment of hope that your suffering may one day give birth to an element of wholeness and a greater wisdom of the heart. Curiously enough, that wisdom, torn from so much pain, becomes one of your buried health points, something you rarely stop to consider as such. For finally it will be your health that will motivate you to take the steps leading to your reentry among the hopeful.

In striving to overcome the suffering produced by anxiety or depression, you need to discover different parts of yourself. You need to know what's real, what's pure fantasy, and what might be possible for you in the future. Your responses to these points can help you sort out emotional tangles that keep you mired in unresolved conflicts and anxiety. Those tangles are so distracting and physically wearing that managing your life can become a daily hassle.

STARTING YOUR REENTRY

Let's turn our attention now to what's real. This needn't be difficult to discover, because it refers to what's actually so. It refers to all the real features of yourself and your experience. It refers to both health points and trouble points. In trying to deal with various points, you can divide reality into segments of doing, feeling, and thinking. For example: (1) What do I actually *do* with my time in any one day? How does an average day progress for me? What are the activities with which I fill my time? Whom do I see and what do I say? (2) What do I actually *feel* as I go through an ordinary day at home, at work, at play, and with family, friends, and strangers? (3) What do I *think* about during the day as I plan and go about my routine chores and encounters?

Try to think about those three points for yourself. You'll be working with them in a little while. Right now I'll discuss each one in more detail.

1. *What do I actually do in an average day?*
You can answer by making a list of your activities. Here are two sample lists. You make your own in your record book. The following one is that of a woman with school-age children.

> Get up
> Get family out
> Have breakfast
> Some days back to bed

— 137 —

Make phone calls
Second cup of coffee
Straighten, clean, laundry,
depending on day of week
Dress
Chores (vary with day of the week)
Lunch home or with someone
See friend, take lesson, class, etc.
Work on project
Children home, snack, talk
Take children to appointments
Odds and ends at home
Prepare supper, serve, clean up
Check schoolwork
Check plans for next day
Settle children for the night
Relax, read, talk, watch TV
Do hair and go to bed

A woman with preschool children will spend more time in the physical care of her children and in playtime. She'll take them to a playground and supervise when they are playing with other children. Her time centers very closely on the routine and the needs of a young child. All those activities would be included on her list. A career woman might make the following list.

Get up
Breakfast
Family out
Dress
Out to work
Office details
Lunch, shop, calls,
    plans for self or family
Office routine
Home, shop, chores
Dinner, etc.

Other house chores for self or family
Plan for next day
Go to bed

You realize how many variations there might be on such a list, depending upon your occupation, age, health, marital and family status, interests, location, skills, and education. Make your list now, detailing as many items as you can. It's easier to do this if you select an actual day that represents a typical one. Was it last Monday, Wednesday, or Thursday? If you can't remember everything you did, that's all right. You'll be surprised at how much comes back to you when you start to set down the items in your record book.

2. *What do I actually feel as I go through the day's activities?*

Take the same day and the same activities. As you list each item again, write next to it a short statement about what you were feeling while you were engaged in the activity. For example:

Get up—feel sleepy, wish I could stay in bed; sort of draggy until
    I wash my face
Get family out of house—all kinds of feelings; angry at children for
    squabbling, not having things ready; impatient with Jim
    for not telling Billy to stop teasing Mikey; feel like killing
    Muffin who jumps around and barks as kids rush around
    getting things together
Have breakfast—very jumpy; read paper and calm down

Et cetera. Some of your comments here may very well read "nothing." Don't hesitate to put that down.

3. *What do I think about during the day as I go through my activities?*

This might be difficult for you to remember. But start in the same way.

Get up—Nothing; thinking just do it
Get family out—How stupid I am that I can't manage better
Back to bed—Sleep or daydream; silly things like being someplace
    else; why did I get married; being a great scientist, a

> beautiful performer, a lover, a sacrificing heroine; making
> brilliant conversation with people I never speak up to

The woman who doesn't find little children especially delightful may have dozens of feelings and thoughts to include on her lists. They could relate to her dissatisfaction with the demands of child rearing. For example, open-ended time with a young child can become boring and tiring unless it's carefully planned. Without that planning, by mid-afternoon these women are ready to "climb the walls." Their boredom and irritation with the activities of baby care have reached the point where they are impatient and angry that they feel so "bogged down." All this could be placed on list number two about feelings.

"Climbing walls" refers to the jumpy, restless feeling of anxiety that builds up each day because of ongoing, unresolved conflict. On the one hand, this woman doesn't want to spend her time as a baby-sitter. She finds it tolerable, or even enjoyable, only for short periods during the day and is bored with it much of the rest of the time. Yet she's unable to acknowledge her feeling, because she feels compelled to think of herself as a "good" mother who cares for her child with patience and love, and without complaints. She thinks she should want to do that with all her heart.

Yet here she is feeling impatient, unloving, irritated, complaining, and bored "out of my mind." Angry with herself for her inability to follow the only pattern of motherhood she can accept, she becomes more irritable, and more in conflict with her inner wish that she be perfectly loving and patient *all the time.* If you think about our second question, you might come up with some of the feelings described here —in your own context, of course. You can already observe how closely feelings accompany activities. I ask you to start with activities because it's easier to remember what you did. That way you have something solid on which to hang your memories of what you felt and thought during the day.

Spelling out this particular conflict (which seems to afflict countless women with young children), a woman might be saying (1) I want to do what I feel like doing as a mature woman—that is, not be a full-time baby-sitter. (2) I want to do what I think I should be doing as a mature woman—be a happy full-time baby-sitter. Opposing wishes like these are not necessarily incompatible, for one resolution to this conflict is a schedule that allows her time of her own and time for the essential care of her child as well.

Although her solution may not be an ideal one, she cannot arrive at any solution at all unless she identifies the underlying conflict that nags her. But she can't identify that because she's afraid to admit that she's not a supermother, but an ordinary one with ordinary needs, shared by any number of other women at one time or another.

Since she's unable to deal with the essentials of solution—that is, identifying the conflict and planning alternatives—by mid-afternoon her irritability and anxiety levels are quite high. Tired from her day's work so far, she knows she still has another five hours or so to put in before she can relax and "go off-duty." Becoming more agitated that she might not be able to make it through the evening, she feels she'll snap and scream or strike her child if anything unpleasant occurs. When it does happen occasionally, it seems to relieve some of her tension. But her guilt lingers on.

As she works with the lists and suggestions made here, she can begin to come closer to herself. As she does that, she can learn what she needs and allow herself to have it if it's reasonable.

No other person, even your child, can eclipse you to the point where you never put yourself before others occasionally. You would be less than human if you really wanted to place second *all the time*, for you'd have to be an angel—or at least a close facsimile.

WHAT'S POSSIBLE

So often, people worry a great deal about the future. They think about themselves in different circumstances and feel they could never deal with them. This kind of thinking is all fantasy, for there is no self of the future. There can only be *plans* for the future, or *assumptions* that may or may not be confirmed later on. Your *self* is all the things you are *right now,* positive and negative. It's you; it's with you now and has been with you all along. It is every asset and limitation you have. Each day, each experience, adds to it so that it is continually growing. That self is what you have to try to *accept* rather than find, because there's no other place you can find it except within yourself —that is, within your mind, body, and feelings—right now.

There's nothing mysterious about the self if you consider that it's all of you all the time, no matter how poorly or how well you treat yourself. You are unhappy when you feel you aren't providing the opportunities you believe you should be able to offer yourself. Yet it is possible to use the *thought energy* you expend in ruminating over your unhappiness and direct it into plans for the opportunities you think you want.

I'm reminded of the jokes about finding "the meaning of life." There can be something humorous in the absurdity of looking far and wide for something that is with you every moment of your existence. Your meaning is your life—deeds, wishes, reactions, experiences— and what you decide to do with it each day, week, or year. You can change that meaning any time you decide to, and any time you are ready to go through the steps essential to change.

Sometimes talk about a "potential" self can be misleading, because what is potential is not real and can quickly take its place among those glorious fantasy expectations of yourself. And so you can be repeatedly disappointed that your potential is not coming to your rescue, not realizing that it's purely imaginary, that it's only a concept in your mind that needs to be transformed into something alive and tangible through your efforts. "I never realized my potential," says a perennial drifter, "because I never finished college."

To shift potential to the realm of reality, you need to ask yourself: What's possible for me with the particular ingredients of my woman-power and the efforts I am willing to make to harness that power to some purpose? You can list those ingredients in your record book and see how they match the idea you're considering. If there's no match at all, except for a passion to get into a new field, then your plans have to include a training period. Viewing potential as part of an active process of planning and movement begins to remove it from the region of vagaries to that of reality.

Any time I've talked with a person who "found" herself, the reaction is very much the same. She will declare, in effect: I've discovered that I wasn't all that awful, that I had it all here all the time. But I just couldn't see it. I kept looking for something else. So I couldn't put together what I already had. I somehow thought there was something out there that I was missing, something I needed to make me feel good, something that everyone else had. I felt I was deprived. I always felt bad and envious that I didn't have it. But I know now I'm the only one who can make me feel good at rock bottom. Any time I'm unhappy I have to use myself to find things that I'll feel satisfied with. But I have to do that with myself, with my own wishes and my own efforts. I can't complain and expect someone else to look out for my happiness.

Without those paper images you hold before you and worship, you are entirely free to look at yourself and to find your self if you will. Then you can begin to plan what's possible for you in the future—that is, tomorrow or next week, not some distant, shadowy future. Recall that the future is also the next hour. That's why you need yourself right now to approach that next piece of living and not let it frighten you.

When you think about what's possible for you in the future, you need to be aware that plans are not the future, and that the future becomes your living present only when those plans are activated. Plans cannot remain as thoughts, for as such they are only assumptions regarding how you might proceed tomorrow to achieve a particular goal. They flow into the deeds and accomplishments of the future only as you follow the steps of your plan with your active woman-power.

Sorting out the points I've made and responding to them is the beginning of your reentry into that region where you'll find small and large parts of your lost (discarded, unaccepted) self. You don't have to celebrate and cherish each part you rediscover if you don't care to. In fact you'll find that you don't like some of them. But you easily can put these aside after you've acknowledged them and decided you have no interest in or use for them in your present life. That process is an alternative to the habit of unconsciously casting elements of yourself into oblivion because they shame you and make you feel anxious or depressed.

WHO ARE YOU?

In this process of finding your lost self, of reentry into the full reality of your person, you have other questions to ask: What kind of person am I? How do I prefer to live? What are my needs? See how many of the characteristics on this list apply to you. Check those that do. If you want to, add the words *occasionally* or *frequently*.

prefer active physical pursuits
need to feel secure
not easily excited
feel strong
get very involved
like to remain neutral
feel weak and uncertain
can establish priorities
want freedom
don't clutter time or mind
like to be a doer
feel dependent
can be practical
keep unentangled
nonassertive
cooperative
come on strong
prefer intellectual pursuits
like to comply or defer
like to win
feel easily ridiculed
disciplined
objective
need constant approval
will compete anytime
prefer domestic pursuits
afraid of getting close
like to dominate
submissive

afraid of losing
afraid of abandonment
independent
a follower
orderly
indifferent

There are many other personal traits that could be included. Think about some others that apply to you and add them to your list. Then group the ones you've checked in three parts marked *A, B,* and *C:*

A. Those you like or admire
B. Those you dislike and deplore
C. Those you don't feel strongly about one way or the other

Now take list B of those you don't like and ask yourself, How much don't I like these traits? Give them one, two, or three plusses.

With this exercise you find out which parts of yourself you don't like and how much you don't like them. In all probability those are the parts of yourself you've tried to "lose," without being aware of how strongly you felt about them or how you try to block them out.

By not letting yourself be aware of them, by not acknowledging their existence, or by pretending they're not around, you lose features of yourself. You might be thinking, What's the good of admitting something you don't want anyway? Well, if you have a small sharp stone in your shoe and it hurts you, you can take off your shoe and remove it. But if you don't pay attention to it, it won't go away, and it will continue to hurt your foot. It may even make you feel so uncomfortable that you might miss something that is important to you.

In the same way, if you insist on ignoring a quality that is causing you trouble (conflict), you won't be able to decide to do something about discarding or changing it in a thoughtful way, so that it no longer adds to your supply of self-hate and keeps hurting you. Sometimes there's nothing you can do to change an unwanted aspect of your personality. In that case you continue to hurt yourself by continuing to worry over it. Rather, you might try turning your womanpower to the work of uncovering features of yourself that please you more. In this process you'll find the impact of disliked features slowly lessening.

Think of the large numbers of persons who are always trying to lose weight. They want to get rid of something, just as you want to get rid of those hated bits of yourself. Suppose a woman wants to lose sixty pounds. After making all kinds of efforts, she finds that if she loses more than thirty pounds she becomes cranky and difficult to live with. She is wise if she relinquishes her goal and works to advance other features of her personality and develop more style in her manner of grooming. The second thirty pounds will not melt away; but if she's satisfied with her efforts, in all likelihood she'll be able to maintain her new weight without great distress. She will have learned something important about who she is and can accept that, if she's willing to keep learning about other aspects of her being.

In some ways nearly everyone is trying to "lose" something she dislikes in herself. It may be poundage, a mannerism, an attitude, a trait. You can be more effective in this if you first acknowledge what it is you want to lose. Then you can work actively and consciously to rid yourself of just that—and not something else you prefer to keep. As I've indicated, when diligent, frontal attempts do not succeed, you can turn your womanpower into some other effort that will bring you a return you can accept.

All the while, you are making decisions, and you're in charge of what you're trying to accomplish. Whether or not you achieve your end doesn't change your connection or closeness to yourself. That closeness lies in your awareness of your decision and what you're doing with yourself. That closeness is what relieves your anxiety and makes you feel more accepting of all the things you are. I hope you realize that I'm not talking about closeness to yourself as a fearful, compulsive, egocentric concern, but as a state of awareness of your perceptions, sensitivities, and attitudes.

A NEW LIFE SYSTEM

Some of you may find it difficult to work with the lists I've given you. You may prefer a more open-ended method. So I'd like to suggest a variation for reentry, for the finding of your lost self. Perhaps you can work better by focusing on these questions. Remember that writing the points in your record book is a good way to make your efforts more productive. Try to answer the following briefly:

1. How do you see yourself?
2. What do you like about yourself?
3. What do you dislike about yourself?
4. What are you satisfied with?
5. What do you feel guilty about?
6. What would you like to be, do, or have in the *near* future?
7. How do you relate to another person?
8. Is there any way you'd like to change that?
9. Is there anything new you'd like to learn?
10. Have you tried it? If not, why not?

In this book I'm asking you to try the methods I'm suggesting. I'm well aware that I'm asking you to commit yourself to a long-term effort. Your best motivation in this work is the knowledge that you will be formulating a different *life system* for yourself, one of optimism and change. You are being asked to try new ways of thinking and behaving, of taking risks. Turning life habits into new directions takes time. Knowing this will encourage you when you feel results are slow in coming. But remember that to whatever degree you succeed, you are more likely to be in a position to deal with future stress in different and more satisfactory ways.

ONE WOMANPOWER

No human experience is ever completely lost or uncounted. This point is the fulcrum about which your work to help yourself will effectively turn. You are going to use your *body power*—your own reactions, interests, intellect, and observations—to regain those lost parts of yourself. All I can give you are explanations, encouragements, and suggestions for the process. You will do the rest. Please don't concern yourself with results as you work. Just try to go along as best you can with the suggestions offered.

It might help you to know, though, that like most persons you use only a very small percentage (5 to 25 percent) of the resources of your body and mind each day. As I've indicated, your mental attitudes can contribute to your strength and endurance (any athlete will confirm that), and a fit body can contribute to the healthy functioning of your intellectual processes. Remember, then, that whatever you feel you are not, you are still *one womanpower* to use as you will. You still have well over 50 percent of your physical and mental resources to employ in recovering your sense of well-being. I'd like to help you put that one full womanpower to work in behalf of lessening your dissatisfactions and anxieties.

If you stop to think about it, your feelings are reactions to a combination of physical, mental, and social (interpersonal) stimuli. While your control of interpersonal input is necessarily limited, you can use your one womanpower to determine the kinds of stimuli that come from your own brain and anatomy. So do yourself a favor. Try to become better acquainted with your very own secret weapon—*your one bodypower.*

CLOSENESS

I think you realize that loss of closeness to the elements of yourself, positive or negative, can create feelings of distance and estrangement from others. That loss can render you utterly miserable when, for example, you think your partner is no longer interested in you, or your employer doesn't consult you enough or your friends show too little concern for you.

You might regret your companions' lack of interest or concern, and long for it. But you don't have to be everlastingly miserable and feel so abused that you aren't getting the reactions you want. Your primary feeling of closeness has to be the outcome of your own concern for yourself. Your misery usually flows from a strong dependence upon another person, who is given, in effect, the guardianship of your ties with your own feelings. Such dependence can result in a shaky security base for you. As soon as external interest or concern in you wavers, you waver as well. Placing yourself in such a vulnerable position is not being fair to yourself, for there's rarely a reliable or sustained external source to supply you with the steadiness of self-regard that everyone needs to feel comfortable.

I know that, realistically, very, very few persons have a completely steady security base that they can maintain without some other person as support. But I want you to know that the *extent* of your need for external support is the factor you need to scrutinize. The degree to which you can support yourself will determine your sense of strength and self-reliance and the effectiveness of your womanpower.

In this context it's still surprising to note the large numbers of women still looking for the "other" to supply them with that support and closeness. "Unless I have someone to share the holiday with, I *know* I'll be miserable," says one of these women. They refuse to give up their insistence on remaining dependent and vulnerable. For them a sense of closeness always depends on a "relationship" as the only possible source of well-being. They permit their choices to narrow down to either a partner or loneliness. They will avail themselves of no other option.

I'm not saying that it's not a good thing to feel close to someone. It's a marvelous feeling. I *am* saying, though, that closeness with another person is a choice, not an inviolable imperative. It is secondary to your own sense of *primary closeness* to yourself, to the sense of self-ownership that you have when you can be alone without feeling deprived.

Primary closeness evolves in early life, in the context of other persons, namely, your family. At some point, however, you need to be able to swim alone. The life process, then, becomes one of separation, rejoining, individuation, and closeness, each at different points in time. Throughout, however, you need to extend and hold that sense of primary closeness to yourself. With it you can never feel totally dependent or abandoned when another person disappoints you by not sharing a closeness you desire. Perhaps a test for mental health might be the extent to which you could choose to be with someone or to be alone, and how well you felt with either choice. While closeness to yourself cannot guarantee the absence of loneliness, it can ensure the absence of ongoing despair.

X

Hang-ups
to Leave Behind

Shoulds can grind you into the ground. They can make you feel depressed, remiss, guilty, anxious, and at least marginally discontented. And that's putting it mildly. Once established as part of a compulsive life system, shoulds become rigid *musts.* You are continuously admonished by your inner judge. Shoulds dictate how you should feel, think, or act, and they expect an impossible best all the time.

According to your shoulds, no goal is unattainable. For example, the student who receives 85 percent on schoolwork is unhappy if she feels she should receive 95 percent. Shoulds drive you to insist upon goals that may be totally unrealistic for *you.* They drive you to believe that anything can be understood, learned, and endured; that relationships with *all* persons should be exemplary; that deviations from these goals are not acceptable.

Related to words like *standards, expectations, oughts, goals, beliefs, imperatives, dictates,* and *mandates,* the word *should* is a commonly utilized expression which captures an underlying quality of self-incrimination and bondedness to your inner demands of yourself. For example, you will feel and exclaim repeatedly: "I should have known that!" "I shouldn't have done that!" In some individuals, such admonishments are endless. When unmet, they are demands which can reduce you to a state of self-loathing. With all that, however, I believe that an understanding of your *should system* can start you on a voyage that will diminish its harmful impact on your regard for yourself.

Some individuals take issue, though, with a notion of the harmfulness of shoulds. "How can you run your life without standards and goals?" they ask. "With difficulty," I would answer. That is not the point however. For you surely need some sense of order and structure to your plans for yourself. The point at issue here is one of *flexibility* regarding the structure you might wish to impose upon yourself. Any goals or standards you have need to be shaped by your abilities, your interests, your needs, your limitations, and be appropriate and relevant to them. Such considerations can keep your expectations within reasonable bounds, and serve to dissipate the absolute arbitrariness of a compulsive *should* system which may be not only unrealistic for you but totally inflexible. You can see where you might be driven by this combination of inflexibility and lack of attention to your personal reality. Too often, an acute depression can follow a sudden sense of failure of your shoulds.

WHAT ARE YOUR SHOULDS?

Driven by shoulds, therefore, you can be deprived of free choice in your dealings with yourself as well as with others. Shoulds become the instruments that urge you to connect with that perfect imaginary you. They compel you to pursue that imaginary image in order to feel acceptable. It's an image that will correspond to whatever characteristics you think most generally valued among your peers.

For example, your *should* system makes you feel you should be "the best" in honor, integrity, dignity, intellect, fair play, and reserve. Or it may dictate that you should be always warm, loving, affectionate, and fun-loving. Or glamorous and sexy. Or an outdoor type. It might drive you to believe that you should be indefatigable, innovative, and enthusiastic without end in your work. Any time you feel you fall short of the image you've established for yourself, which will be frequently, you will feel like a wretched failure. While failure is an in-built feature of living for everyone, wretchedness need not be.

Among other very common, recognizable shoulds are some of the following stereotypes: "Loving" mothers should and must always care for their families, even if they are in a sickbed. "Loyal" assistants should and must be available at any time, regardless of their personal needs. "Dependable" friends should and must be rocks, even when they need support themselves. "Serious" thinkers shouldn't and mustn't ever do or say anything foolish. And so on. You can further illuminate the concept for yourself if you think of people you know who fit these or similar descriptions.

What I'm describing is for the most part an unconscious, compulsive process. Still, I believe that you can "get a handle" on it. As you become aware of its workings, you will learn how to loosen its grip on you. Disposing of it entirely is not our goal; it would be unrealistic to expect that. Rather, I am interested first in helping you to expose and scrutinize your *should* system. Then, as you accomplish that, you can begin to reduce its destructive impact on the quality of your existence.

I am encouraged by what I have seen in this regard. As soon as you can identify with what I'm describing, you can start to unravel the web that shoulds weave about your spirit and your will. From there to the next step is a matter of time and practice. Time is needed for you to grow familiar with how the system works after you have identified various shoulds within yourself. Then you have to be willing to accept your part in keeping it alive for all these years. At that point of recognition you might be very hard on yourself with thoughts such as these: How could you be so stupid, so unaware, so naive, as not to see what you were expecting of yourself, how you were hurting yourself, how you were groveling before your own idols?

Now just look at what is happening when you do that. Once more shoulds are admonishing, saying that you *should* have known what you were doing all along so that you could have avoided it. See how quickly new shoulds can climb up on the shoulders of old ones you think you understand and are putting to rest. This is merely the *should shuffle,* where you push more obvious old-time shoulds into the background and let new ones dictate to you. You see how slippery they are. But that's all right—it's what usually happens. I'm telling you now so that you can expect it, and perhaps not be fooled when it takes place.

But I have to warn you again immediately, because it's so easy to be lulled into thinking you're on top of everything. Then you'll feel disgust with yourself for allowing yourself to be fooled anyway. Another should rears its head: You shouldn't be fooled by something you've been told to expect! See how it works? There are always dozens of little shoulds lurking in the shadows, ready to run out and replace the one you've already exposed.

How, then, can you keep ahead of them? By keeping at it. By emphasizing your womanpower. By believing that *you—all* of you—are stronger than those many minor and major shoulds. By remembering that they will weaken as you maintain your resolve to expose them to the truth of your reality. By being determined not to worship arrogant, false idols. By learning something about humility in admitting your limitations. By taking a kindly view of your falterings as first you understand, then try to shuffle, and finally let go of your own demand for a pathetic glory. This is the cure for the overcoming of any compulsive drive in your personality.

Let me remind you that this process may arouse anxiety. But that's to be expected. Don't let it stop you, for it's anxiety born of a hesitation (conflict) about constructive change. You'll live through it, and as you find yourself going through the steps I've described, you'll begin to feel less tense. At that point, you'll know that you've begun to take charge, and that your shoulds are starting to melt down like the Wicked Witch of the West.

WHY A SHOULD SYSTEM?

In the context of describing neurotic behavior dynamically, the term *shoulds* was first used in the 1930s by Dr. Karen Horney. It is her dynamic interpretation of shoulds that has filtered down through the years in the academic and mental health communities. And it was principally her followers who applied her concept of the "tyranny of the shoulds" to their clinical work, and who repeatedly have been able to demonstrate its validity. That concept was one that Horney lectured and wrote about throughout her career as a psychiatrist and psychoanalyst. To understand its many facets is to understand one of the basic features of the neurotic process. In more recent years writers have also grasped much of its meaning and have capitalized on the impact of the concept by popularizing it in their writings. At times its clinical origins have been obscured and overlooked because of such popularizations, which have nevertheless been necessary in transposing important information and bringing it to the attention of the public.

But why a *should* system at all? As you read through the material here, you will find that a very large number of people have poor feelings about themselves, developed early in life. Simply put, they do not feel good about themselves in many respects. They actually look down upon their natural or acquired abilities. Poor self-esteem makes it difficult for them to accept themselves as they are. They have constant, lingering feelings that they are never quite good enough as workers, parents, friends, students, or partners.

I'm not inferring that you are caught in a *should* system if you try to make yourself and your condition more to your liking. You may do this because it pleases you to see growth and evidence of change in yourself, not because you feel you are a terrible person. A *should* system is evolved only when you start from a position of self-rejection. It is designed to produce (with your imagination) a person that you find tolerable. (The process of insisting upon seeing yourself through rose-colored glasses was described earlier in the section "Dynamics of Conflict and Anxiety" in Chapter Three.)

The wish for acceptability and approval is a natural one and develops very early in life. It is part of the need for *positive affirmation* that every child must have. It also contributes significantly to unfolding feelings of self-identity. In a positively affirming environment, the child's errors of judgment, mistakes, forgetfulness, disobedience, and other shortcomings do not damage that identity. Most of what a child does can be taken as a matter of course in the maturation process and needs to be neither credited nor discredited.

In such an atmosphere, then, children can grow freely, curiously, and spontaneously, learning in the process to know themselves, their abilities, their limitations, and respecting the efforts they are encouraged to make. Such children develop little fear of disapproval or rejection, and little dependence upon praise for a sense of well-being. A steady flow of environmental affirmation—not praise—teaches them that they are accepted for whatever they are.

The overuse of praise is dangerous. If children become dependent on praise for a sense of worth, they may feel that something is wrong with them when it is not forthcoming. It's like becoming accustomed to a rich diet. When you don't have it, your food may taste flat. Since the external environment is unlikely to offer the "gobs" of praise that family environments often do, children may learn to seek social satisfactions at home to the exclusion of seeking them elsewhere. In so doing, they miss out on social development with peers, one important element of the maturation process.

On the other hand, where the environment is largely a nonaffirming or a negatively affirming one, so-called mistakes are deplored, and the child can develop a sense of being generally "bad." Suitable rules are essential to some kind of orderly living. But an overabundance of rules and regulations, too many parental frowns and scoldings, and too much family tension and anger may be viewed by the child as signs of disapproval and rejection. Please remember, however, that parental disapproval is a fact of life. I'm referring here only to an imbalance, where the negative parental output far exceeds the positive.

Too much disapproval, then, makes the child feel uncomfortable, "bad"; and she cannot tolerate those feelings for too long. (Just think how long *you* might be able to stand such disapproval.) She is then required to learn what to do to be considered "good"—that is, approved of. Children have the ability to learn that lesson very quickly, even when they fail to practice it.

At a very early age, then, a child has learned that there is an acceptable (good) way to be and an unacceptable (bad) way to be. It's clear to her that the way she is expected to be and should be is "good," and so she makes efforts directed toward that end. Like anyone else, though, she makes many mistakes. If those failures are reinforced by too many harsh parental responses, she comes to fear them and to strive more and more to live up to her pitiful little shoulds, which she really can't fulfill because she's so inexperienced.

By later childhood, however, she is more adept, and already she has a better-functioning set of shoulds. They become more elaborate, more restrictive, and more controlling if the environment remains primarily a judgmental one. She is constantly whipped into shape by her *should* system, because of her recurring fear that she will be met by disapproval and rejection if she slips. These points are among the early developments that determine the quality of confidence, trust, and self-esteem that a person will carry into adulthood. They will affect the nature of her conflicts and the manner in which she tries to resolve them.

Let me point out that no parent is out to deliberately effect a detrimental development in a child. It can happen, though, because of the much less than ideal conditions in which parents themselves have been raised and then pass on to offspring. Certainly most parents make every effort to do their very best with their children. And it is in fact their very best. Little service is afforded them by pointing out how poor that best may be.

I am not suggesting that children are best "let be." *Positive child affirmation* is a very active process and something parents need to understand, learn, and apply in order to change the quality of their parenting, so that their children can grow with confidence to take their place among their peers. Affirmation is entirely compatible with essential discipline and restrictive parental moves. Children do not suffer from discipline that is just and kindly imposed. They have a strong sense of what's fair or necessary. Even punishment that is not imposed with a hurtful or humiliating intent can be accepted, though not enjoyed. Once more I need to remind you that the spirit of a parent's approach has a much greater impact on a child's view of herself than has the specific content of the approach.

In order to implement new thinking along these lines, parent education is becoming part of educational systems in some parts of the country. It ought to be investigated if you have an interest in the subject.

RULES OF THE SYSTEM

Shoulds, then, form a network of conscious and unconscious goadings and restrictions, which frequently oppose or extend too far beyond your natural inner strivings. That network provides the substance of a *should* system, which *in its extreme form* can tyrannize you and rule your every moment. Any wish to change, any questioning, any failure to fulfill its demands, can arouse your anxiety.

I have indicated how your *should* system is composed of a very large number of *rigid rules and regulations* that you began to establish early in life. You keep adding to them from time to time, and they are not negotiable. Shoulds are derived from your cultural, social, and familial heritage, as well as from the imperatives of your peers, the immediate social climate, and your own intrapsychic pressures. For some of you, there is a should for every occasion, for every thought, wish, or deed.

You might be wondering what can be so damaging about that. Nothing, if you are free to choose and use the rule *when it is appropriate and suitable.* There's nothing wrong about developing and using your own personal rules and regulations *if you can accept yourself when you don't live up to them.* In other words, if you can take them or leave them, as is relevant, then you are not shackled by a *should* system.

But a multitude of women cannot do this. And so they carry an enormous burden of guilt as they see themselves less than perfect performers according to the mandates set up by their *should* system. If they do not live up to the letter of the should, they feel uneasy and even unworthy. When a discrepancy arises between the quality of their being and that dictated by their *should* system, they feel dissatisfied and frustrated. This kind of reaction is one you must identify in yourself and refuse to honor as you have in the past.

SHOULDS AS A LIFE SYSTEM

Once it's well formulated in adulthood, a *should* system is consistent and predictable, unless you are willing to work to dissolve its power over you—which is possible, as I've mentioned above. Helping you to weaken some aspect of that life system is one of the principal goals of this book. There are, however, unknown numbers of women (and men) who seem content to live according to that predictable, dependable, unchanging, and *rigid life system.* But there are also countless numbers who feel stifled and frustrated by their *should* system, because it leaves no space for deviation or innovation, for risk taking or adventure.

When you do deviate—and since you're only human, it happens repeatedly—you suffer from the guilt I've already spoken of many times. You cannot avoid feeling troubled that you haven't adhered to the inner commands on which so much of a sense of identity and security depends.

Here again are the familiar elements of inner conflict. You want to break away from the stifling effects of a fixed *should* system; yet you want to remain with the seeming safety and dependability of that system and keep your image of a "good" person untarnished. To weaken its hold, therefore, you need to realize that the safety you've invested in your *should* system is a specious one, manufactured by your imagination. With that insight you can begin to work your way free of it—that is, if you aren't overwhelmed by your disappointment in its illusory nature. At that point your work with the twenty-step program will be given a strong boost toward success.

Until you have this insight, your *should* system makes you feel that you must always be equipped and ready with the proper feeling or response for any occasion. If your personality is such that you enjoy pleasing others, your *should* system does not permit you to please selectively, as you might wish. You are obliged to please indiscriminately and all the time. There's that absolute again—*all the time.*

Please remember, though, that I'm describing extreme forms here. There are *degrees* of involvement in your *should* system, and a broad range of possible formulations. There is no doubt that you are not totally bound by the restrictions of your *should* system. There are features of your life that are open and free and spontaneous. When you are relaxing or playing, you are more likely to be free of shoulds. When you are involved with music, art, or beauty of any sort, you may also be free of them. Even when you try something new, you may be free of your *should* system. For example, lots of people describe a great sense of freedom when they travel. In that case no one knows them, how they feel, or what they expect. No one can expect anything of them, they feel. There's a sense of freedom from the mandate of the shoulds. The censor has been left at home, and they are left with a pleasant easiness.

I want to repeat that I am not speaking against standards, or against orderly and disciplined living, when I speak of how your shoulds can tyrannize your lives. Self-discipline is something you consciously devise to help you order your life and achieve certain goals. Self-discipline becomes part of your *should* system only if it becomes an inflexible, compulsive set of rules that robs you of any preference. It has become part of your *should* system only when you find it ruling you, when you find yourself responding without enthusiasm, interest, or initiating will.

Rose is one woman who describes the burden of her *should* system at work. She speaks: "I feel edgy most of the time. It isn't that my job is so demanding, or all that important. Yet I'm always a little worried about what I do. It's ridiculous, really, because it's an easy job. But I worry about what the people in the place think of me, of what I say, what I wear. When I get home, I feel so much better. I can't wait to get into my little apartment, where I can do as I please, and not what I think someone else wants me to do. It's such a relief to feel *even*—no ups or downs. No uncomfortable uneasiness that I feel all day. I can eat, sleep, sit around. It's so relaxing. It's the only way I can make the day. If I didn't have that to look forward to, I don't know what would happen. But I can achieve that even state because I'm alone. As soon as I have someone over, or go out and socialize somewhere, the motor—anxiety—starts running again. Although I like to get out to have fun at times, I know I have to pay for it."

Rose is describing her constant concern with her shoulds. They stand around her on all sides like soldiers. She is always aware of something that she feels is out there watching her. She doesn't realize that those external expectations are only reflections of her own inner demands of herself. Failing to fulfill them, she feels "edgy" all day. What she means is that she feels anxious, and feels relieved only when she's away from people.

There can be different sources of anxiety in dealing with your *should* system. You can feel anxious, as Rose does, because you don't feel you are "making it," and you believe you'll be criticized by your peers. Or having "made it," you're not sure you can maintain it. Or you can feel anxious because you unconsciously hate the restrictions your *should* system imposes on you, and you're fighting it all the time. But you feel that it's dangerous to fight your "mother" *should* system because you might be subjected to "unknown and terrible retaliations" if you don't obey like a lamb. If you identify with what I'm saying, you're beginning to undermine your *should* system.

The maintenance of a fantasy self-image depends upon the proper working of a *should* system. If you can't be "good" according to your system, then you often feel totally "bad." You must have noticed how suddenly you can feel very much "in the pits" when you're disappointed in something you did. That's the feeling you fight to avoid. It's that bad feeling you dread, the feeling of shame, guilt, stupidity, or the quick shift into depression.

You feel that the "goodness" your shoulds demand can save you from feeling "bad" or from being unimportant and ordinary. But it can't. And until you decide to disrupt it with constructive actions, you're caught in the middle of a sea of anxiety—whether you fail, or whether you go with your *should* system and "succeed." But your determination to live more independently will break that chain of events when you cry out, "Enough! It's time for a change!"

It's a poignant struggle, and persons of all ages, women and men, are caught in it. Rose feels (and perhaps you do, too) as if a dozen or more people are always standing around judging her, criticizing how she looks, sounds, behaves. She is totally unaware that those judgments she imagines are all expressions of her own self-critical apparatus. Nor is she aware that most people have neither the time nor the interest to occupy themselves that way. That insight can afford her some relief. On the other hand, she might feel devastated if she senses such total disinterest in her. So she externalizes her own critical self-judgment outward onto them by fantasizing that they are critical of her. Then she keeps busy with her troubled reactions to self-made negative fantasies of herself.

While I want to emphasize the inflexibility of the system, I want you to know as well that it can be made to bow before your persistent efforts toward a different form of existence. That inflexibility can feed doubt and fear in you upon any new undertaking that has no preexisting shoulds established for it. You've heard the expression, "I didn't know what I should say in that situation. I didn't know how I should feel."

FEELINGS VS. SHOULDS

Goodness! How can you know how to feel in a new situation? You will feel the way you will feel. Feelings suddenly spring alive and are with you before you can "permit" them. You can't avoid having them; they're inevitable and unpredictable. But you can certainly decide what you will say or do about a feeling. It's always your choice. For example, if you think you might be tactless, or you don't want to risk certain consequences, you can remain silent. But that's your decision to make. Not every feeling needs to be openly expressed. Only your awareness of it is required for you to deal with it appropriately.

Many people have great difficulty with what-should-I-do and how-should-I-feel when a dear one is dying. They do not want to visit because they feel so "badly." One of the reasons they feel bad, or anxious, is that they feel unprepared for a change that will occur. They don't trust their natural responsiveness and they become anxious.

"Should I try to be cheerful?" they ask. "Should I stay a little while or a long while? Should I read, or try to talk? What should I say if he says he's dying? Should I cry if I feel like it?" Answers to these questions come best from your own sensibilities. But kindness, tenderness, even humor, can go a long way in solving your dilemma. The dying are frequently lonely and depressed, and terribly anxious as well, and your presence just might relieve those feelings.

Try to think of what you might feel or want if you were in a similar position. Couldn't you just touch him, to relieve his sense of isolation? Couldn't you help him with a drink, wipe the perspiration from his face, move his arms or head to relieve his stiffness, tell him there's a bird singing on a tree branch outside the window?

Think of how we comfort each other in distress. Is dying any different, except that it's more mysterious, more final? When you say, "I don't know what I should do or say," is that really true? Aren't you giving yourself too little credit? Haven't you ever comforted anyone before? Haven't you ever been in a situation where a person could hardly move to help herself? Can you use your feelings of sorrow and your common sense to raise these questions and teach yourself what to do, even though it may be the first time?

You don't need shoulds or rules for such a situation, or for many other circumstances. Nor do you need to feel ill equipped. You have all the answers and resources in your own being, in your own compassionate responses to misery and fearfulness. You might make some mistakes. But I think I can say that you'd learn quickly what to repeat and what to avoid. I also think you'd feel good regarding what you'd learned about yourself and caring.

FEELINGS AND CHOICE

You know by now that I am not an advocate of indiscriminate change. I am not for letting *any* feeling or thought fall out of your mouth regardless of its possible harmful effects on you or anyone else. Surely we've all noted how unsettling, even devastating, that can be in personal relationships. What's more, I'm not for promoting haphazard approaches to solutions or reckless activity on behalf of change.

But I *am* for encouraging you to try to be aware of what your feeling or opinion really is. I am for encouraging you to try to make a considered decision about what you want. These are marks of *autonomy*. They are also part of the *privilege* you have been demanding but which some of you are hesitant or afraid to assume and practice. This is the privilege of choosing your own move in your own time. It is a privilege men have assumed and practiced throughout their history. I've indicated, however, that while men have had that privilege in many sectors of their existence—certainly more so than women— they, too, have been similarly bound by the restrictions of their *should* systems. And they, too, can learn how to benefit by gradually undermining their shoulds.

When you decide you've had enough, you can begin to diminish the impact of your *should* system so that it doesn't hold so much power over you. Using the twenty-step method is one way of doing that. You can find new sources of well-being in acceptance of yourself as a person with both advantages and limitations. That knowledge can be used as a strong weapon against a *should* system that constantly mars a reasonable freedom. You need to learn to accept that most of us fall short of the images we secretly construct for ourselves. In real life both accomplishment and nonaccomplishment are part of our human inheritance. Whether you can or cannot accomplish, you are still one of us.

As a member of the human race you can be "great" in some respects and awful in others. You are wonderful in the fact that each human being is a marvel of creation. Although you are not personally responsible for that, you are personally responsible for keeping that marvel in good condition, so that it can live well and usefully and unafraid to meet the changes and challenges of the times. Your greatest satisfaction can be found in the power you can develop and hold to rule your own life. The choice is yours. But you need to be willing to confront your fear of change. In the next section you'll find some explanations for that fear and several steps you can take to overcome it.

XI

Anxiety and the Anatomy of Change

A change from the practice of pessimistic and self-destructive life patterns to more hopeful ones is certainly a positive move. Yet, for all the need to change, just contemplating it can strike fear into your heart. That fear is one of the deepest roots of conflict, anxiety, and depression.

Fear of change is commonly referred to as fear of the unknown. But there's a difference between these two, for change can be regarded from other points of view. You can make a change to something that is, in fact, unknown and unpredictable. It may be something you've never experienced, thought of, or even heard about.

You can also make a change to something that you do know about, something that is common in the experience of those in your environment. It might be an attitude or an activity. You could not say it was unknown in a strict sense. Nevertheless, if you were to move into a known position, *but new for you*, your anxiety could very well be aroused.

There is also the situation where the fear is related more to leaving behind something that is familiar and habitual. Giving up the sense of security that familiar habits hold for you can make you feel uneasy, frequently leading to a depression. You may then resist the change in order to avoid new anxiety that is aroused and the depression that might follow. The approach described here can help you to reduce that anxiety to some extent.

APPROACHING CHANGE

Each kind of change entails a movement away from what you're involved with at the moment. It requires you to shift your position by considering several points before any action can take place. Therefore, in order to make a change you have to consider these points:

1. Make the decision to change in some way.
2. Select the change you want to make.
3. Plan how you're going to undertake your move.
4. Anticipate the risk of failure when you make your attempt.
5. Overcome the inertia of your present position.

Please write these five points in your record book and start responding to them in an easy way. Try not to get all wound up with them. Move on if any one is troublesome.

What do I mean when I speak of changing something? *Something* can be anything: an attitude, a thought, a prejudice, an action, a feeling, a value, a wish. It can refer to items like a job, car, school, garden, home, style, friend, lover. But it also refers to the changing of harmful or useless and time-consuming life habits that impair your well-being in some way. In order to help yourself, you need to learn to avoid scattering your *anxiety energy* and put it to work productively by planning constructive moves. Anxiety energy is there to be used and it will drive you in any event. Therefore, *you* might as well be the one to decide *how* it drives you. This was discussed in more detail in Chapter Six. See if you can put your anxiety energy to work by raising these questions based on the five steps just mentioned.

1. Do I think I *want* to make a change? (No point in frustrating yourself at the outset if you aren't interested just now.)
2. *What* is it I want to change? What single unit of concern can I isolate that I want to change?
3. Once I've decided what I want to change, *how* am I going to

go about it? What specific, concrete plans do I have to make
to begin to effect the change I've selected?

4. Can I prepare myself for *failure* as well as success? Can I
   remember that no matter what small move I contemplate,
   there are at least two possible outcomes—success or failure?
5. What will my very first move be? *Which* step will overcome
   my present position of inertia and get me moving in the direction I want to go? How can I summon up the courage to take
   that step?

You will have to think a bit about these points. When you're ready,
you can work with them in an active way by writing the questions in
your record book and trying to set down your first responses to them.
Working with these preliminary questions can begin to give you a
sense of autonomy over your life and prepare you to work more
effectively with the twenty-step program outlined in Part Two.

I keep urging you to use a record book because it's almost impossible to hold all your questions, thoughts, and plans in your mind, even
under the best of circumstances. When you feel anxious, thoughts
bounce about and collide at random. Frequently, they can't be dealt
with in an orderly fashion, and I can assure you that there's no virtue
in making your task more anxiety producing. That's something you
certainly don't need!

WHICH CHANGE FOR YOU?

The women's movement has to do with change of course—change for
women, men, families, industry, religion, politics. No one and nothing
escapes the flak of an enthusiastic (and essential) exploding of the old
myths and mystiques of womanhood. Awarenesses have become shar-
pened regarding attitudes, opinions, prejudices, values, wishes, needs,
abilities, options, and talents. Proponents and dissenters create a
paradox, among women of all ages and positions, that gives rise to
extraordinary uneasiness, to family disruptions, to confusion, and to
uncertainty.

In raising their consciousness level many women have also raised
their anxiety level. Shifting attitudes point to the anxiety of change.

As a positive feature of change, however, you become involved in countless new activities, new careers, new associations, new thoughts and feelings.

There are all shapes, forms, and manners of moving toward the modifications you are determined to make. Be assured that there's a way for each one of you who wants to be different, new, in some way. But for your efforts to be most effective, the way you choose has to be compatible with your particular style, your personality, your position and circumstances. The first thing you have to do is to *find a way that is suitable, comfortable, and convenient for you*—not simply one that happens to be popular at the moment.

SERENITY LOST

Whichever path is followed, and whatever gains are made, change almost invariably leads to the loss of serenity, which generates new anxiety in women of all ages. It's especially high among adolescents and young women. This group feels obliged to consider questions that lay dormant for generations: Do you want to marry or remain single? Do you want children or not? Do you want to divorce or remain married? Do you want to work outside the home as well as in it? Do you want to work at a *job*, or do you plan to build a career? Do you want volunteer, part-time, or full-time work? Do you want to live alone or with others?

Other women are considering these questions: Do you want to further your education regardless of your age or position? How much responsibility do you want to take or to share? How much leadership are you willing to assume? How much ownership are you going to demand? Will you invest your own money? How many rights and privileges will you expect? How much power will you seek?

Some of you are asking: What choices do I want to make regarding my activities, my behavior, my relationships, my work, my play? How can I decide what will be most productive or satisfying for me? What are the changing needs of those who depend upon me? How can I meet them reasonably without undermining my own needs? What are my talents and assets? How can I exploit them to the fullest? How can I categorize options open to me so that I make sound decisions?

How can I establish priorities if my home or work situation keeps shifting? How do I know when to move and when to stay?

These questions cannot be answered *now*. They can only be considered at appropriate times. Women who raise too many of them become frenzied by the variety of new options. That's because they feel impelled to accept each new concept, each new question, as an undeniable imperative. Such anxiety can be avoided by pausing to sift them through a thoughtful, selective system.

This is what's done by women who have learned to make decisions and who value their opinions. They are the least fearful of departures from precedent. They are the women who have held responsible positions in the marketplace or at home. They know whether or not they approve of something. They are confident enough to accept or reject innovation. While even these women have felt a compulsive need to be compliant and agreeable, they can now enjoy changes in attitude that relieve them of the guilt they often felt when they exercised their authority in the past. I mention these women as persons who have already gone through the process I am suggesting that you try.

NEW SHOULDS

As I've already indicated, there are many troubled "new women" who experience new anxiety from their acquiring of *new shoulds* and from their inability to discharge their anger. They are experientially aware of still existing discriminatory practices at work, school, or home and are not meek in their reactions. But even as they express their indignation, they continue to feel *anger anxiety* in direct proportion to their struggle with their residual guilt. That guilt keeps anger from being effectively discharged. As anger increases, more of that *female residual guilt* is aroused. As long as such guilt persists, so does anger anxiety.

These women feel guilty because they are in conflict over their right to express angry feelings. They are still attached to their old image of womanliness and are still unwittingly trying to maintain some of its features. This is another instance of unconsciously wanting it both ways—to be outspoken with your indignation and anger, and to be loved for being a good, forbearing woman—that is, one who does not express so-called negative emotions. The conflict remains a virulent one, because these women have moved too quickly in acquiring new shoulds, rather than new strengths, and because they still cling to some of their old shoulds. In addition, one of those new shoulds leads them to believe that they have to go "all the way" and express their anger each and every time it is aroused. Because that is socially impossible, their guilt and their fear of retaliation regenerate, and they enter a quandary over which should to follow, the old or the new.

On the positive side, however, is another possibility. Although attitudinal changes are slow to come, sometimes new shoulds can serve to loosen the old and make way for something else that might eventually be more constructive. But only small increments of change can be expected with each segment of effort. And when we deal with deeply ingrained personal and cultural attitudes, the smallest changes are to be welcomed for the courage they represent.

New shoulds are also found in those women who do not suffer especially from discriminatory practices, but who have evolved new sets of unrealistic inner and outer demands. These demands are often inappropriate or incompatible with the circumstances in which the women find themselves; and their own expectations of their performance can be overwhelming. They give themselves tasks to accomplish that take the strength and endurance of superpersons. Ellen is one of these young women. She works in the media and shares an apartment with another woman. She works very hard, and after-hours she puts in another "shift" several evenings a week.

Ellen talks about herself: "I never have the feeling that I can go home and think about relaxing all evening. I'm on the go all day. I do want to get ahead. It's rough, because sometimes you're ignored. They want your ideas, and when you have some, they say they don't like them. I don't know if it's like that every place. But there's a lot of tension and competition where I work.

"Then I've got to get home, shop, cook, eat, wash my hair, and get dressed. There are so many places to go. You've got to keep on the go to meet people. I'm out two or three times during the week and on the weekend. It's very expensive to keep that up. I stay out a few hours, come back, and have to get ready for the next day before I go to bed.

"I can't afford to go away for weekends to relax. But I made a great discovery recently. I can go to my parents' home for the weekend. It's quiet there. They don't expect anything of me. There's good food, and it's easy to get my laundry done. I have a friend who's horrified that I want to go there once in a while to retreat and get away from it all. But I tell her not to knock it before she's tried it. The secret of harmony that I've discovered with my parents is not to expect them to have your views. After all, if you want them to respect your views, you've got to be willing to respect theirs. You can't argue with them. It seems to work for me."

She continues about her life in the city. "I have a lot of energy. But I still feel so tired sometimes. At times, I wonder if it's all worth it."

What you hear in Ellen is how a person follows a set of new shoulds for the way a young career woman in a city is supposed to conduct herself. What she does with her time is not always in keeping with her wishes, but with a picture (image) of what she should be doing with it.

Of course this is not true for all young women in her position. But there are many of them. It is disheartening to see such youth, energy, and productiveness thrown away on activities that aren't enjoyed and about which there is conflict. I must emphasize that it's not the specific activity that is at issue here. It is the element of choice that seems to be absent. Without that, Ellen cannot choose a change to something different.

If Ellen is freely choosing to live her life as she does, and if she is not self-destructive, it would be difficult to fault her in terms of healthful living. You may not agree with her, but individual tastes are often beyond question. But if Ellen subjects herself to this "on the go" kind of life because of the compulsiveness of her new shoulds, then she needs to hold her actions up for scrutiny.

Ellen is afraid of being bored, a great national fear in this decade. No one must ever be bored, according to some unwritten law. For some persons it's as if they'll break out in an incurable rash if—perish the thought—they should be bored for a while. Ellen feels she must be continuously "challenged." She feels bound not to let a challenge escape untouched. She doesn't understand that running from boredom so frantically is not too different from being bored, for there can be anxiety in both. She doesn't understand that boredom is part of life and that if it's troubling you, constructive steps can be taken to deal with it.

Ellen's image of the new woman depicts a perpetual fight for freedom or autonomy. New shoulds dictate: Don't let anyone tell you what to do. Don't let anyone guide or help you; you can do it all by yourself. She's not aware that her "great discovery" about being able to relax at home with her parents has put one of those new shoulds to rest: Don't have anything to do with your parents. Stay away from them. Don't share anything with them because they'll spoil it. Despite such imperatives Ellen is beginning to rediscover the peace and special warmth she can find only in the ready and enduring embrace of her family.

Clara, too, illustrates this point. She accepted a position as a teacher's assistant in the fourth grade. She was miserable from the beginning because she was expected to *assist,* and she felt that was demeaning. "I've been trained to be a teacher, and he won't let me do what I know I can do." Her new shoulds kept her completely alienated from the fact that *she'd been hired to be assistant,* and the assistant's duties were different from those of the classroom teacher. She expected equal duties and equal responsibility. These were not written into her contract. Nor was she being paid the wage that those responsibilities and that position demanded.

Both of these young women have an unwarranted sense of obligation toward themselves, which does not necessarily relate to the realities of their positions. Both feel that they should always be doing the best for themselves. Again, you cannot dispute that. But when that "best" collides destructively with other factors that have to be taken into consideration, you do have to wonder about it.

Ellen feels she should be rushing about getting "into" anything that's new and exciting. Her word is *challenging.* For example, she takes on new sexual formulae like new fashion fads. She has to "try" them, whether or not they're compatible with her desires or style. She feels she must ever expand her range of activities, her interests, her circle of friends. She should travel. She should never, God forbid, be dependent upon the support system her family has been willing to provide her. Was she ever surprised at how good it felt to visit with them!

Before that should was exploded, she insisted that only friends were dependable for support, for comfort, for companionship. She was often irritated when they proved not to be so reliable or available, not recognizing that they were all into their own problems as she was into hers. She said she was willing to support them, but they had to support her when she needed it. No provision was made for the time when they had the same need at the same time.

If you're financially self-supporting, you can easily be led to believe in a myth of independence, another new should. That myth, coupled with the demand for interdependence among peers, brings many confused and troubled young women into treatment. Their abject dependency is in considerable contrast to their imaginary images of themselves. With slogans of liberation swirling about in their heads, they have assumed that they are indeed autonomous. They have taken those slogans as the banner of freedom. Then why, they ask, are they so anxious, so depressed, so unhappy?

Though these women are hard-working and able, they haven't learned that breaking molds (old shoulds) takes care and skill. You can't merely substitute new shoulds for old. They have not learned that there are limits to what they can accomplish in any direction they choose for themselves. They have no sense that they must select, must establish priorities, that they can't do everything that pops into their heads.

They need to find out many things. They can't fulfill all their bursting expectations in jobs, social life, or sex; they cannot maintain perpetual action. All jobs aren't great or well-paying, no matter what they were told. Most jobs are ordinary, routine, and won't take the place of the work that they must do to develop into substantial well-grounded persons. These women will tire like anyone else. They'll become disinterested. They'll find that they can't keep up with their own pushing, something that frequently throws them into a panic.

They blame themselves—the system—anything. "What's wrong with me?" they ask. "Everyone else is doing it. Why can't I?" When they reach a certain level of tension, they may resort to drugs to help them to relax. They don't entertain the notion that they're trying to do too much, for they've conditioned themselves through the shoulds of a new image, which become as much of a bind as old shoulds have been.

New shoulds include exaggerations of all kinds. In addition to those just mentioned, there's the endless emphasis on "communicating," "competing," "relating," "challenging," "supporting," "sharing," "rights." Certain of these women believe that their liberty overrides any other consideration, which frequently makes them appear arrogant, rude, inconsiderate, and self-destructive, especially when they insist on "confronting" in offensive ways. They expect catch phrases, smatterings of erudition, and the use of "psychobabble" to establish their position as persons in the know, persons to be reckoned with. They often develop an unpleasantly hostile manner that turns off the very persons of whom they are making demands.

Their associates sometimes look upon their vain efforts in favor of self-prescribed rights as so much nonsense, not to be taken seriously, an attitude which enrages them. They feel abused and coerced by a need to cooperate, compromise, or accommodate, as the case may be. They see such requirements as acts of humiliating submission.

Women like Ellen and Clara have little understanding of the principle of combined effort for accomplishing a task or project. They have little idea of how to work, live, or talk with employers, parents, teachers, co-workers, partners. They feel they can blurt out anything that's on their minds in the interest of being honest and "letting it all hang out."

Values are distorted and confused. They range from the inappropriately familiar to the strident. The possible effect of an inappropriate familiarity is lost on them. Then they are offended if a stranger responds to them in what *they* consider too familiar a manner. They have not grasped the distinction between friendliness and familiarity. They have not appreciated that all situations are not "equal" according to their own evaluation, that they must judge each encounter according to its actual features and not according to their fantasies of what those features should be. They firmly believe that *their* grievances should be *your* concerns.

Such young women have difficulty finding a "suitable" person with whom to share their lives. *Suitable* points to a person who must fulfill expectations that are for the most part naively unrealistic. They assume that to express their displeasure, automatically ensures their partner's understanding acquiesence.

Dealing with middle-aged men in power can also cause grief for this group of women. They become argumentative and stand on their "rights." The men then hesitate to help, support, or advance them even if it's in their power to do so. When this occurs, the women are exasperated at the slow pace of their progress and become more impatient, more angry, and less confident. Only those with exceptional skills or talents, who will sincerely extend themselves in the interest of their work, can counter their petulant, rudely outspoken, and hostile new attitudes.

As these women become aware that they are setting blocks before themselves, however, they can learn to be assertive and appropriately demanding without being offensive. For there is no rule stating that to be assertive is to be rude, abrasive, or hostile.

CHANGING

Relationships with men have acquired new sets of shoulds, which may be at some distance from a woman's true feelings and wishes. Consider Julia, a woman in her thirties, in this regard. She speaks: "I was into all the crazies of sex for years. I felt obliged to sleep with every man I went out with. I thought they expected it. I expected it of myself. I know now that I didn't want to every time.

"One weekend I found myself in bed with a guy who turned out to be an utter bore. I didn't think I could get through the weekend. I don't remember how I had gotten into that spot. But I felt I couldn't ask him to leave. He was obviously ready to spend the rest of the weekend in my apartment. He ate, sat around, watched television, ate some more, and wanted to make love. Love? Yuk!

"And here I was going along like a little lamb. But that weekend did it. I did a lot of thinking in the next few weeks. I thought I was such a modern gal, with it all together, calling all the shots. What a joke that was.

"I gradually changed my habits. It was hard, I can assure you. It's like giving up smoking. You get so used to it, you feel that something is missing. My friends were shocked when I told them I'd had it with

'ad lib' sex. That wasn't where I was at anymore. I didn't have to prove
how great I was anymore. If I really liked someone and I felt like
making love, then I'd do it. Well, what happened was that I didn't
meet anyone I liked well enough for that.

"But I did meet some people who were fun, and I enjoyed being
with them, talking, eating, playing. But I honestly wasn't interested
in becoming intimate. After a while I realized I had just been following a pattern before—these are the things a gal does in the big city.
They were a set of rules I was following. Just the way we all wore the
same kinds of pants or shoes when I was in school. It was all kid stuff.
Doing what the crowd was doing.

"I realized much later how I felt, on another level, about what I
was doing. It had something to do with the way my parents look at
the way I've lived my life. I think they think I'm a 'tramp,' and I can't
get away from that feeling. That's what makes it so hard to visit them.
I know how they feel way down deep, and it makes me feel guilty.
It's impossible, I think, to get away from those early attitudes that you
know your parents hold, no matter what they say. Of course, they
became more accepting of my life-style. But I know that it makes
them unhappy all the time, and they can't help it. Because they love
me, they pretend that the way I live is okay with them. But it's not,
and never will be. I don't know what's going to happen with family
feelings in my generation. We can't stand the guilt we feel when we're
with our parents. Yet we want to go home sometimes.

"Their sad faces and forced smiles are hard to take. It's too bad,
because I think we need all the love we can get. So we have to reject
their love, because it hurts too much to feel that we've disappointed
them so much. Is there anything that can be done about that?

"There *is* a double standard for men and women. And my parents
just can't get over it. I suppose the best thing is that I won't feel the
same way with my daughter, if I have one. But who knows where the
next generation will be at."

Julia continues. "I haven't had sex now with anyone for over two
years. And I'm quite happy about it. I don't miss it. I don't feel
deprived. Sometimes my friends howl when I tell them that's the way
I feel. I remind them that only a generation ago, most women didn't
have sex until they were married, so what was the big commotion. If

they were unhappy, it wasn't necessarily a problem with sex. If they were able to survive without sex then, I don't see why I can't. And I am. I don't see how women can be *so* different in such a short time.

"I think now that women have been sold a bill of goods"—new shoulds—"about all the wonders and need for sex. Look, I think it's great. I'm not saying it's not. But it isn't essential to survival the way some people seem to think it is. And men especially have been pretty quick to pick up that aspect of the new thinking. It suits them fine to have you think that you need sex in order to feel good and be happy.

"I've done a lot of thinking about it. I go out on dates. I let a guy know right away where I stand, because I don't want him to feel that I've led him on. After the first surprise, they settle down, and we have a good time. It's really great. So relaxed. We're not thinking about later, or trying to build up to it in all those phony seductive ways I used to use—with the hair being tossed over the shoulder, and the mouth half-open like those sexy ads. God! It looks as if all those women in the beauty ads are looking to flop into bed with some guy. Well, that's the way I used to feel. I thought I had to feel that way. It was an obsession. The time I spent on it!

"It's a funny thing. The guys appreciate the plain, good fun we have now when that's out of the way. That reminds me of something I heard years ago. After we'd had sex for the first time, this guy said to me, 'Now that that's out of the way, I'd like to get to know you.' I didn't ask him what he meant. But now, I'm amazed he could have said that. Can you imagine that? Getting sex out of the way?

"I've come to believe that sex can spoil a perfectly good relationship. No, I'm not being a prude. It's too late for that. I've seen it all. But I feel that I was just on a kind of long detour, thinking I had to behave the way I was supposed to, or no one would accept me."

Julia refers again and again to her shoulds in terms of sexual activity. She thought she was "expected to" or "supposed to" behave this way or that. She describes quite well how she felt trapped and helpless with those new shoulds. When she began to question whether or not she really went along with such behavior, her answers led to a change in attitude. She saw clearly that she had not been making choices about the way she was living, yet thought that she was. Furthermore, she was appalled at the time and energy she gave it.

Julia is a good example of a woman who had shifted her shoulds from old to new and felt conflict over thinking she had to adhere to those new imperatives categorically. She had not really made any inroads toward freedom of choice, because she was just as rigidly bound by her new look in sex behavior.

As I said earlier, "new women" fall into different groups. There are the women with new shoulds who need to be *winners.* They can't show themselves to be vulnerable at all, to need help, to be weak or soft. They worship ambition, drive, and success. They have "marvelous" jobs, high salaries. They don't like to share responsibility with anyone and therefore lose touch with others. They feel obliged to compete in all ways, not just in their work.

"WORKING" MOTHERS

Career women who have families are even more harried if they are caught in the drive for success and yet have to "keep it all together" at home. That can point to expectations of themselves that are unrealistic and exhausting. They feel disgraced by having to cut corners. They feel they should be able to do it all.

This family woman is a new woman caught in an old bind. Rushing out to work may have been her choice. Or it may have been a new should for her. But she continues to support her old expectations of doing everything she should do for her family. No fundamental change has taken place when she simply plies herself with more shoulds. Previously she was beating herself to be a supermom. Now she's beating herself to be both supermom and superworkingwoman. In order to change in a real sense, she has to begin to look at her expectations of herself and her family in a different way. She has to recognize that she has limits of time, energy, and enthusiasm; to look upon her family as having a share in family responsibilities; to stop viewing them as helpless people who have to wait for Mom to make dinner for them every night.

If you are one of these women and your reasons for working aren't clear to you, you will have trouble planning your time. That can lead to your becoming overburdened, tired, guilty, conflicted, tense, and irritable. Some quick suggestions might help you to evaluate what you are doing and decide if you are really exercising the freedom of choice you so dearly cherish. Here are ten suggestions for harried working parents.

1. Understand *your reasons* for working.
2. Make *no apology* for working or for time spent at work.
3. *Establish priorities* each day, keeping your own convenience in mind as one of those priorities.
4. Plan activities with built-in *flexibility*.
5. If there's a conflict at any time, ask yourself which item is the most important *right now*.
6. Try to *make decisions* as things come up. You can always change your mind.
7. Plan small units of *quality time* with your children. They don't need hours of time to know that Mommy loves them.
8. Give children as many *responsibilities* as they can reasonably manage. Change them when appropriate.
9. Make your children *feel needed*, because they really are when your time is limited. Even if they grumble, they usually feel good about your being dependent upon their help.
10. Accept your partner's cooperation *without criticizing* it. He's always doing his best—even though you may not think so. You can make suggestions later to improve the quality of his help.

Because it might be particularly useful for the mother who works outside the home, I want to elaborate on points eight and nine above. There is some agreement that one of our social tragedies regards children who have no sense of responsibility. Many of them have not been able to develop it because of several factors. Among these factors are the accoutrements of affluence that have made children's un-skilled household help unnecessary. Another factor points to parents who haven't taken the time to help children learn how to be responsi-ble. (It doesn't really take a great deal of time. But it does take some.) In this respect financially impoverished families have an advantage, because they have been more willing to encourage their children to earn or to help at home.

Too often children are no longer *needed* as they were in the past, when family work had to be shared because of its volume. There is still an ongoing volume of work to be done in any family. But some parents hesitate to share it with children, because they don't like the way the work is done, or because they feel guilty about "imposing adult's work on children"! Children are sometimes told, "Your job is to study and get good grades." So children who don't get good grades necessarily fail at their job, and are left with no other means through which they can feel a worthy and contributing member of the family. I need not remind you how sad a state it is when a child cannot feel accepted by the family.

Being part of a family that accepts and needs them for something other than good grades is what helps children develop self-confidence and positive self-esteem. If they can't do one thing, they can always do another. But they can't feel your love if they think you're disappointed because of a poor academic, social, or athletic showing. Once they sense your disappointment and develop a feeling of inferiority in relation to the point at issue, it's difficult for them to recover entirely from that feeling. Responsibility must not exceed a child's ability, however, for the whole point is to give the child an experience of success, so that self-confidence can be allowed to grow and follow the child into adolescence and adulthood. You'll be aware when it's time for something more difficult, for they will let you know one way or another.

Speaking of children's needs is no different from speaking of adult's needs. There is little doubt that you, too, want to be needed for something, by someone, so that you can add to your feeling of your own substance, of your own womanpower. Feeling that you are needed, you can put the mind, heart, and muscle of that one womanpower into service whenever you choose to do so. Each such unit of effort that you make becomes a building block in the course of overcoming your fear of change. Success there furthers a development that permits you to live and enjoy to the limits of your unique possibilities.

Now we'll move to Part Two, where you'll begin to work with the twenty-step method I've referred to in Part One. I've already told you that there are examples of persons who used the method to help themselves. Reading about them may encourage you to work with the program as well.

PART TWO

TWENTY STEPS TO MANAGE ANXIETY AND DEPRESSION

XII

The Twenty-Step
Program

Our recent history seems more and more characterized by evidence of anxiety and depression. As pressures build, greater numbers of persons find it almost impossible to maintain an equilibrium of physical and emotional comfort that is essential to well-being. The self-help program here is one that you can learn to utilize when you feel that your *comfort/discomfort equilibrium* (CDE) is no longer an equilibrium, but a condition of discomfort more often than not.

Part of the anxiety you have to deal with is generated by an external environment, one over which you have little control unless you're willing to take legal, political, or collective social action. You're subjected to heightened assaults of stimuli: louder music and noisier machines; greater numbers of tastes, foods, smells, corruptions, clothes, people, automobiles, primaries, homes, TVs, records, newscasts, careers, trips, life-styles; bigger everything and more of it.

Other elements of the environment over which you have even less control are those of a more global character: widespread economic failures; rapid changes in familial and sociological attitudes and practices; disillusionment in political and democratic processes; poverty and warfare; fear of atomic power—and even, strange as it may seem, the beginnings of fear of invasion from other planets!

In reacting to this too-muchness, one woman recalled: "I remember that, when I was a child, a skyrocket on the Fourth of July was a skinny, wobbly little streak of light in the sky, with a dozen puny stars popping out at the end of it. But how we thrilled to it! Now, the whole sky explodes with visual effects and bombardments, breathtaking in a way, but overwhelming in another, and so much that it leaves you stunned."

Is a sky packed full of exploding color analogous to the explosions of innumerable stimuli reaching every crevice of one's being? More stimuli than you can reasonably process, either emotionally or intellectually, can lead to a sense of attack, a feeling of helplessness, and finally a numbness. In a helpless state, you will feel more vulnerable and *are* more vulnerable. No segment of society seems to remain unaffected before this onslaught of too much. I sometimes wonder what will happen to the last "nature man," the "gentle Tasaday," now that he's been anointed by the touch of civilization. How long will he escape? Will he finally fall victim to anxiety's fallout, which rumbles its way inexorably across continents and oceans to ferret out every last human being who might be susceptible to its infectiousness?

You have learned in Part One that anxiety generated by an outer environment is only part of the story. For anxiety is produced by a constant interplay between the forces of your inner and outer environments. You know that in order to tolerate anxiety, people devote a large part of their energies to the development of defenses against it. But not all defenses are neurotic ones by any means. At times defenses are essential protective devices and can result in productive living. Too often, however, they serve to drain interest, energy, and creativity, leaving you too tired, too disillusioned, too bitter, to rally your resources for the activities that nourish you and help you to achieve your goals. One of the aims of this book is to help you deal with some of the common events in your life that evoke tension and anxiety and lead to depression and other fruitless defensiveness.

DISGUISED ANXIETY

These common events are what block Connie, a woman who wants to start work on a project and who says, "I know what I want to do, but I just don't get started. When I think of getting started, something happens to me. I find lots of other things to do—things that have to be done right away, that minute. Phone calls to be made, mail opened, friends to contact. Dozens of little things that steal my hours. Sometimes I'm aware of being a little nervous. But not usually. Only at the end of the day do I realize, I've done it again! And then it's too late to do anything about it until the next day. You know, I've wasted weeks and months that way, trying to get something done that could have been finished in a couple of days, or even a couple of hours."

Anticipation of working on a project arouses a mild *effort anxiety* in Connie and produces her procrastinating behavior. Such anxiety can be disguised also as edginess, irritability, impatience, or outright anger. It can masquerade as thoughtlessness, tactlessness, lack of consideration. Any mannerism, deed, thought, or attitude may be a cover for anxiety. Nevertheless, anxiety can be gradually and gently exposed as you move to identify and uncover its many disguises.

TWENTY STEPS TO RESOLUTION

These steps can help you expose the conflicts that create anxiety and lead to stumbling blocks in your relationships, your work, and your general progress. You will learn how you can work with these steps as you read how others used them. If you choose, you can learn how to change features of your life that might threaten your psychic integrity. You can learn, too, how to try to strengthen qualities that are lying dormant within you and can give you new hope. Here are the twenty steps:

> *STEP 1:* Select a single troublesome issue that causes you to feel anxious and depressed, or that creates repeated tension, guilt, anger, or conflict. (This is Issue Number One.)

STEP 2:   Determine how Issue Number One is causing you or someone else to suffer.

STEP 3:   State whether or not you have tried to disregard the issue.

STEP 4:   State whether or not you have tried to deal with the issue.

STEP 5:   State your willingness to reduce your suffering.

STEP 6:   State the ways in which you've tried to deal with the issue.

STEP 7:   Decide why your efforts at solution have not been effective.

STEP 8:   Find out how you react to change in regard to that issue.

STEP 9:   Decide if you want to run the risk of trying to make a change.

STEP 10: Enumerate what you can lose and what you can gain by making a change in the issue you've selected.

STEP 11: Choose a possible solution in dealing with the issue (Alternative Number One).

STEP 12: Put Alternative Number One into action.

STEP 13: Collect input from others regarding the efforts you've made.

STEP 14: Evaluate your new action (Alternative Number One) in terms of losses and gains.

STEP 15: Decide on another solution (Alternative Number Two) if Alternative Number One has been ineffective.

STEP 16: Repeat the evaluation process for Alternative Number Two.

STEP 17: Continue with the selection of new alternatives if previous ones are impractical, inconvenient, or ineffective.

STEP 18: Try to determine whether you've reached your limit regarding the issue you're working on.

STEP 19: Try to find the end point of any single issue *before* you become too discouraged with your efforts.

STEP 20: Feel free to return at another time to an issue you've already worked on.

As you read over these steps, I think you can tell that their main purpose is to keep your attention on only one trouble point at a time, rather than scattering it over several issues. That way you are left with some sense of accomplishment, for efforts directed at one point only are more likely to clarify something for you. When your efforts are scattered and you jump from one thing to another, you may come to feel that you can't deal with any of them. And you probably can't, for you're actually trying to do a nearly impossible job.

Responses to these twenty steps are detailed in subsequent chapters so that you can tell what others have done to build, for example, a *one-year plan to better mental health.* You will learn how an unemployed artist agonized over her "incompetence" and finally found a new way to earn a living; how a writer learned to evaluate herself more realistically and overcame her writing block; how a teacher fought with her discouragement in dealing with discipline in the classroom; how a divorced mother struggled to teach her adolescent boy the pleasures and advantages of parent/child cooperation; how two women worked on marriages that were dissolving and were able to bring their problems to a partial resolution; how middle-aged people who were able to maintain hope could enrich their lives even while limiting them realistically; how the twenty steps can be used to overcome depression. Their stories may differ greatly from yours. But you'll recognize their despair, their anxiety, and the real efforts they made.

ELEMENTS OF EFFORT

You know that if you want to accomplish anything, you have to *do* something, consciously and deliberately. This is a simple, basic principle that you probably accept in theory. Yet you're often busy trying to accomplish something by simply thinking about it, without making any visible effort. If you find yourself doing that, you're in very crowded company, you can be sure.

In ordinary routine matters like going to work or school in the morning, you have to get out of bed, dress, eat, and get on your way, or you'll never get there. But first you have to find out *what* you want to do. You don't usually have to decide that every day, because much of what you do is repetitious. But you have to *make an effort* every day just to accomplish your routine. For some persons, however, just thinking about making an effort can lead to the feelings that I call *effort anxiety*.

Effort anxiety can be caused by three factors: fear of change, resistance toward the actual effort you have to make, and anticipation of failure. Do you see how these three factors depend upon each other? If you fear change, you'll resist making an effort to make that change. If you resist effort, you'll certainly fail at what you want to accomplish. If you anticipate failure, you won't be interested in making a change—and on and on.

Please understand that not all persons react in this way. But when you do, you're always involved in the following equations:

$$\text{WANT} + \text{EFFORT} \longrightarrow \text{POSSIBLE SUCCESS}$$

I have to say *possible* success, because there are no guarantees that your efforts will lead to the success you want. Almost guaranteeable, however, is the equation:

$$\text{WANT} + \text{NO EFFORT} \longrightarrow \text{NO SUCCESS}$$

Your anxiety can be relieved slightly if you can state a *specific want.* In doing this you've made a decision (always revokable), and that's usually encouraging. You've also used your mind, feelings, and experience in making that decision. That feels encouraging, too. It doesn't matter how minor the decision is.

The good feeling you have with this first step of decision is a *now satisfaction.* When you are troubled, there are very few of these now satisfactions around, so grab one whenever you can. After you've decided what you want, you need to start your *planning effort* and then the *action effort* necessary to place those plans into action. You may have difficulty in planning for action effort, because the action might be frightening to you.

At this point you need to ask yourself: What is the worst thing that can happen if I do such and such? Something benign may flash through your mind, or something horrendous. Try to state out loud what has crossed your mind. Listen to your words and then say aloud, "Now is that really a good possibility?" By this time you may feel that what you thought would strike you dead is not likely to occur, or that it's something of an absurdity. If that happens, you can move on. If not, you will have to plan for further action efforts until you find one that doesn't frighten you so much.

One element of your fear lies in a past that establishes expectations of success or failure for the present. If you've succeeded in the past, you may be afraid that you can't repeat your performance with a new action effort. If you've failed in the past, you fear you'll fail again. It's not entirely unreasonable to feel that way. But in either case your *now effort* will be undermined by anticipated disappointment in future performances. This can keep you busy thinking about your specific want, but it won't be helping you to make now efforts.

Wanda illustrates this point. For an entire summer she thought about renting an apartment she needed in order to work at her new job in the fall. Her anticipation of failure kept her from making a true now effort. Logic had little to do with her feelings. She had to use most of her salary for hotel accommodations until she finally found a suitable place. This happened only when a friend assured her that something was available. At that point she was able to make an effort and did succeed.

Using one step at a time, however, you can deal with each issue in a new way, which can help relieve your anxiety. For example: You will not be asked to decide what you want to do with your life or how to work to rid yourself of major anxieties. You will be asked only to state a *single small issue* that has been troublesome and has been causing conflict and anxiety. (Should you say this or that? Is it better you go or stay? Can you buy that item or not?) Using very small units of now efforts, you can become an active participant in this process.

Because you care so much about your own healing, your *active participation* in the program will be the strongest ally you can have. You have noted that much of the material here is repeated in different contexts so that your understanding of anxiety and the dynamic causation of human behavior is gradually added to. Suggestions are made to help you find ways of accomplishing something you want to do but are having difficulty in starting. In working with only one issue at a time, part of your anxiety can be overcome bit by bit. And when it comes to anxiety, even a little relief can feel very good.

If you do not like the procedures presented here, or cannot go along with them, try to design your own set of procedures. But whatever you decide to do, you still have to go through steps similar to these:

1. *Involve yourself* by thinking about one thing you specifically want to accomplish.
2. *Make an effort* to find out what advantages you already have that can help you to accomplish your particular goal.
3. *Plan and do something specific* to achieve what you want.

NEVER TOO LATE

Yes, it takes time and effort. But no matter what your age, time is on your side. If that puzzles you, consider this. Let's say that in the next year you just go along doing whatever you usually do. Now let's suppose that in this same next year you try to put into effect a one-year plan for better mental health in terms of reduced anxiety in one area, or better family relations with one person, or more effective work habits. If you can follow some of the suggestions made here, chances are you'll be in a slightly different position by the end of the year. I want to emphasize the word *slightly,* for no matter how slight the change, that year has been used to your advantage. But if you just go along, and make no effort whatever in your behalf, it's doubtful that much will be changed from last year.

To put it a little differently, nothing is going to happen if you don't make it happen. Then, if you can decide that the year has been well used, and you can see some small change, you might feel sufficiently optimistic to repeat the performance the next year and the next. Just think how all those *small* increments in growth will add up after five years—after ten years! So you see, time *is* on your side if you will use it *for* rather than *against* yourself.

If you have reached middle age, you already know that one year, then five years, then ten years, can go by quite swiftly—and faster and faster as you grow older. So you might just as well do something that will be liberating, starting right now! After all, what do you have to do that's more important?

Remember that, ultimately, liberation for all women and men originates primarily within each human spirit. The responsibility for that ultimate individual liberation belongs to each one of us. Mature adults can no longer point a finger at someone and say, "You're to blame for my heartbreak!" If you feel you've had a "jailer" who has retarded your progress as a whole human being, remind yourself that the jailer guarding the prisoner is a prisoner as well.

Collective liberation can be publicly fought for and legislated. And it surely helps to direct your efforts toward that end. But *individual liberation* does not come from others' opinions and efforts, nor from legislation, action groups, or even your own therapist. In the final analysis it always comes from yourself, from your own desire and effort to free yourself. All that I want to accomplish here is to bring you yet another way to proceed on a journey of self-discovery and finally of self-liberation.

MOVES FOR CHANGE

Existence can be one of profound joy with an infinite capacity for reaching out. Or it may be one of tethered gropings in a world of little boxes. Women are leaving self-limiting roles through successive waves of change, all leading to a hard-won transition from anxiety, frustration, and should-bound, compulsive living to a more wholesome, resilient life. One of the most difficult tasks facing them is to transform their way of relating to events as they arise.

If it has been your custom to react in troubled, frustrating ways, you will be bound to continue in the same manner *at first*, fiercely resistant to your best intentions for change. Your resistance places you among an indefinite number of women who, through the years of self-effacing expressions of anxiety, have propelled themselves into *behavior ruts*. These ruts are like magnets, keeping you immobilized (yet secure) when you want to alter some aspect of rigid behavior, or when you try to undertake an entirely new course.

Ordinary activities such as packing or unpacking, calling for an appointment, taking medication or exercise regularly, can meet with that resistance. Because she was afraid she couldn't decide what to keep or discard, one woman kept her bedroom filled with unpacked cartons for two years after moving (effort anxiety). For an entire year a student resisted his impulse to ask a classmate for a date, because he was afraid she would reject him. A patient needed to call her doctor every day to ask how many pills she should take, because she was afraid to take any responsibility for her treatment. Another woman collected recipes for making bread, and after four years she found out that she was afraid to face the fact that she didn't really want to make bread, thinking all along that she should be eager to do it.

These were activities they believed they wanted to deal with. But the process of actually doing them seemed insurmountable and shrouded with fear. Because they seemed like such small matters, the persons involved felt disgusted with themselves for not being able to "just go ahead and do them." There are many matters like these where you'll find yourself feeling the same way. As you continue to think, plan, and act in old, habituated ways, you, too, will continue to get the old results of tension, anxiety, procrastination, inertia, disgust, guilt, and depression.

How, then, can it change if you want it to? My answer has to be that *it* cannot change. *It*—the task, the situation, the encounter—has no autonomy of its own. *It* can do nothing. Only *you* can effect a change. The old, habituated, troubled, anxious way will not change by your intending it to change or willing it to change.

You might be easier on yourself if you can recognize that your resistance is an element of fear and not just pigheadedness or laziness. That is a first step. Then you need to know that fear is a perfectly valid human response, and that much of the world's business is conducted in concert with it. So you are in good company.

What does this mean, then, as far as you're concerned? It means that *even while you're afraid you can act.* While afraid, you can state what you'd like to do. While afraid, you can plan how to achieve your goal. While afraid, you can start to activate that plan. After a first move you'll realize that fear and action can coexist very well, and it will give you the courage to keep moving. With each step you take to overcome your resistance, you'll find your fear just a little bit diminished.

That effort against fear is what eventually leads to a self-reeducation program helping you to become more accountable to yourself for the changes you wish to bring about. With such a program you can learn to deal with, and alter, ineffective ways you have of meeting troublesome issues, as well as routine matters that require your intervention. In Chapter Thirteen I'll tell you about Bonnie, a young artist living alone in the city, and how she applied the twenty steps to her reeducation.

XII

Applying the Twenty Steps

Good or bad, whatever you do is done with the purpose of satisfying one of your needs and making yourself feel better. That is to say, your intentions toward yourself are usually honorable ones, even though you may use harmful means to achieve them. Very often, blatantly self-destructive actions are intended not to hurt, punish, or destroy, but to help relieve an intolerable feeling of anguish. Sometimes you don't even know how much anxiety you are trying to deal with. Or if you do, you may not realize how ineffective your present methods of coping might be.

Some people cry, "But I've tried everything!" More likely they've tried minor variations of the same pattern over and over. But they're left with the impression that they've really worked on doing something positive for themselves. The efforts they make are commendable, but they find that no positive steps are taken. If you have any doubt about this point, all you need to do is to look around you—at family members, at friends, at yourself. You will find them practicing repetitious, compulsive patterns, year in and year out, unless persistent, deliberate attempts are made to change them.

PREPARATIONS

In working with the program, you need to make such deliberate attempts, and certain preparations as well. Making those preparations often helps you overcome the initial blocks when you are ready to begin your work. Here are some points that have been generally helpful.

1. A loose-leaf record book is the most practical entry book to use. It permits easy entry of later thoughts or skipped steps.
2. A regular time for working is a dependable and time-saving device. You can always change it if necessary. This will give you practice in learning to change a pattern without undue anxiety.
3. Try to decide where and how you want to work. If you don't want to be disturbed, make it known. This is your time for yourself, and it is not to be shared if that's what you prefer.
4. When you have made your arrangements and are ready, try not to rush. You don't have to get everything down. Choose your own pace.
5. Make a list of the twenty steps and keep them available in your record book so that you can refer to them easily.

As you work, you will gradually become aware that your words are subject to no one else's perusal, judgment, or evaluation. They stand exactly as you set them down. They don't have to be approved, validated, or graded. No word you write ever has to be changed or wondered about. Changes will take place only by addition, not by obliteration.

Incidentally, this point is a basic element of self-acceptance. What you hate or want to deny in yourself does not have to be rooted out and obliterated; it can be left alone. But as you add new, preferred experiences, feelings, or attitudes, you will effect a change, because some of the old hates wither away from disuse. Self-hatred, which is always linked to nonacceptance, has to be continuously fed. If you are nourishing and encouraging other more gratifying aspects of yourself, self-hatred cannot exert its original power over you.

What may strike you as ludicrous about applying a self-help method to the human condition is the enormity and complexity of the subject matter. But remember that this work is limited in scope. It is designed to inform, encourage, relieve, and strengthen. It is designed to put you in touch with the wellsprings of your own *personpower*, something every woman, man, and child inherits without asking.

That personpower is unintentionally but systematically weakened through frustrations produced by compulsive roles, including those of submission and nonassertiveness. Such roles are established by social and family customs and internalized by neurotic needs for approval, acceptance, and love. I want to see you put an end to that systematic weakening process and turn it about by a deliberate, systematic strengthening of your personpower.

CHOOSING AN ISSUE

The first step of this program involves clarifying your troublesome issue—that is, what you want to work on. Certain issues are more easily identified than others, so there is often a shifting of the issue you are considering. A clear issue facilitates the selection process of Step One. Where your issue is fuzzy, or more complex, the system tends to break down, for it is meant to deal with just *one* specific trouble point at a time. If you find that you feel irritated with the questions, you may be trying to deal with too large a trouble point— that is, an issue that consists of several subissues. In that case, the subissues have to be identified and dealt with singly.

For example, a parent found herself liking her son less and less. She selected this as Issue Number One and became bogged down almost immediately. The subissues she subsequently found were that she didn't like his appearance, his friends, his schoolwork, table manners, indifference to chores, rudeness, attitudes, and values. There was just too much to deal with. She finally decided to focus on the way he behaved at the dinner table. That became Trouble Point Number One, and her findings in using the steps were illuminating for them both.

Another woman found the issue of her child's TV watching too amorphous. She narrowed it down to TV watching on school days. After she dealt with that, she felt more confident to tackle weekend watching and specific programs of which she disapproved.

A third woman, complaining of "poor communication" with her husband, chose to work on conversations in the bathroom, where they almost invariably argued over some detail of intimate living. I can assure you that she had difficulty "communicating" in every room of her home. But restricting the location helped to narrow the content, and thus permitted her to deal with only one unit of dissension instead of an extensive problem involving every facet of their relationship.

An important sign of too broad an issue will be your inability to follow it through to a workable solution. Even when you find a single, clear-cut item, using the twenty steps might be upsetting for you at one point or another. But there are usually small satisfactions along the way, and I can only encourage you to try to keep going, even when you feel you've reached a blank wall. Sometimes a little "break" helps you come back to it again with less resistance. At times you'll find you want to skip one or more steps and return to them later.

I just mentioned resistance. Don't think that you won't be resistant to following the outline. That may be your greatest handicap in working with the program. You may very well put off, procrastinate, be busy—in other words, experience effort anxiety. It's really a good idea to have everything in order for yourself, so that you can't use the excuse that you don't have the right materials to proceed. Remember, if you want to try, and have decided to do so despite your effort anxiety, you have to make the first effort of getting ready to work.

PURPOSE OF THE STEPS

It may be helpful now if I go through each of the steps with you, using a woman's brief entries to demonstrate their use. Becky, a divorced woman in her thirties, was given a vacation, and she found herself feeling sad and teary as the time approached.

> *Step 1: The issue.* I feel terrible about my coming Christmas holiday. I don't know why, but I'm very tense about it.

This is a useful illustration, because it is contained in a specific time segment and concerns only one person, Becky herself, so far. Steps Two, Three, and Four help to familiarize her with her feelings as they pertain to the issue. Step Two immediately presents her with the fact that there is suffering involved in her unhappiness. That's something she may not be aware of, even though she says she feels "terrible" and "tense." Steps Three and Four clarify the issue and introduce her reaction to it by raising the question: Is she doing anything about it? And Step Six asks what she is doing, if anything. Together with Step Five (Do you want to reduce your suffering?), you see how Becky is drawn into an immediate involvement with her issue in terms of whether or not she wants to help herself and what she has or hasn't done so far.

Step 2: How is the issue causing me to suffer? How? It is just making me feel awful whenever I think of it. The other day some people in the office who have the same time off were talking about taking a cruise. I had to leave because the tears were spilling out of my eyes.

Step 3: Am I disregarding the issue? I suppose not, now that I'm trying to write this all down. I'm not even sure what the issue is. I feel terribly lonely when there's talk about holidays. Maybe that's the issue—feeling lonely on the holiday. Being all alone. I guess that's the real issue. Feeling that there's no one to spend the holidays with. I don't think I've answered the question. I don't think I've tried to disregard the issue. I just didn't know what it was.

Step 4: Am I dealing with the issue? No. Just feeling bad.

Step 5: Do I want to reduce my suffering? Yes.

Step 6: How have I tried to deal with it? I haven't.

Step 7: My efforts haven't worked because I haven't made any.

Step 8: There hasn't been any change in regard to the issue. I still feel depressed about it. I don't know how I'd feel because I haven't even contemplated a change.

Steps Seven and Eight help Becky to evaluate her involvement to date. She's able to see that there are no results because she hasn't done anything yet. There is a clear cause and effect apparent here, which can be quite relieving: Nothing happens if I don't make any effort. When I do, something might change.

Some women feel helpless because they don't understand their own contribution to their helplessness through inertia and resistance to change. They keep thinking that there's some magical curse on them, rather than acknowledge that there's been a real absence of effort to overcome dependency.

> *Step 9:* Yes, I'll run the risk of a change. But I don't know what change to make. I have a Christmas vacation, and I'm depressed over the prospect of wasting it by being alone and not able to enjoy a trip or something.

This Step Nine is a pivotal one, because it's the step of commitment. Becky has put herself on the line here: Yes, she says, I am willing to do what I must, and I am willing to risk change if I have to.

> *Step 10: What can I lose or gain in making a change?* The only change I can make is to spend some money I haven't got. So I can lose money. But maybe I can gain some fun—unless I'm worrying about the money. These questions are hard to answer.

Getting past Step Ten opens the way for specific action regarding your trouble point. This step is also an evaluating one and helps to bring to consciousness advantages and disadvantages that may never have been considered before. It also brings out unknown fears and possible guilts, which tend to lose much of their impact when they are seen written on a page. Significant discoveries can be made in Step Ten that may be of considerable interest to you.

> *Step 11: Choose a possible solution.* I don't know how I can do this. If the issue is feeling so lonely, I don't know what alternative I can find for that except to plan something to do.

It's obvious that Step Eleven begins the process of laying definite plans for concrete actions. Here Becky looked up holiday programs and activities in which she could participate. She was surprised at the number of events that were scheduled and that she could attend.

> *Step 12: Putting Alternative Number One into action.* I can't because the holiday isn't here yet. I can only plan it.

Resistance may be seen at any step, but previous steps may involve only thinking and writing about the issue. Step Twelve demands action that goes beyond the use of a record book and may be resisted because of a rise in anxiety level (effort anxiety). Usually, however, working on the previous steps helps to arouse interest that can motivate action in Step Twelve. Becky seemed to be balking here. Sometimes Step Twelve is postponed, and Steps Thirteen and Fourteen, both evaluative and supportive steps, help to ready you for Twelve.

> *Step 13: Input from others.* I've told several people what I'm planning, and even included some in my plans. They think my idea is great, because there are many good musical programs during the holidays and they are looking forward to them. Wendy says she'll have a party if I help her. So there would be plenty to do.
>
> *Step 14: Evaluate.* I don't feel so sad about it anymore. But I don't really feel good. I still have this heavy feeling. I just don't know what I want. Maybe I should ask myself that. What do I really want?

Steps Ten and Fourteen present opportunities for a free flow of imagination. You will see how the spontaneous raising of the question, "What do I really want?" led to Becky's solution, which she recognized the moment she thought of it.

> *Step 15:* I couldn't answer that question, but it kept popping up all week. And when Suzi said, "What do you want to do?" I said, "I want to go home and see my mother," just like that. I was so surprised to hear myself say that. Suzi laughed at me. But I said

it anyway. That's what I want to do. And then I started to cry because I can't afford the air fare. She lives two thousand miles away. Suzi said it would take me a half-hour to get a loan at the bank. I hesitated but knew that I wanted to do it. So at lunch, I got the loan and I'll get a ticket tomorrow. That's my Alternative Number Two. I didn't really like my Alternative Number One, but I didn't know why. Is it so strange to want to see your mother for the holidays? I don't really care, though, because I'm going anyway.

Step 16: Evaluating Alternative Number Two. Good. I don't have to ask anyone about it. It feels good and I know that's what I want to do.

Another opportunity is presented with Step Sixteen to think more deeply about any solutions you have for your issue. Repeated steps for evaluating help to develop confidence in your own ideas for coping with an issue. Becky had no hesitation by this time and knew she had managed her dilemma quite well.

Having found her solution, Becky obviously didn't have to continue on with Steps Seventeen to Twenty. What is probably becoming clear to you are the following points: (1) Not all the steps may be pertinent for everyone; (2) they may be responded to loosely; and (3) there is a point at which an issue may be resolved and there is no need to finish responding to the rest of the steps. Steps Seventeen to Twenty are for repeated efforts at finding alternatives when previous ones are found to be generally unworkable.

Becky's issue was not a major one and was therefore easily resolved once she started to work directly with it. Steps Seventeen to Twenty apply more to issues that are difficult to resolve. They are designed to minimize discouragement and the arousal of self-hatred over the failure to activate applicable alternatives.

A rather profound alternative was discovered by Jed, a man in his forties, who was doing good work as a research engineer, but felt that he was "drying up." He found innumerable things to complain about, but had remained passive over the issues for a number of years. One day he discovered that he could talk about wanting to make a change for the next twenty years, until his retirement, but that he never would make a change unless he did something besides think about it. After using the twenty steps over a period of several months, he was able to put together a résumé, which he submitted to an agency specializing in his field. He was eventually offered something he liked at some distance away and at a lower salary. Considering the advantages and disadvantages to both himself and his family, a decision was made (not without trepidation) to make the move, and he has not regretted it.

One other young woman was criticizing herself because she couldn't drive. In using the twenty steps she came up with the alternatives of taking lessons, getting a license, and purchasing a small, inexpensive used car that was within her means.

Here, then, you have had an introduction to how the program can work. In following chapters you will read of others who have used the twenty steps, and something of the motivating forces behind their various issues and resolutions.

XIV

You Can't Predict
What Will Happen

Women can be their own worst critics. Lugging about emotional tote bags filled with shoulds, they are the least forgiving when they find they can't apply those shoulds as they have predicted. One purpose of living by your shoulds is to maintain a quality of predictability for the events in your life. If that quality is removed, your shoulds lose their power to give you a sense of security. Even under the best of circumstances that sense of security is precariously balanced and can easily tumble into the dust when your predictions (expectations) don't come to pass.

Bonnie's story is the common one shared by those young women who flounder in a morass of loneliness, new shoulds, and new anxieties produced by changing attitudes and practices relating to nearly every aspect of their lives. The following diagram depicts their position.

$$New\ Poorly\ Formulated\ Attitudes\ +\ New\ Practices$$
$$\downarrow$$
$$New\ Unrealistic\ Expectations\ (New\ Shoulds)$$
$$\downarrow$$
$$New\ Failures$$
$$\downarrow$$
$$New\ Conflicts$$
$$\downarrow$$
$$New\ Anxieties$$
$$\downarrow$$
$$Helplessness\ +\ Guilt\ +\ Anger$$
$$\downarrow$$
$$Self\text{-}Hate$$
$$\downarrow$$
$$Loneliness\ +\ Poor\ Problem\ Resolution\ +\ Hopelessness$$
$$\downarrow$$
$$Depression$$

An only child, Bonnie had been raised in a small town and attended a nearby college. "I was a good student," she relates, "and I liked to talk to teachers or anyone I could learn from. I liked challenges, but I wasn't really a striver. I tried only in subjects I liked."

Bonnie had built a lifetime fantasy about going to the "big city" and amazing her family and friends with a quick success. She found work as a commercial artist, but considered the work beneath her. She assumed the attitude that it was a challenge, however, and began to learn to live independently. Her social life was restricted, and on weekends she usually remained in her apartment, feeling lonely, neglected, and unloved.

Her story continues. "After I had worked there for four years, there was a reorganization, and several of us had to go. The idea of getting another job was very scary to me. When I'd think about going out in the morning, my heart would begin to pound and I'd even feel dizzy."

As her savings diminished, Bonnie began to put our more feelers for work, but she was unwilling to take "just any job." She gradually withdrew, until she rarely went out or saw anyone. After a particularly anxiety-ridden weekend, Bonnie decided she couldn't wait any longer to see what would turn up. "I felt I just had to do something to help myself. I couldn't be passive and wait for my unemployment to run out." That weekend had been so frightening that it broke through her resistance to change. "I knew I was afraid to act. But I also knew I couldn't stand another weekend like that one. I had to do something."

USING THE PROGRAM

The twenty-step reorientation program was suggested to Bonnie, and she began to work on it. She seemed somewhat intrigued by it, but frequently felt exasperated because she thought that "nothing was happening."

Step 1: Select a single troublesome issue (Issue Number One) *that causes you to feel anxious or depressed, or that creates repeated tension, guilt, anger, or conflict.* Everything I do creates repeated tension, guilt, or conflict. Where do I start? Everything I don't do creates tension too. I'm damned if I do and I'm damned if I don't. What earthly good can that do? A stupid question isn't going to help me. Select a troublesome issue? Impossible! All my issues are troublesome.

I wrote the above and gave up in disgust. But decided I have nothing better to do, so will start again. Really have nothing to lose. Okay, here goes. What is the first step? Select an issue. Just writing that down makes me feel scared. How can I select just one? Nothing comes to me. I'm a blank. Maybe I should put everything down. No dates, nothing to do, no one to talk to, no money to spend, no job, no sex, no future, lonely, lonely. But if I have to select one, I'll say that my issue is not having a job.

Step 2: Determine how Issue Number One is causing you or some-one else to suffer. Suffer? That's a laugh. That's all I do. Sit here and suffer. Because I don't know what else to call this crummy life I live. But everything makes me suffer. Mostly the feeling that no one wants to be with me. That's worst of all. Is my not having a job causing suffering? It sure is. Maybe that's why I feel so wound up all the time, so tired. I can't even say yes or no to something. I always have to make a big deal out of everything I do. I think I have to cover all bases, all the time—but all the time, not just once in a while. No wonder I have trouble finishing anything. Every little pocket has to be turned inside out.

Step 3: State whether or not you have tried to disregard the issue. I talk about getting a job with everyone I meet. I look in the paper. Is that disregarding the issue? I don't know. I'm sure as hell not getting a job. That I know. How can I be disregarding it if I think about it so much? Okay, I'll say no, I'm not disregarding it. I'm regarding it every minute, in fact.

Step 4: State whether or not you have tried to deal with the issue. Now that's a stupid question. I answered that in step 3. I said I regard it all day.

Bonnie was not able to make the distinction at that time between thinking about her problem and dealing with it in a definite way. Still defensive, she tore at her passivity and fears. Finally, she begrudgingly admitted that she was doing very little about dealing with the issue of finding work. Bonnie struggled with each step (only a sampling of her comments are recorded here), but her admission that her thinking about it was not dealing with the issue was perhaps the most difficult step for her to take.

Step 5: State your willingness to reduce your suffering. Yes, I'm willing. But if I am, why don't I? What keeps me from going out and getting a job? That would stop my suffering.

Step 6: State the ways in which you've tried to deal with the issue. There haven't been many ways, and they certainly haven't been effective. If there are no openings that I want, I have to deal with getting a different kind of job, and I haven't dealt with that. So I really have nothing to say here. Maybe I'll defeat this system by not having anything to say. What am I doing here? Who am I fighting with? This system is supposed to help me and I'm supposed to be trying to help myself, and I talk about defeating the system. Sick, sick!

Step 7: Decide why your efforts at solution have not been effective.
They haven't been effective because I'm trying to do something
that has almost no chance for success. I'm limiting my job hunt-
ing, such as it is, to a very narrow area. I'm completely disregarding other kinds of jobs for making a living. I'm considering myself
an experienced artist who is being tragically overlooked. I feel I
should be sought out and given work. That's really the crux of it,
and it's so unrealistic, it's even funny.

Step 8: Find out how you react to change in regard to that issue.
Scared! I don't even want to think about looking for any job. I
feel so anxious I don't know what to do with myself. I think just
the idea of any job, even one I might like, makes me uptight. I
tried for one in a brokerage office, but I managed not to get it even
though I think the guy wanted to give it to me. It was for a kind
of a runner, and I told him I was an artist and not interested in
that kind of work. He said he didn't understand why I was applying for it. I said I needed work. And all he said was that he didn't
think there was anything I'd like. There it was. A job in my hand.
And I just shoved it away. What is so wrong about working as a
runner. I act as if I'd be doomed if I took the job. And I act as
if someone is going to take care of me forever.

*Step 9: Decide if you want to run the risk of trying to make a
change.* I guess I don't and that's that. I don't see any reason to
go on if I don't want to make changes. There's really no point to
it. I'll just wait until my unemployment runs out and then maybe
I can get on welfare. I won't starve.

   At this point Bonnie again is expressing her feeling of hopelessness.
She tends to overlook what she has already done in working with the
method. So many people feel that they are absolutely obliged to
change whenever a change is mentioned. If they find they can't,
they're very hard on themselves. That's what Bonnie did. She was
thoroughly disgusted with herself because she responded to the idea
of change with anxiety.
   Since she had no way of predicting how any happening would turn
out, she could not expose herself to the trauma of the unknown. She
felt she had reached an impasse, because she could not consciously

accept the concept of changing. Although she had worked with the program on and off for some weeks, she had not given herself a scheduled time to make entries, and so several days went by between them. During that time she thought about working at it, but procrastinated and then felt guilty because she wasn't doing anything to help herself. That created resentment toward the whole idea of writing in her record book, and it contributed further to her passivity.

Making no effort to continue with Step Ten, Bonnie felt annoyed, discouraged, and spent hours dreaming and musing. Fortunately, her parents wrote during this interval and asked her to come home for a visit. She decided to go, and just before leaving her apartment, she threw her record book into her bag.

At her parents' home she took it out one day and began to read it. She felt dismayed at its querulous tone but was surprised at the lengthy notations she had made. Although Bonnie was not one to pat herself on the back, she later admitted that she felt pleased at the work she had done. Nevertheless she referred to it as "crap." After a gap of many weeks, she started with Step Ten.

> *Step 10: Enumerate what you can lose and what you can gain by making a change in the issue you've selected.* Wow! What can I lose? Here goes. I can lose this horrible stagnant feeling of having nothing to do, nowhere to go, and no one to talk to. I can lose the fear of running through my savings. I can lose my disgust at not being able to get work. I can lose my dream of being a great creative artist. I can lose my having to lie when I say I'm working in my apartment. What can I gain? A regular check. Inviting someone to a restaurant if I want to. Going to the theatre. Visiting people more, and being able to bring them something. Having some dates. Having a sense of purpose to my day. I'm really fed up with this open-ended time. I've had it. I'll have to wash and dress regularly. I'll have my teeth looked after. I'll have a good reason to call people I haven't talked to in ages and tell them about my job. I suppose I'll feel better about myself.

With her peers Bonnie shares a common contempt of being "conventional." She is of the school that thinks having a "purpose" to the day and being concerned about self-esteem are impossibly "square" concerns. In recognizing the conventional cast of her possible gains, she feels some revulsion. At this time, however, her mood was not a bitter one, and her distaste was tinged with humor. But she was afraid of being too conventional in thinking she was gaining so much in finding a regular job. She felt she shouldn't be reacting that way. By now, several months had passed since she had started with Step Number One. She was able to continue.

Step 11: Choose a possible solution in dealing with the issue. I suppose my only alternative to not looking for a job is looking for one.

And she did just that by contacting persons who were working to inquire if there were openings. She said she didn't know she could contact so many people who worked. She had been under the impression that most of them didn't have regular jobs. This is an example of how removed Bonnie was from the simple reality of making a living.

Step 12: Put Alternative Number One into action. What a turn of events. I went to a store with an opening, but couldn't see myself working there. I talked with the assistant art buyer though. He said he'd like to see my work. So I came back and took out some old paintings. Now I'm in the pits because there's really nothing I can use. I think they want little things—still lifes. I can make some of those, but that's not my idea of what I want to do.

Bonnie called a friend, Terri, who suggested that Bonnie paint a simple still life in acrylic. Terri also impressed Bonnie by saying, "If you get out of your apartment, things begin to happen." With that, Bonnie began to get out more often, and started to reverse her habit of withdrawing.

Step 13: Collect input from others regarding the efforts you've made. I saw Jake in the deli and asked him what he thought about painting for an art shop. He said, "It's better than selling. Why don't you do it?" I said, "You don't think it's prostituting my art?" He said, "It won't be the first time for money." He suggested that if I'm having trouble getting started, I should walk around to other places where they were mass selling and I could get a few ideas. That sounded like a good thing to me, and I'll try to do it. Even though I haven't really done anything yet, I feel better than I did before I left the city.

Step 14: Evaluate your new action in terms of losses and gains. If I paint a still life what do I gain? Well, at least I'll be active. I'll be doing something I know. I'll be brushing up. Haven't done anything in art for months. I might even sell it. If I can do one thing, maybe I can do others. Maybe I'll even start painting what I want to. But I'm still evading the issue of getting a job. What do I lose? Will I lose my self-respect if I make these things for the store? Will I lose my touch? Will I lose my motivation to do good work? I don't know what difference it makes really. I haven't been motivated to do anything on my own since I've been here. So there isn't much to lose there.

Bonnie operates on the *principle of extremes:* Either you're great or you're at the bottom of the pile. Since she has no evidence for a claim to fame, she can only believe that she is "at the bottom of the barrel" of competence. This belief is immobilizing, and it keeps her from making efforts, because "it wouldn't be any use." Although she realizes that any effort would not catapult her into instant fame, she still feels there's no point in trying anything. Regarding her work, her fear has to do with fear of failure to achieve that instant fame. This is a position that can certainly not be overcome by inactivity. Even seemingly pointless activity can help to loosen the rigid cast of that attitude and lighten some of the dead weight of inertia.

Note that as soon as Bonnie began to make actual physical moves, her mood became less pessimistic. At some point she began to get a glimpse of her fantasy preoccupations. Such a glimpse can sometimes puncture excessive fantasizing and reduce it to more reasonable proportions that neither overwhelm the imagination nor interfere with reality testing.

As long as Bonnie remains isolated and without some specific purpose and activity, she has to elaborate an extensive fantasy life. Fantasies serve her as a substitute existence. As her daily living becomes more "real" and acquires more substance, she has less need for excessive fantasizing. I refer here to a quantity of fantasy that displaces productive living. However, the weaving of fantasies, in and of itself, is an ordinary, common, and often necessary pastime.

One day as she was making her rounds of art shops, Bonnie came across a rather large collection of shells of all sizes, shapes, and colors. She was fascinated by their textures and etched configurations and decided to make an investment by buying the whole lot. She felt as if she had a new toy and began to experiment with shell arrangements glued to textured backgrounds. She searched for inexpensive materials, and even went to the beach, woods, streams, and fields to find natural materials she could use as supporting backgrounds. She was still writing in her record book.

Step 15: Decide on another solution. My new alternative has been put into action, because I have made several shell collages and I like them. I don't know if they'll sell, and I'm afraid to find out. I think I'd be happy just sitting here playing with my shells and going out to find all sorts of materials to work with. I'm sure I can work the shells into other things for more color and interest.

Step 16: Repeat the evaluation process for Alternative Number Two and get input from others. I don't think I can put this evaluation process off much longer. I have several pieces ready now, and I suppose I could ask some people what they think of them. But I still have to take them someplace and try to sell them. God! The idea of that really turns me off. I feel so scared when I think of it. What am I trying to do? I've done some work and I do feel better. The next step is pretty obvious. There's no point in going on to Step Seventeen (which suggests continuing with the selection of new solutions). I've already found a good solution. I can make these collages and I like them. Maybe I've reached Steps Eighteen and Nineteen.

Step 18: Try to determine whether you've reached your limit regarding the issue you're working on. Is that it? Have I reached my limit in trying to find a job? I've really found a job to do. But the rest of the job is to sell what I've designed. Maybe I can work at making the collages, but I can't work at selling them.

Step 19: Try to find the end point for any single issue before you become discouraged. Maybe I should call this my end point, or I certainly will become discouraged. I don't want to get into that terrible condition I was in months ago. Maybe that's what I ought to try to avoid. Because if I get so depressed again, I won't do anything at all. At least now I'm producing, even though I'm not selling. And I don't want to stop.

Step 20: Feel free to return at another time to an issue you've already worked on. But I can't do that, because without getting a job, or at least being paid for my work, I don't see what other issue I can go to. *I've simply got to finish this issue.* I can't leave it. I can't just say it's my end point. I can't let myself get discouraged. I've put too much into it.

At that point Bonnie realized that she was blocked because she wanted someone else to sell her collages. She didn't want to have to go out and "peddle" her work. The idea repelled her. She was afraid "they" would laugh at her work and ridicule her, and she felt she couldn't stand that.

And so here's Bonnie, having produced some acceptable work, still caught in ambivalence caused by a dreadful fear of humiliating failure. Remember that she wants her first attempt to be immediately praised, accepted, and purchased. Remember her need to see only extremes. Realistically she knows her work isn't the greatest. But because she can't predict what might happen to it, she can't help but feel that it might be totally unacceptable. She feels she can't face that inevitable rejection. You see her predicting failure here, for realistically she cannot predict great success. She still gives herself only two alternatives, humiliating failure or great success.

Bonnie seesawed on this sharp edge for some time, unwilling to give up what she had gained and unable to go forward to the next step. She finds it so difficult to see herself as she actually is—a young, inexperienced, untried, unknown artist, who has to scratch around like most others to do her work and make a living.

While wallowing in this new despair Bonnie was invited to a wedding. She decided to go and bring the couple one of her works. They were very pleased with it. Another guest admired it and asked if she could buy one. And so, quite inadvertently, the mountain had come to Mohammed! This experience provided the push Bonnie needed to make the move to risk rejection.

With people like Bonnie the following questions invariably arise: How much did she really help herself? Wasn't she "lucky" in the help she received from others? First there was the invitation from her parents, which served to change the setting by physically removing her from the isolation she had imposed upon herself. Then there was Terri, who urged her to get out more. Finally there was the woman at the wedding who was her first "customer."

All of this is true. But surely no one functions in a vacuum. You are constantly interdependent with all the persons and events of your environment. And many outcomes would never take place without something preceding, initiating, or stimulating an action on your part, which in turn can lead to another and another.

As time passed, Bonnie thought of the particular course she had taken. She feels now she could not have foreseen that her first creative work would have taken the form that it did. That was purely accidental. What can usually be foreseen, however, is that some such accident is likely to occur if efforts are maintained.

The accident of opportunity is usually not predictable and is an endlessly fascinating occurrence. People who don't have to struggle as Bonnie has learn to identify the *unpredictable accident of opportunity,* sometimes under the least likely of conditions. But there are many, many Bonnies who have to begin to learn to believe that their efforts might lead to an outcome that may only remotely resemble their original goals, and learn to accept the shift in direction when it occurs.

It's clear that Bonnie had no special plan as she went along. There were just two things in her mind: the necessity to do something, *anything;* and her vacillating willingness to make any effort. Her response to the suggestions of a self-help program was one way of mobilizing herself, of becoming more involved with her problem. You saw how tentative her efforts were, how difficult it was for her to work consistently, to keep at her problem, to be confident that she could accomplish anything at all.

Even the most successful use of a self-help method is rarely uphill all the way. It follows an up-and-down course, no less rocky than most other experiences you have. It isn't likely that you can act consistently, optimistically, and enthusiastically over a plan of action if you are generally not that kind of person.

Ordinarily you will continue to be very much the way you always have been even while making your best efforts. The two main differences are that you are willing to make a new effort, a different effort, and that you feel a smidgen of wavering trust in your ability to help yourself. That's all you need to get started. Just that little smidgen. If you need outside urging along the way, and you can get it, that's all to your credit. If you regress badly, you can relegate that regression to the past and make another *now effort* in the present. That's all part of the process.

There's no miracle that will make you keep moving. But if you absolutely need to believe in a miracle, I'll offer you something like one. That is the miracle of your persistent need to survive and grow, which will ultimately drive out your despair and hopelessness.

XV

To Be or Not to Be

In some marriages a barren, leaden bond between the two partners is formed. It's an inevitable result of a style of living that each partner has evolved long before, as well as during, the marriage. Profoundly indifferent to their own growth, they stop supplying themselves and each other with the emotional sustenance that a person needs to give and receive in order to maintain a maturing process. (This point was described as a base-line need in Chapter Four.) While the marriage is destined to become the focus of the problem, it is in fact just one feature of a neglected investment in living.

WILL THIS MARRIAGE LAST?

Here is the story of two women, Tarra and Gaill, who, each in her own way, contributed to the development of relationships that are common prototypes in marriage. Tarra's was one in which husband and wife lived parallel lives, touching only as custom or convenience demanded. When the marriage exploded, there followed a series of events that proved the most stimulating of the entire time this couple had lived together. Gaill's marital habits and attitudes relate to another large segment of women, whose husbands expect and demand the primary role in the family and will tolerate no more than a secondary role for their partners—all the while criticizing them for their "spinelessness." If this sounds familiar, read on and discover how Gaill eventually accepted that though she couldn't "change" her husband, she could start to pay some unbiased attention to changing something in herself—without casting away too much of what she cherished.

Tarra, an attractive, middle-aged businesswoman, became greatly agitated when she couldn't decide whether or not to divorce her husband. He had discovered her intimacy with a colleague of hers and was despondent. He had believed that theirs was a sound marriage, but in her opinion it was shaky at best. From that point of view she thought that it might be more honest to leave him, but she was in acute conflict over the issue.

Tarra wondered if their child was justification enough to maintain what she considered a flat and stale relationship. Her husband, Todd, pleaded with her not to be hasty in making a decision, and prevailed upon her to try to work on improving the marriage. In seeking help, therefore, they decided to focus on the issue of whether or not to continue with the marriage, and began to work with the program.

For Step One Tarra wrote: "I find this difficult to do. The issue seems to be a very complex one. If I say it's a marital problem, where do I start? If I state the parts of the problem, there's more than one issue:

1. Do I want to break up my marriage?
2. Can I stand to hurt Todd if I decide to leave?
3. Should I deprive my child of a stable home?
4. If I divorce and remarry, do I want to make him a stepchild?
5. Do I want to marry the man I've had an affair with?
6. Should I keep my son with me, or let him live with my husband?

"I feel so upset because I can't decide how to proceed. Then there's Todd, who's upset also. He's worse off than I am. He seems almost incapacitated. He hasn't been able to go to work for several days, and he says he'll die if I leave him. He's terribly depressed. I feel rotten that I've hurt him so. I never intended that. But now that it's come out, I have to decide if I want to go or stay. That must be my issue for the moment."

Tarra felt engulfed by her feeling of guilt and incapable of deciding something that would affect her entire future. Angry also at having to deal with it, she wished he had never found out. Her ambivalence was a most difficult thing to tolerate. At times she felt she could try to make a go of it and felt relieved for a while. Then she'd swing away from that decision and feel torn again. Both she and Todd were suffering from acute anxiety over a conflict that had been precipitously exposed and that neither was prepared to manage.

Like a kid on a holiday, Tarra had known that her affair would end one day, and that would be that. She never considered having to make a momentous decision regarding it. She couldn't understand why she didn't let the whole thing drop now that it had come out. She felt no loyalty to her lover, nor any great love. But she seemed to be hanging on to her distressed state.

In working with Step Four, Tarra realized that her life had been pretty static for a long time and wondered if that had something to do with her inability to let go. Was she using this to do something about a situation that she'd never really thought about before? Had she been wanting to disrupt the marriage? Was that why she had the affair?

It was an exciting though disturbing time for Tarra. Perhaps not the way most people think of excitement. But what she was going through now was certainly a far cry from the dull, safe repetition of her life with Todd. That had always been predictable, routine, secure —but so dull!

She wrote in her record book: "Maybe it's the excitement that I want. A change. Maybe I'm afraid I'll sink into that routine torpor again. But isn't there anything in between?" In their marriage this couple had honored an unspoken agreement not to upset the apple cart; to do all the "correct" things to show their son how to behave in society; to come together only as might be expected; to maintain a comfortable home; to entertain and to keep alive friendships and activities that would continue to foster and maintain this setup. It was a self-perpetuating system, but it had become deadening for Tarra.

"As I think about it, it seems so sterile, so lacking in warmth, like a void. We did things together, but everything became so routine. There wasn't a scrap of uncertainty or excitement or passion in anything we did. We anticipated everything, so that nothing could go wrong."

Considering her willingness to risk change, Tarra wrote: "Here I am in middle age almost and I don't even feel that I've ever been young. I can't blame this on my marriage, though. It's been like this all along. My parents always worked hard and didn't do very much. My mother went to her local club. My father had a couple of cronies he'd visit. Otherwise they were always together. There were no friends who came to our home. We weren't even close to relatives, although we saw them at holidays.

"I feel I missed a lot in my family. I keep thinking about a lost childhood. I never had time for after-school activities, because I had a job after school. I wasn't inspired to do well in school, either. I was bright enough, but I did very little work. I'd reach a certain level and seem satisfied to remain there. My parents did encourage me to play the piano, but after learning the basics, I seemed to make no progress. I liked it, but couldn't seem to make the effort to work at it. I imagined that the music would just flow into my head if I looked at the notes long enough. I really would like to take it up again someday.

"In my family there was no communication, no conversation about goals and aspirations. No one asked about what you wanted to do later in life. We used to live one day at a time. If I hadn't sent myself to college, no one would have suggested that I go, or helped me to plan a course of action. There seemed to be a poverty of spirit, a lack of interest about what happened.

"I think I've lived my life the same way. Our lives have that element of changelessness also, and while I want to burst out of it, I still cling to it. That's why I must have had the affair. It was such a change. So daring! I really couldn't resist the opportunity even though I never planned it. It was like being snatched from the arms of death, of sameness, of routine. But I don't think I ever thought about it in that way.

"He said he was madly in love with me, and that was very heady for me. It made me feel desirable, needed. I didn't feel guilty with him because I believed I had suffered for a long time. It was justified. I deserved it. I had apparently felt neglected in some way. I never really tried to talk with Todd to explain what I felt, what was wrong. It seemed impossible to talk with him. I thought we were poles apart, but I keep wondering if we really were."

TALKING AGAIN

One day Tarra asked Todd to meet her after work for dinner. She realized that they rarely did anything without their son. He was always included. "We love him very much, but there's no way you can have an adult conversation that's private and intimate with a youngster around," she commented. "Maybe we felt we had no conversation left —so it didn't matter anyway."

She had planned to talk about the "problem" with Todd. But somehow she didn't. It was a pleasant dinner in a quiet restaurant he'd selected. Since Todd reacted so well, she suggested they try the same thing again, "to talk." During the following week the atmosphere at home was less heavy, and Tarra felt less agitated than she had in weeks.

Even though Tarra and Todd didn't "have a chance to talk" about their marital problems when they started to have dinner together, they were trying to be together in a different way. Their new interest was a guarded one, but each was more curious about the other. There was no denying it. This marital upheaval was without question the most painful yet the most stirring event that had ever occurred in their marriage. Neither could resist watching for signs of resolution, and their interest in each other was sharper than it had been for years. Although both remained anxious about the situation, there seemed to be tendrils of excitement that were not altogether unpleasant.

Nothing was taken for granted in those early troubled weeks. Though they were worried and unhappy, a certain alertness had replaced the habitual flatness of their relationship. That flatness had come partly from their efforts to maintain a reasonable, comfortable equilibrium in their home at all times. In a sense they had achieved the ultimate of equilibrium. There were rarely those swings between comfort and discomfort that characterize the comfort/discomfort equilibrium I described earlier.

In most families there are frequent wide swings, sometimes violent ones, into the discomfort zone. Then efforts are made to swing back into the comfort zone and to establish a comfortable equilibrium. It's an ongoing process in the natural course of human encounters. With Tarra and Todd, however, little was ever permitted to disturb the established equilibrium. Therefore, little sense of difference was experienced, little sense of variety, of changing shades of existence. They had lived rather in a comfort zone of constant early "twilight," neither too dark nor too light, and almost entirely predictable, for each day was molded into the image of each preceding day. That was the mold Tarra had shattered, and she had been unprepared for the force of the feelings that followed.

This couple continued to work with the program, but they didn't try to change their general style of living to any great extent. Small changes gave them the sense that they were being sufficiently active with their efforts. This way of proceeding was compatible with their style and served to keep further anxiety arousal in check.

A decision to try to remain in a marriage doesn't automatically make one feel satisfied with it. Sudden changes in feeling, pro or con, are characteristic, and Tarra was confused by the contradictions and inconsistencies that arose. But, she was willing to consider the problem from a different point of view, and that's an important first move that must be taken when you've decided to substitute positive mental health practices for negative ones.

Tarra was applying the use of her health points to turn about a condition that had arisen from the habitual use of interpersonal neglectfulness. Tarra and Todd had neglected their marriage, and yet they were disappointed that it hadn't nourished them in a way that would make them feel alive. Whatever creativity or enthusiasm they possessed regarding personal relations, they had put into their affection for, interest in, and time with their child. Little was extended to each other, a factor contributing to their dissatisfaction and lingering loneliness.

Of her life with Todd Tarra says, "We almost never talked about ourselves, our dreams, our ambitions. We didn't even gossip." It seems as if she had unconsciously selected a partner with whom she could live in the same way her family had lived. It felt familiar to her, and therefore comfortable. If this is so, then why did she find it so oppressive after a time?

It appears that Tarra had undergone several transitions in her attitude and in her view of herself, even though she had "never thought about it." What had been comfortable and suitable for her when she married couldn't continue to satisfy her, for she wasn't the same person she'd been a few years earlier. Yet she failed to make these changes known. Remember that neither one was strong on "making waves." So instead of noting and sharing small changes as they occurred, Tarra expected Todd to know what was going on within her, to know how her needs and wants were changing.

Not totally unaware, Todd had noted certain shifts in his wife's views, but he became intimidated by emerging new facets of her personality and began to withdraw. Seeing her changes only as rejections of himself, he couldn't understand that they were related primarily to her own development, and not to him. Also in the dark, Tarra viewed his withdrawal as disapproval and rejection of her new concerns. Both, therefore, resented the other for these mutually imagined rejections and grew still farther apart. Unknowing, neither could realize that their initial lack of communication and sharing had given rise to suspicions and the fear of abandonment that finally led to the crisis confronting them.

Gradually, however, this couple began to be able to talk about what had happened to them. At first they needed to leave their home to keep the talks from becoming rancorous or guilt producing. But very slowly—and I underscore the *slowly*—they were able to address themselves to single items that had always been bones of contention. At times they addressed themselves to small issues about which neither had guessed the other was concerned.

I should emphasize, too, that they were frequently discouraged, experiencing many "dry runs" in their efforts. But they found they could also discuss some of their differences with friends. One friend suggested a "marriage weekend"—just the two of them for an entire weekend.

Using the suggestion as a possible alternative, they explored their feelings about it. What emerged was a deep fear of closeness. They admitted to feeling "trapped" with each other. Afraid to make a commitment to such a weekend, they felt they might not be able to stand each other for two entire days and nights. "She'll go up the wall if she has to talk only with me for two days," Todd explained. "I may not be able to hold my tongue," Tarra said. "And he'll fall apart if I'm unkind."

Tarra believed that such sustained closeness would reveal her propensity for "bitchiness." Todd believed she wouldn't be able to tolerate his "lack of imagination and fussiness" for two days. It was the same fear experienced in different ways: I am not a decent enough person for my spouse to be alone with for two whole days.

And so we have two people needing the same things—acceptance, kindness, affection—but feeling within themselves incapable of having those needs met because of their own inherent deficiencies. It was this need that Tarra had felt was fulfilled with her lover. She felt he had accepted her as she was, expecting nothing more. She didn't believe that need could be fulfilled with Todd, because she felt he could never accept her manner.

Nevertheless, all the while, each one's efforts were having an effect on the other. When one was considerate, the other noted it consciously, and often made some reference to it. Formerly they had "expected" such acts, feeling that they were entitled to them as part of an unwritten marriage agreement. Their new awareness made them more appreciative of the common, small fragments of human intercourse that inevitably leave a residue of well-being—as long as one does not demand them as a right, nor is suspicious of underlying motivations.

It is useful to keep in mind, though, that any feature of behavior can be distorted by exaggeration. I am not suggesting, therefore, that every positive act is to be specifically noted and recorded, for you will find that certain features of close relationships are savored best in your private thoughts. Each partner has the task of deciding what, how, where, and when certain thoughts, dreams, fantasies, desires, and needs may be shared. To feel that everything has to be shared in order to keep a marriage open and alive would be going to another extreme. Each partner must assume the responsibility to be thoughtfully selective in deciding what to share. Otherwise the relationship may fall into a mutual evaluation system and run the risk of losing the spontaneous features that it deserves.

In time Tarra was better able to acknowledge something of her fear of closeness and of her ambivalence over change. Appreciating her physical and emotional response to the restrictive nature of the relationship, and the way she had contributed to its narrow uneventfulness, her resentment against Todd diminished. Backed up by his slow awakening, she was able to uphold her efforts toward greater self-acceptance and to value a fragile promise of affection and trust.

EXPECTATIONS CAN BREAK YOUR HEART

Another woman, Gaill, had no doubt about her marriage. She wanted to keep it and felt it was the only way to live. She was content with her children and home, but wasn't satisfied with the hollowness of her relationship with her husband. Her goal was to enrich it. She sounded rueful when she said that. "I've been trying to enrich the relationship ever since I've been married. I don't know why I say that's my goal *now.*"

Gaill was aware that the marriage had rarely been trouble-free. Trying to "make things better" had become second nature to her. She didn't know that she and her husband, Ellsworth, had become ensnared in the most common of poor marriages. It was one in which the neurotic needs of both partners had led them to select a spouse with whom they could act out the familiar defenses each of them brought to the relationship. To continue to use these defenses may possibly minimize their anxiety, but it also promises the least happiness for them.

Ambivalence reigned in Gaill's feelings and thoughts about her husband. According to her, Ellsworth was "all man." He had to have his way about everything that was going on, had to criticize anything that did not originate with him, and had to make final decisions about many things that did not really concern him. All this had initially been reassuring to Gaill. She expected that such a "strong" man would "take care of" her and relieve her of many of life's burdens.

She was willing to become the "good little wife," and her attitude was one of patient compliance. She showed no interest in developing responsibility for herself. She would be content if the "world went by," as long as she could be happy with her husband. Ellsworth suited her, for he seemed to embody qualities of forthrightness, assertiveness, dependability, and strength, qualities in which she felt deficient.

And Gaill suited Ellsworth, for she was the kind of woman with whom he felt he could have his way unequivocally, the kind who would put up with his critical but "honest" comments, his arbitrary whims and decisions. He felt she was malleable enough so that he could "develop" her into a truly "worthwhile" individual, one worthy of partnership with *him*. It's possible that he could have helped her to grow, for her self-effacing tendencies had brought her into adulthood as a naive, undeveloped person. But the concept of his Henry Higgins to her Eliza was all in his head, for he made no real effort to extract from himself the industry essential to such a plan. Overlooking that small detail, he was left with the feeling of failure, disappointment, and frustration at her recalcitrance in cooperating with his grand design.

And so it was that he found himself constantly critical of her efforts to please him and her timid moves at being assertive. "It doesn't matter what I do," she remarked. "I cannot please him. I can't remember anything I've ever done on my own that he has not ridiculed or been furious about. Ridicule is his kinder response." When discussing her willingness to maintain the marriage, she said, "I'm not the divorcing kind. That's something I would never do."

Gaill's timidity annoyed Ellsworth. Yet when she tried to speak out, he chided her for "talking nonsense and being long-winded." As she gradually learned to deal with him and became more assertive, he called her "bitchy." That accusation would almost destroy her; but when she tried to control her bitchiness, he said she was "mushy like oatmeal." "But there have been many *good* times," she declared, though one is hard put to discern where those good times were.

Although the personalities involved are different, there are factors at play which are similar to those described earlier in Tarra and Todd.

You see here guilt over not being the kind of woman Gaill expects herself to be, fear of change, and avoidance of the anxiety any significant move entails.

THE POWER OF PREJUDICE

There are countless marriages in which you can identify the two personality types found in Gaill and Ellsworth. It might seem to you that perhaps such relationships no longer exist in days of liberated womanhood. But I'm sorry to report that they do, and to a very considerable extent. Among middle-aged and elderly couples, among women who never expected "equal" partnership, this kind of relationship has flourished and still does. Although some of these women are demanding certain changes, their roles remain essentially the same.

What is more surprising, however, is the number of younger couples who complain about exactly the same things their elders have complained about. Young women complain of certain attitudes and unreasonable demands in their husbands. They call it "chauvinism." Young men complain that their wives don't keep the house or the checkbook the way it should be kept. All of this points to the fact that prejudices die hard. Many young men in their twenties have already picked up so-called "masculine" attitudes and beliefs from their middle-aged fathers. And young women follow the "feminine" attitudes of their middle-aged mothers. They are both in conflict, therefore, in that they can become saddled with outmoded, fantasy images while still striving to espouse and experience a freedom they aren't convinced they want or deserve.

That these young people often deplore worthless, denigrating, culturally transmittable attitudes does not immediately alter their dilemma or change their practices. What is encouraging, though, is the extent to which they can, more than their parents, gradually free themselves of such transmitted beliefs and make changes that offer their partners and themselves more autonomy. Those who cannot free themselves sufficiently from old ways, or blend them with the new, are frequently overcome with anxiety, and they find their way to divorce courts hoping to put an end to their suffering.

But Gaill was not thinking of divorce, for she held to her expectation of loving and being loved. But it was a fantasy wish, totally inconsistent with her partner's personality. Because Ellsworth was so rejecting of her moves toward harmony, Gaill wondered: "It takes two to produce any kind of relationship—good or bad. There is something I am or am not doing that makes it possible for a poor relationship to be perpetuated."

NEED FOR CHANGE

Here is the old *mea culpa** theme again, and Gaill kept dedicating her energy to urge Ellsworth to be the kind of husband she thought he should be. Nevertheless, her wish to explore her part in this master/slave combination led her to the use of the twenty steps. She was quick with her work, responding to several steps at one sitting. Her entries kept to the themes: "There should be more I can do. Why is he so disgruntled? I don't want to feel angry with him. It upsets me. I resent trying so hard and still have nothing work with him."

Exasperated by her failures, she kept probing. "Does he enjoy finding something to pick on? Maybe that makes him feel good. If that's so, I shouldn't complain. But it's certainly a downer to listen to him. He can squeeze the fun out of anything." She described how she had tried to improve the marriage. "I've tried to deal with him in so many ways. I've asked, begged, demanded. I've tried to cajole, entertain, persuade, teach. I've gotten hysterical or withdrawn. When I do that, he gets hysterical or withdrawn too. It's like a graveyard duet.

"Then he complains that nothing ever happens—as if a little genie is going to pop out and ask the master what he desires. He's had his little genie, and it's been me. But that hasn't worked either. And I'm beginning to think that maybe I don't want to be a genie any longer.

"I've noticed that he's so much nicer to others. With me he doesn't have to bother. I think I have to learn to talk to him without caring so much what he says or does. If I care, I can be hurt, and I feel guilty. If I don't care, it won't hurt. Maybe there's a time not to care."

*It's my fault.

REAL DIFFERENCES

When Gaill came to Step Twelve, she wrote: "I really haven't the slightest idea how to go about this. What I really want is to get closer to Ellsworth, yet it seems like a losing battle." Her involvement with her thoughts and feelings, though, clarified her part in the marriage. She began to think how different she and Ellsworth were. "Maybe that's why we don't agree on much. Men have 'manly' concerns that women don't care about. Maybe that's why it's so hard for men and women to live together. Most people can't live together without really trying—both of them. It isn't much good if only one person is trying. Both have to.

"I know I complain that he never listens to me. He replies that I have nothing to say that interests him. I tell him I always listen to him. He says then, 'Why don't you learn anything?' Last week, I suddenly realized that I do listen to him, but I'm not interested in what he's saying. It bores me. But I've always tried to be responsive and ask questions. He's right, though. I can't learn anything from him because I'm not interested. That's all he's saying to me, that he's not interested in what I'm thinking about or enjoying. He's more honest than I am. But I try harder!"

Gaill has brought out a point of difference that has always exasperated couples. It is true that what intrigues and excites one partner may hold no real interest for the other. And there's no reason that it should, for tastes differ widely in all areas of living. Nevertheless, couples who are compatible to any degree can listen to and can respond to each other's concerns because they find pleasure in a partner's involvement and enthusiasm, even while not sharing it and without a true interest in the subject.

After some time Gaill began to see that her husband held very traditional views, and that he had absolutely no interest in changing his attitudes or behavior patterns. She saw how fruitless were her attempts with one whose goals were so divergent from hers. "Maybe he's not putting me down. Maybe he just isn't thinking about me at all? Is that why he can't be close? You can't be close to someone you're not even thinking about. I don't think Ellsworth knows anything about closeness. He seems to treat me as if I'm an intruder, as if all

I want to do is to bother him. That's the way it sounds. I'm not really a nagging wife. I just want to be friendly, close. He has to have the upper hand all the time.

"I guess this is men's competitiveness. It's an inbuilt thing in some men. They can't overcome it. They don't even know it's there sometimes. He thinks competing is good. Men are supposed to compete. It's like a religion with them. I know Ellsworth always has to feel he's number one, no matter whom he's with. I just wonder if there's any hope to get close to a man like that. I suppose I have to give up trying to change Ellsworth from being the kind of person he is. I have to find a common ground whenever I can and be satisfied with that" (Step Eighteen).

At Step Nineteen Gaill wrote: "I guess I've reached my end point in knowing that I can't really help Ellsworth with something he's not willing to change. I guess he can't afford to admit that a change would be good for him and for the family. That would mean to him that he's been wrong all along. And that's something he could never stand. He's got to be right—all the time. If he can believe that, he will feel he has no need to change. I just have to forget wanting to help him with this and just make the best of it."

As Gaill learned about the limits of what she could expect from her husband, she began to turn from a compulsive search to achieve closeness and harmony with him. She started to think in terms of trying her wings elsewhere, where someone might appreciate the work she was willing to do. She didn't want to abandon her family in any sense. But she felt it might be a good thing for all concerned if she spent less time fussing over what she thought they needed.

LOOK TO YOURSELF

A striking feature of these notes is the central position in which Gaill placed her husband. Although she complained about many elements of his personality, he remained the center of her existence. It was difficult for her to take him as he was, for she has been too dependent on him and too sensitive to his likes, dislikes, and moods. Her well-being has been bound to her need for *his* approval, *his* decisions. Separating herself from this dependent position aroused too much anxiety in her.

Ellsworth has been dependent on her as well, for he needs a "willing victim" to acknowledge and respond to his often irrational demands. The mutuality of this dependency provides the adhesive that binds such partners together. They both suffer from that bondedness, but without strong efforts they are unable to extricate themselves from a situation that harms them both. Though the view is different from each one's side, neither view exists in reality.

Toward the end of her work with the program Gaill began to feel hopeful, began to see that she might have a place for herself in all this, a place independent of the whims of a husband or a child. She doesn't *have* to be such a good mommy and homemaker. She can try her wings. She can look to herself. She can occupy herself with activities unrelated to the concerns that have been her life for over ten years.

Like others, Gaill now questions the intensity of her attention to those family concerns, and she's working to appreciate that the *sharing* marriage of her dreams is not compatible with the kind of relationship she and her husband have established. This helps her to acknowledge the impossibility of her quest. But it will take some time before she can accept that without feeling responsible for its failure.

When Gaill comes to that point of recognition, it will be a relieving one for her. She's waited for years hoping that something would happen to "change" her husband. That patient vigil has deflected her attention from the issues: How can I find satisfaction for myself without feeling so neglected and abused, without feeling "bad," without disrupting my family life? How can I avoid feeling "put down" by a partner who feels his position of authority threatened by my new unwillingness to be intimidated? How can I find something for myself, even though my husband has no interest in what interests me? How can I enlarge and enrich my existence?

Interestingly enough, when a woman like Gaill can make a positive transition in the direction of such issues, it has a liberating effect on the entire family, including the husband (even though he may never admit it). Gaill can learn how it is possible to remain "your own person" and yet continue to honor commitments made in the marriage. Both children and spouse often respond with mixed feelings at first to shifts in "Mommy." But when they see that their safety is not jeopardized, they can respond positively to her new attitude. She may then find herself free of resentment, free of impossible, heartbreaking expectations, and therefore less guilt-ridden.

If Gaill can maintain her determination to do something just for herself, she'll discover that there are all kinds of changes possible, not just the elusive ones she's been carrying around in her imagination. That discovery will be truly liberating, for she'll have more of an incentive to look for opportunities. That liberation will permit her to look to herself with a new optimism. Yet she won't have to leave her family—for remember what she said at the outset: "I'm not the divorcing kind." That's her style and that's what she's chosen. That's all you can ask. She won't have Heaven; but she can have more of all this.

XVI

If Your Efforts
Are Blocked

Real efforts cannot be blocked unless your motivation is. And if you read "blocked" as *conflicted*, you can understand what it really means. You are blocked when you are not clear about your priority at any given moment. Remember—simply stated, a conflict is a condition of wanting and not wanting something *at the same time.* Keeping that point in mind can allow you to select what comes first, right now. When you can choose only *one* course to pursue in any one time unit, then you can begin to make practical plans followed by reasonable actions.

It is difficult at first for some people to become committed to the twenty-step method. You may find yourself resisting as you start on your own program to manage anxiety. Some persons resist because they feel "ridiculous," or they don't want to be "disappointed again." Others don't see "how it can work." While they recognize and admit to the practice of poor mental health habits, they are frightened to use such a direct method, which places responsibility on them for their own welfare. For such persons, however, the concept of a one-year mental health program proves sufficiently appealing to motivate them. It helps them to feel that they needn't expect instant results, and so keeps additional anxiety from being generated.

In this section you'll read of three women who were blocked in making moves that were essential to their well-being. Adale, a writer, despaired that she would never write her stories because of her writer's block, which related to fear over an uncertain reception of her work. Jasma, a high school teacher, couldn't seem to discipline a particular student because of her mixed feelings toward him in the classroom. And Eileen, a widowed mother, knew she had to be firm with her twelve-year-old son, but felt guilty that she didn't want to "service" him. She was also afraid that she'd lose his love if she became less permissive.

WRITER'S BLOCK

Adale makes her living as a writer in an advertising agency, but she has always wanted to write short stories. Deciding that she had a serious writing block, she was willing to try the twenty steps to try to overcome it. At thirty-eight Adale felt she'd missed her chance and was anxious about her future. As she wrote, memories tumbled out. She remembered that an English teacher, in commending her work, once told her that writing had to become second nature to her, a kind of *happy habit.*

Other memories flow: "When I was a child, I had a baby-sitter who was in her sixties. She used to talk with me about all the things she was going to do before she died. I thought she was very old at the time, and I wondered why she was waiting to do all those wonderful things. She used to say: I'm going to travel all over the world when my ship comes in; I'm going to get this or that when my ship comes in. Once I asked my mother if *her* ship had come in. She laughed and said, 'It comes in and out. Where did you hear that?' and I told her.

"I have the feeling that I'm like that old woman. I seem to be waiting for a ship to come in that never will, just as I know it never came in for old Mrs. Mills. But she seemed content waiting for it and believing that it might just happen. Even as I write this, I'm shaken that I seem to be on this same pathway—passing the time until something else comes along. That may have been all right for Mrs. Mills, or for anyone who doesn't want any more for herself. But I can't be content with that. The thought of it terrifies me. Yet I wait and

I have waited all these years. I seem to be in a dream—waiting for something out there to happen, as if I'm going to be rescued. One of my stories will be sold somehow, and then the publisher will want another and another, and then I'll be famous. Is it possible that I've made this fantasy my reality? I can't even think of that because I think I'll go crazy if I do."

As Adale wrote about Mrs. Mills, it occurred to her that there might be a story there, a small snail-shell-like story about a person who lives an entire life within herself, her little apartment, her little neighborhood. "Yes," thinks Adale. "This might make a good story. Just a short one about a baby-sitter, who can seem so close to a child. But when she leaves, she seems to take everything of herself with her, leaving hardly a memory, until the next time."

NOBODY'S WATCHING

Adale wrote voluminously. She continued with the steps, unable to respond to any one of them with only a few lines. When she came to Step Eleven, she wrote: "WRITE!" She then took a sheet of paper and wrote at the top, "The Baby Sitter." And she wrote and wrote, remembering what her high school teacher had said to her: Just write. Don't worry about the perfect word. Nobody's watching. You can refine later.

Adale found herself looking forward to getting home and working on her story. Doing that, she became more aware of her previous hawklike, self-judgmental attitude that made her so critical, so dissatisfied, and interfered with her flow of words. Always proud of her high standards, she complains: "But what good have they been when they keep me from doing anything?"

The story was finished and rewritten several times in the same open way, letting her fantasies flow directly into the writing, without passing through the censor in her mind. She knew she had come upon a method that worked for her, but she was a little apprehensive that she might lose it.

Adale was wondering and curious about what was happening: "In the beginning, I wrote with a flourish, a wave of enthusiasm, drawn from my notebook writing. There, I saw myself able to write pages and pages of what I considered nonsense. Who cares about what I write? That is the fact. No one does. But someone has to care or I can't write. So that leaves me. Only *I* have to care. It's nice to have someone else caring, but it's not critical. I've seemed to care too much, though. And to be honest, I felt that everyone else I talked with had to care the way I did, or there wasn't any point to it. I have to admit that writing all that nonsense got me into the swing of it.

"As I wrote one thing I had observed in Mrs. Mills, other thoughts seemed to come from nowhere. Most often they were just germs of an idea which I jotted down. It seemed to me that if I didn't write them instantly, they would just disappear, and I couldn't recapture them. Then I'd go back to them after I'd finished the thought I was with and find that they did have a place in what I was writing. But I had to expand them to make them fit into the story. I found that these expanded germ ideas turned out to be the parts I liked best. Yet they would never have appeared in an outline, or been anticipated in any way.

"Once I started to work with them, they seemed to acquire a life of their own and just grew. It was the most exciting part of the work, especially because I actually had no idea how any one of them would turn out. It was scary at times, because I seemed to be tumbling ahead into unknown territory, just following one idea that would stimulate a second, and that would stimulate a third, and so on. There was no way of knowing where it would all end."

To simplify Adale's problem to a consideration of only one of its elements may seem sketchy to you. But it can be useful for the purposes of our work here. I cannot possibly point out all of the features of her writing block, but I think it's clear that one of the strongest features of the block was the *inner censorship* demanded by her shoulds, even *before* she had a finished product to edit. Adale's willingness to respond to the twenty steps and to permit herself to write her "nonsense" was enough to break through the block and release her from an inner self-condemning judge and jury who held a relentless grip on that part of her mind and feelings that she calls her creativity.

This is not the outcome in every case. But some "loosening up" can take place if you have the courage to use this procedure for yourself. Remember, too, that while I'm speaking of a writer's block here as an illustration, I'm talking about blocks of all kinds. As you work with the twenty steps in the context of your own issue (*your* block) your musings might lead you away from a frozen, rigid circle of self-destructive habits, and into an open plain of possibilities.

PLEASE NOTICE ME

From Adale's personal problem with blocked efforts we shift now to one that involves two persons. Stymied in her efforts to help a student who desperately wanted attention, Jasma, a history teacher, defeated herself by becoming angry with her failure to discipline a student.

"Oh, you don't know what you're talking about." This was muttered under the student's breath, and Jasma wasn't sure whether the remark was meant for her or for another. The student was Bert, a thorn in Jasma's side for some time. Disruption was the name of Bert's game, either overt or covert. It was all the same to him. But disrupt he would, and there seemed no way Jasma could control the situation and conduct the class as she knew she should.

She found Bert's sullenness, alternating with clownishness, quite offensive. But he seemed determined to harass, annoy, and exasperate. Deciding to remain cool and maintain control, Jasma felt she could get Bert to become more cooperative if she tried hard enough. But Bert had not responded to any of Jasma's attempts to engage him. She now found herself angry, tense, and anxious when he was in class.

DON'T GIVE UP

Jasma felt she'd tried everything when she decided to use the twenty steps in coping with Bert. She followed a different format of four steps however, because she thought it would be more useful for her. These are the comments she entered in her record book.

1. *Identification of the trouble point:* I have known Bert for several years. Originally he was one of my advisees. At that time he proved to be opposed to every suggestion I would make as his teacher-counselor. He was not a likable student. He would nag most of his teachers and show his craving for attention by surly, hostile behavior. In my class now, I find him not much different. His hand is constantly raised to participate in discussions, so it is difficult to ignore him. To do so results in sullen behavior, where he slams books, slides down in his seat, and makes rude comments. Altogether, this type of behavior destroys morale in the class. Much of the time the rest of the class is more interested in how I handle him than in the work we are doing.

At one point I spoke to Bert about his attitude. He explained it by accusing me of favoring the other students, of not recognizing his "opinions," of "picking" on him. I gently disputed every one of his arguments and asked him if he liked the class. He said that he felt the class was too easy for him and wanted to be recommended to an honors class. I felt that the work there would put too much pressure on him, but I encouraged him to work, cooperate in class, try to respect the ideas of the other students, keep an open mind, and I would review his work at the end of the term and make a decision. He seemed satisfied with this. At the same time I stressed the importance of attitude and behavior, emphasizing the fact that in an honors class he would come in contact with more able students and he would not be able to intimidate them so easily. He paid attention to this and his behavior improved for the rest of the term.

At the end of the semester he asked me if I was recommending him for the honors class. Although I felt that Bert could not do the work in the other class, I told him that we would try it. I warned him of the competition, of the pressure he would experience, but he desperately wanted to try it. I told him that he could probably make a grade of B in a regular class, but that in honors the work would be very much more demanding. He reminded me that his attitude had changed, that he would apply himself, and that he had learned to pay attention and not sulk whenever things did not go his way. I wanted to believe him. I know he is a very unhappy and anxious boy and that he made me feel anxious about my authority in the classroom. But I wanted to help him and myself as well. His behavior had changed, and I felt that since he wanted this so badly, it was worth giving him a chance, even though I was in conflict, thinking that such a move went against my better judgment as a teacher.

At the beginning of the next term, Bert appeared in my honors class. During the entire month of September his behavior was marked by surly, flippant remarks. One week he came late to class every day. I would interrupt whatever work we had begun and ask him for a late pass. He would reply, "I don't have one and I can't get one!"

The next time I decided to ignore the lateness. That resulted in the slamming of books on the desk, noisy shuffling through a notebook, muttering. When I spoke to him about disturbing the class, he retorted, "You're always pickin' on me—I was only looking for something." I spoke with him after class and warned him that any more latenesses would have to be reported to the dean. The lateness routine stopped.

At about this time, Bert started to berate the other students in the class. He interrupted their discussions and laughed at some of their remarks, or grinned grotesquely whenever a wrong answer was given. My patience was running out. I accused him of rudeness in front of the whole class. I deliberately ignored him. I raised my eyebrows at him. I stared at him whenever his behavior was particularly odious. I glared at him. I tried to recognize his hand as infrequently as possible. Nothing worked. He does everything just short of becoming a serious disciplinary problem.

2. *Planning a solution:* On a day when Bert's behavior was not so obstreperous, I seized the opportunity to ask him to see me in my office later in the day. He was completely taken aback. He hadn't done anything "wrong" in class and couldn't figure out what I wanted. I planned to limit our meeting to twenty minutes and to talk only about class progress, not about behavior or attitude. At this time I decided that a short meeting each week would give Bert some attention and that perhaps his hostility would subside.

3. *Taking action:* Bert appeared in my office at the appointed hour, cautiously subdued, testing me, watching for some ulterior motive on my part. I asked how his schoolwork was progressing in general. I avoided any particular reference to my class where

his work was below level. We discussed his plans for college next year. Following that talk, Bert's behavior in class was awful. He disrupted classwork several times by being late, calling out, and trying to engage the girl next to him in talking whenever my back was turned.

Several days later I asked Bert to meet me again in my office. We continued our discussion of the previous week. I did not mention the behavior at all. At this time we discussed the pros and cons of going away to college. Again, it was a short interview. The next day Bert's behavior in class was characterized by noisily sliding down in his seat and keeping his eyes closed. He raised his head occasionally to show me how he was suffering. I decided to ignore this. After class, he slammed his books together and stormed out.

The following day Bert was calmer, and I decided not to mention the outburst of the day before. I figured he was hoping I would request another interview because of his behavior, but I didn't. I was determined that the interview technique would be used only for general discussions about academic progress and plans for college. In this way I hoped to provide him with a modicum of the attention he needed without getting too involved in coping with his obviously serious emotional problems. My primary concern is to maintain a healthy, vital, enthusiastic, and vibrant atmosphere in my classroom. Bert has the capacity to destroy such an environment.

Bert and I met again. At this time we discussed some photographs he had taken for the school paper. He asked me if I would look at them and comment on his selection. I said I would. During class the next day, I noticed a marked change in Bert. He arrived early. He opened his text and notebook before class began. He contributed to class discussions by making worthwhile remarks and observations. At the next interview he asked if I would read a short essay he had written and make some corrections. I said I would. During this interview Bert told me how he came to write the essay. It was something we had discussed in class once that had inspired him. His behavior continued to show improvement.

After class one day, Bert told me that his essay had been accepted by the newspaper. He was pleased. I told him that I thought it was good. By now I felt that my low-key attitude had been far more effective than a more enthusiastic response to his constructive moves. I think that might have made him feel that I would be disappointed if he could not "produce."

4. *Evaluation:* I feel that my efforts were successful. Bert is a disturbed youngster. I was faced with the problem of coping with his emotional upheaval and its effects on me and other teenagers. I am not qualified to handle the "psychological" nature of Bert's behavior. For that reason I decided to show him attention of a different kind from what he was eliciting in me and in other teachers. I wanted to show him that I cared about him in some way, but not to get involved in opening Pandora's box by discussing his past or personal matters. As long as I acknowledge him for a few minutes once or twice a week, he seems to be satisfied, and has continued to be cooperative in class.

POSITIVE AFFIRMATION

All youngsters have a strong common need, which is not considered neurotic. It is a need for ongoing *positive affirmation,* a requirement for their continuing development of self-confidence. They seem to be saying: "I cannot exist in a vacuum. If I feel, think, and act in any way, I need someone to feel myself against. I need someone to hear me, to affirm my existence, or else I have no sense of substance, no sense of self-trust, no confidence in my abilities and strengths. I cannot do this by myself. I must have *some caring person* there to acknowledge me, to say, 'Yes, I see you and hear you as you are, and I receive you into this world of people. Come and walk with me. I will hold your hand and guide you so that you will learn the ways of your fellows and learn how to live with them. If you are afraid, I will teach you to trust.' "

Bert, too, has this natural need for affirmation. Because of his anxiety, however, he distorts it into a relentless, compulsive need to elicit and grab every scrap of attention he can arouse, positive or negative. Only in this way can Bert relieve his terrible anxiety, even though the relief is never really successful or lasting. By disrupting the class, such a youngster often feels a spurious and fragile pride at how well he has succeeded in eliciting an acknowledgment. But it becomes a sad and hollow victory for him.

Only when he received attention that he clearly recognized as acceptance instead of rejection could Bert relinquish his need to disrupt. He was apparently getting his needed dose of affirmation in the few minutes that Jasma gave him in the office, and it had the unmistakable quality of positive attention. Bert no longer needed the attention he had fought for in the classroom, an attention he felt he could command only by being negative.

The play between Bert and Jasma illustrates several points. First, there is the wisdom of diverting attention away from destructive patterns. Tremendously curious about a new approach to him, Bert could not resist following through to see where it led. Second, there is the predictable response to change by the arousal of secondary anxiety. Although it pleased him, Jasma's new approach made him anxious for the very fact that it was new—a change in what he was accustomed to experiencing. An increase in anxiety following the first meetings (worse behavior in class) pointed distinctly to his *fear of change*—even though this change was so decidedly a positive one, one that didn't refer to his obnoxiousness at all, didn't put him down, and in fact helped him unequivocally.

Third, by her positive but low-key reaction to his work Jasma kept the arousal of secondary anxiety to a minimum. Had she been too lavish with her praise, Bert's expectation could have shot up, becoming so unrealistic as to swamp him. His anxious reaction to something he feels he can't handle leads him to disruptive behavior. That cycle was interrupted by her managing to keep his goals within bounds he could maintain.

Fourth, Bert's feedback to Jasma illustrates the principle of self-healing by reference to constructive forces rather than to deeply ingrained destructive practices. What is out of the ordinary here is the rapidity of change over a period of only weeks of effort on Jasma's part. Yet that rapidity is understandable if you believe that people don't usually prefer to be mean, unkind, or disliked.

In terms of dynamics, Bert had the unusual experience of engaging in an encounter with a teacher who didn't feed his tremendous pool of unconscious self-hatred. You recall my previous explanation that such a pool must be continuously fed by your own self-contempt over the many failures of your fantasy shoulds. Jasma's reference to matters that were considerably removed from his poor classroom behavior gave Bert an opportunity to practice positive mental health habits in a sufficiently unrelated area. That way, old practices were not automatically triggered as they had been in the classroom.

In obtaining affirmation and obvious approval from a positive exchange with Jasma, Bert was not driven to resort to the obnoxious behavior to which he was addicted. In reducing his practice of such poor habits, he accumulates less self-hate and allows his self-esteem to grow.

A fifth point is that of changing the scene in order to encourage untried positive responses. Good or bad, old familiar habits usually thrive best in old familiar places. And so, changing the place can help to change the habit. You'll remember how Tarra, a woman on the edge of divorce, used this technique to introduce a new pattern of conversation with her husband.

A success similar to Jasma's can be achieved with adults as well. But because of certain long-standing rigidities, your efforts may need to be more extensive, and you may be much longer in obtaining such positive results. In the case of a relative stranger you may not think the effort worth your while. But in dealing with someone close to you, someone with whom you'll have a relationship for many years to come, you need to consider whether one or two years of such effort are worth a possibly improved relationship for the next twenty or more years. This was a factor in Eileen's efforts to establish a less troubled atmosphere for herself and her son.

DO YOU LOVE ME, MOM?

Living in a small apartment in a large midwestern city, Eileen felt herself dominated by her twelve-year-old son, Doug. "He demands more companionship from me than I'm willing to give. He wants to be waited on and he refuses to help in the running of the household. I appreciate that any boy of his age might feel the same way. But I think that his persistent demands are spoiling a relationship that's been generally good.

"I'm a widow raising a child alone, working, going to school, and trying to keep up with a social life. I have a time and energy crisis of my own. And I just can't go along with all of his demands." It was clear from her manner and tone of voice that Eileen felt she *should* be going along with them. After all, a mother's first obligation is to her child, isn't it, regardless of unreasonable demands? She doesn't want to "traumatize" him, does she, by denying him?

It was also clear that with the program she had set for herself, Eileen could not be a handmaiden for her son, as well as provider, full-time housekeeper, cook, chauffeur, and playmate. However, she had to deal with the feelings of guilt and anxiety that she was failing him whenever she felt irritated or refused to indulge him. She was thrown into conflict over her wish to see to her own needs and yet be the kind of mother she expected herself to be. By now you're familiar with this conflict, which thousands of parents have.

"I've discussed mutual cooperation with him many times," Eileen goes on. "But I don't feel I'm getting through to him. I do think that there's something wrong with my communication that causes his lack of cooperation." She was eager to try the twenty steps.

WHO THROWS OUT THE GARBAGE?

Eileen wrote:

> *Step 1: Select a troublesome issue that causes repeated tension, guilt, anger, or anxiety.* The way Doug cooperates with me is very unreliable, to say the least. I seem to be irritated and angry with him so much of the time. I don't want to, because I love him so much. He's the only family I have and I want to be able to enjoy being with him. I want to respect his views and opinions as he grows into young manhood. It won't be very long! I don't want him to be an unkind, unpleasant teenager like some I see. I want him to talk things over with me and not hesitate to ask for advice if he needs it. I want him to know that I am and will continue to be the one person who has his interest most at heart and who can be depended upon.

out of his clothes and into the shower and ready for bed. "Good night, Mom." Kiss. No more Doug. The garbage is still there.

Step 13: Get input regarding efforts made. I can only evaluate this myself. I don't talk to anyone about it. On the morning after that night, he was gone early. The next time I saw him, later that night, he was in his pajamas. I insisted that the garbage go out. He got very angry and said, "Do you want me to go out without my clothes on?" I said, "That's up to you. Go in your pajamas, or get dressed. This garbage is not going to stick around here any longer." He put on his pants and took it to the incinerator.

Step 14: Evaluate your new action in terms of losses and gains. It seems that when I am really firm, I always gain. That happened about two weeks ago. So far, the garbage has been going out on request, which is the way I want it. But I always have a little pang (anxiety) that he won't love me if I make him do these things. Yet it's funny. We have been feeling more affectionate toward each other than usual. It must be that I'm not angry with him for not cooperating, and he's not angry with me for bothering him so much. I suppose he feels guilty, too, when he doesn't cooperate. It looks to me that he enjoys pleasing me. But he sure wasn't about to help out unless I made him. I have to be willing to run the risk of losing that affection. But it hasn't worked that way so far.

Step 15: Decide on another solution if Alternative Number One has not been effective. I'm going to decide on another area of cooperation now, because I've been successful with two others already. This one has to do with the laundry. I've agreed to do his laundry for him. But he has to help because, after all, the laundry is for him. When he runs out of clean clothing, he tells me. If it's not convenient for me to do it right away, I tell him to do it or to manage for a few days. He pleads incompetence. I say that it's easy. I've shown him several times how to do it, but he won't. He doesn't want to, that's all. He nags me to do it. Finally, I do it when it's convenient. I get annoyed with his nagging and I'd like to get him to do it himself sometimes.

Step 16: Repeat the evaluation process. It almost looks like a game or something. He won't empty the garbage and I won't wash his clothes. But I don't think it is. I really don't mind doing the laundry. The timing is the only difference between us. I also want him to be *able* to do it. I think there is a lot going on here that is good for both of us.

One day, at Doug's urging, the laundry was being done. He helped get the piles assorted. I did the first batch. We hang the laundry up to dry. Doug was full of instructions on how he wanted it hung so his pants would dry for the next day. He had no other clean ones to wear. However, when the first batch was ready to hang, I said, "Okay, Doug. It's time for us to hang the laundry now." "Us?" he said. I replied, "Well, would you rather do it yourself?" He was quite surprised. But realizing his plight, he came right in to do it, although not too cheerfully. I felt I had made my point.

Step 17: Continue with selection of new solutions. There's another problem we've had to solve for some time. It concerns our food shopping. I couldn't get Doug to help me with it at first. Then I decided to wait until we could find a time to do it together. He can be a big help with this and he knows it. But he would always procrastinate. Now he accepts helping me regularly, and with putting away the purchases. Otherwise it doesn't get done. The lack of "snackables" in the house drives him (not me) up the wall. Now he occasionally volunteers, "Let's go food shopping, Mom." Sometimes we have a snack out before the shopping. It has become a nice little outing. We have a good time eating and talking away from home. It's a pleasant change for me as well as for him.

Step 18: Try to determine when you have reached your own limit with regard to the issue. I realize that, with any one of these things, I have to know when to push and when not to. Some days certain things seem so much more important than other days. And I have to mean it when I say I want him to do something. I have to decide how important any single issue is and if it's worth some kind of fuss. Some days it is. Some days it isn't.

Step 20: Other issues I want to deal with. This do-for-me attitude keeps coming up in reference to *my* responsibility—as Doug sees it. He has often been rude and critical of me if I don't do what he wants. I stress that I do not consider myself "irresponsible" on these occasions, as he implied. But, having so many responsibilities, I have different priorities. He seemed to accept this.

Tonight, just as I was writing this last portion, Doug came into my room and asked what ideas I had about dinner. I replied, "None yet." "I have a suggestion," he went on. "I haven't been out all day, and I want to get something at the store. How about if I pick up some hamburgers?" "Great idea," I say, not even hungry, but grateful for the solution. "I'm hungry, but in no rush," says he. "Tell me when you're hungry and I'll go then."

This is the kind of thing that's been happening more and more often, between bouts of laziness, uncooperativeness, and do-for-me. That makes me feel better about our relationship now. Perhaps I have been more aware of the need to set up situations that spare me from having to get angry and impatient with him and anxious about not being a "good" mother. Not that I don't still get angry, but I am a little more aware of what's going on. The question that comes to my mind most frequently is: *How important is it?* Very often just raising that question defuses a situation that threatens to explode for both of us. If I decide it's not important at that time, I can just let it go and no issue is made. When I decide that it is important, I'm better equipped to do what I have to do and accept the consequences. I notice that even when I get angry, I don't seem to remain angry as long as I used to. It's not such a hopeless anger either.

Eileen has used the program in several ways, reinterpreting some of the steps to suit her needs. This demonstrates again that the method is as flexible as you want to make it. It's yours to use in ways that you see fit. The four steps that Jasma used with Bert can be especially useful when you feel too depressed and lack the energy to tackle all twenty steps. You'll notice that those four are steps One, Eleven, Twelve, and Fourteen.

Your Partner Is in Trouble—What Can You Do?

Understanding your partner helps you as well as him, for whatever influences one of you will influence the other. Because of that, if you are living with a man who is chronically troubled, your well-being can be seriously compromised. What's more, when nothing is done to illuminate the problem and attend to it, it may very well worsen. And so you need to learn as much as you can about your partner if you are to be instrumental in maintaining a compatible environment in your home.

You need to know also that women aren't the only ones to invest their pride in, and to suffer from, compulsive, perfectionistic standards. Some men organize their entire existence about such shoulds. Like women, they, too, have their rigid, uncompromising patterns of conditioned responses. They, too, have accepted without question traditional teachings as to how they should feel, think, and develop.

WHAT MAKES HIM RUN?

Taught not to admit to deep personal needs or longings, certain men are obliged to hide their feelings for fear of being ridiculed. Evidence of vulnerability is unacceptable to them, appearing as a weakness of character. Defending themselves against it by hostile or rejecting moves, they hope to mask their fear and insecurity from others, including their partners.

To their minds, any human limitation can damage a man's reputation for strength, fearless purpose, or sterling character. These men need to believe that they are in command and control at all times. Needing to appear completely decisive, they cannot ask for help when they really need it. The men who fall into this group believe in a myth that they are always responsible, supportive, and dependable, regardless of circumstances.

Such qualifications for successful manhood require an extraordinary self-centeredness, for so much is felt to be at stake with each decision, each plan, each action. Trying to maintain that kind of unrealistic image requires a great deal of energy, intelligence, and time. In pursuit of that image they easily lose touch with anyone who cannot help them preserve the myth. They lose touch as well with their own limitations, which they cannot afford to notice, for it would shake their basic premise of invincibility, thus leading to anxiety arousal.

Having been "blessed" with "first-class manhood," then, such men are obliged to pay for their status by preserving a facade that they're all-powerful, all-knowing, and invincible. One woman complained, "He won't admit that he doesn't know the time, even when he's not wearing his watch."

Attempts to convince themselves and others of the veracity of a perfect fantasy image requires them to rationalize blatant inconsistencies and deny outright lacks and ordinary deficiencies. Their uncomprehending partners are too often taken in by the facade, for they can't imagine that anyone would go through such charades each and every day in an attempt to make the fantasy seem real. The woman who sees through this self-imposed male burden early in her marriage is fortunate. She can then be spared the disappointment of continually expecting her husband to be more than he is. She can be spared the feeling that *she* is always falling short, that in some mysterious way *she* is responsible for his real inadequacies, which he's usually trying to hide or ignore. She is spared as well some part of the common problems and heartache that inevitably arise from such a conflict-ridden "manliness."

In a sense such men become unconscious and habitual liars regarding the reality of their personality, character, and ability. That habit can sever them from their genuine needs and feelings. It can sever them from their humaneness. Unless interrupted, that process finally produces cardboardlike bodies without warmth or compassion. This results from the urgings of a fantasy image of perfection, an image imposed on these men by the collective, heedless whims of civilization. As long as both men and women feel obliged to support such cardboard images, their very humanity will be constantly shredded by their self-perpetuated neurotic pride.

In the past men have generally been more anxiety-ridden than women, because of their excessive concern for basic survival. The men of whom I speak still conduct their lives as if their survival were at stake each day. To defend themselves against the resultant pressure, they frequently turn their attention to socially acceptable and often enjoyable pursuits. They involve themselves in high-tension activities. Unconscious mental defenses afford them some protection from anxiety and help them withstand the real or fancied pressures to which they expose themselves. They sometimes drink hard, play hard, and work hard to allay their tension and agitation.

Nevertheless, a seething undercurrent of anxiety robs them of the serenity and sense of security they strive for so diligently, and which they must have in order to maintain their bodies and minds in an optimum condition. Their entire system is habitually geared to resist any response of weakness to the stress imposed by continual anxiety.

In order to relieve that anxiety, shortcomings and failures that a man cannot admit in himself are often, and unintentionally, viewed as shortcomings in the partner. This maneuver is designed to spare the man's pride in his imaginary image. At the same time, the traditional woman, whose pride is heavily invested in her own perfection and whose identity is centered in her husband's opinion of her, is quick to assume the responsibility of blame, thereby reinforcing his position. That's why so many women easily become guilty scapegoats to their partner's criticism. They still depend on their spouse's supposed strength and support for a sense of security. Awareness of a partner's limitations and fears can help women deal with that portion of their anxiety which often beclouds their marital relationships.

These are issues regarding herself and her partner that the woman in transition must come to understand and learn to manage. Feeling responsible for someone else's problems can be totally undermining and demoralizing, because you're relatively helpless to do anything about them. So you're caught in a flow of *responsibility guilt* that has no end unless your partner solves his problems. You need to decide, then, if you want to free yourself from that needless burden. If you do, remember that you can still remain caring—even more so, since you've been freed also of the resentment and self-hate that always accompany undeserving guilt.

The women living with Myron and Fred were in such a position, the older and more experienced one, Sally, to a much lesser degree. Both men suffered from their special rigid perfectionisms. Myron responded with depression and Fred with his fear of aging. They resisted helping themselves for a time, unable to recognize that their problems were real and weren't going to "go away."

COVERT DEPRESSION

"I sit at my desk all day. I feel completely cut off from everyone and everything. Everyone thinks I'm concentrating, but much of the time I'm just sitting here thinking what a fool I am. No one knows how rotten I feel. The only reason I can drag myself to work is that I have a family to take care of. As long as the company is willing to pay me for the little I do, I'll try to get into the office every day. But I don't know how much longer I can stand it."

These comments come from Myron, the sole supporter of a wife and three children. His story is included because it underscores a common but hidden problem in family life. Merri, his wife, is willing to help him. But not knowing what he is suffering, she assumes he's just impossibly cranky and uncaring. Nevertheless, she feels responsible and becomes guilty that she can be of no help. She may even become depressed herself if the pressures make her feel too helpless. If she could understand a little better what her partner is experiencing, she might be able to give him the support he needs. It would be very reassuring for her to know that she's not responsible for his mood. She might also urge him to find help or do something to help himself.

Because Myron's condition was neither discussed nor attended to, it came to the point where he could no longer stand it and had to seek help. The thought of possibly not being able to go to work and support his family provided a strong incentive to do that. He was found to have typical symptoms of depression: fatigue, difficulty in sleeping, loss of weight, loss of interest in most of his usual activities, including sex. He felt worried, irritated, and pessimistic, and seemed to derive no satisfaction or pleasure from anything.

"On weekends," he says, "I wish I could remain in bed with the covers over my head. I feel utterly dragged out. There's nothing I want to do. But then I get so restless, I can't stay there and I have to get up. So I prowl around the house. Or I sit and watch TV. I snap at anyone who talks to me. I must be driving my family crazy. They'd be better off without me. It's such an effort even to get dressed."

Myron was describing an agitated condition where, in breaking through defenses, anxiety adds to the misery of depression. There was no way to motivate Myron to start using the twenty steps at first. Fortunately, however, he was able to take a vacation at the time, and was persuaded to enter a hospital for a thorough check-up. As a result, he was placed on antidepressant medication and responded well. Fearful, though, that he might relapse into his former depressed state, he expressed a willingness to go beyond medication as a preventive.

THOSE SHOULDS AGAIN

Because of his personality Myron was a meticulous worker, but was always becoming swamped with the burden of repetitious details. That involvement helped him to bind his anxiety, but it was distracting him from enjoying his work or his family. It also interfered with his getting started with the program. So his wife prepared a record book and encouraged him to set up a time to write in it. When he finally did, he still felt anxious about doing it.

In his book he described how he worked in a ritualistic way, making sure every detail was perfect. Interruptions were intolerable because they interfered with this process and made him more tense. Over and over, his words pointed to a man who was bright and capable, but who believed that his daily performance had to achieve certain heights in order to be acceptable. In describing how he worked so thoroughly, he began to have small glimmerings of how he contributed to his own "uptightness."

At one point he described his wish to "do everything perfectly" as a "disease that is gradually strangling me." With this comes the germ of a thought that perhaps his brand of perfectionism is self-defeating. But it's too early for him to feel relieved to know that the carrot at the end of the stick is unattainable, and so he views his insight only as another failure. He truly believes that there is only one way to survive, and that is to try to be perfect in *all* respects. If he can't do that, there is nothing else, for he will be held up to ridicule should he fall short of an absolute standard. He is deeply ashamed of his failures, and feels guilty that he cannot do the impossible. You recognize that Myron is describing his own brand of shoulds.

No doubt you know men who make the same demands. Conflicting perfectionistic demands can drive them to thankless extremes of performance. Furthermore, families become caught in similar externalized demands that are imposed upon them. You can see how a family's tension level might grow until it can burst out into open and mutual hostility. A young man described an extreme form of this when he told me: "I don't think you can believe that I had to listen to or participate in the most horrendous, hysterical outbursts in my home every day of my life for twenty-seven years, until I moved out to my own place."

Understanding the inner driving need that such a person must accommodate does not by any means do away with it. But as I've indicated above, it does permit partners to keep themselves free of blame, thus putting them in a better position to be of some help in relieving pressure in the home. They can also remain free of the distraction from their own work that such a burden of false responsibility can impose.

AGING PARTNERS

Woman's work is never done! For their own sense of security and peace of mind, women in late middle age need to understand the changing "facts of life" as they relate to elements which motivate their aging partners. Without learning something of such motivations, these women can add to their own burden of aging those of an increasingly irritable, restless, complaining, and anxious partner—and long before any infirmities begin to significantly narrow the bounds of his style of living.

Here again, understanding that your partner's unhappiness, pessimism, or depression is not your doing—not even directly related to you—helps you to be more accepting and helpful without feeling responsible for his suffering. Freedom from that responsibility relieves guilt and a subsequent wish for vindication.

But a persistent belief that you are a central cause of his suffering becomes one of your poor mental health practices. In this instance they include your insistence that you're primarily responsible for his improvement; feeling ashamed that you're "unkind" because you're annoyed with him; feeling angry at your helplessness to serve him as you think you should. This can become another opportunity, however, for you to turn those practices into positive ones and be more compassionate toward yourself as well as your partner.

This section addresses that large segment of women who have made the decision to keep themselves, their homes, and their families as they always have, and who face the problems of aging in their partners as well as in themselves. In presenting Fred, I'll describe a few of the details of his private concerns and fears, which had inevitable repercussions on his wife Sally's emotional well-being. Those details came to light following an extremely insignificant incident, which bounded through his consciousness to arouse a considerable anxiety reaction in him. Fred speaks:

"It's all over. It's finished. It's been a struggle all along and it's been worthwhile most of the time. But now I don't feel that it's worthwhile any longer. Sometimes I feel as if I'm hanging in limbo. I don't seem to quite make contact. The other day I was about to cross the street and I had this terribly frightening sensation as I was stepping off the curb. I thought, What am I doing here? What are all these noises about? Where are all these people rushing? Where am I going?

"I had just left my office for lunch. I've worked at my job for over thirty years. I know it very well and I'm depended upon. They call me the 'information desk' at work, because so many of the other people ask me for all kinds of information that would take a lot of time to look up. I happen to know the answers, because I've been around a long time and I remember events, places, and dates pretty well.

"Lately I've gotten quite cranky. I don't want to be bothered with details anymore. I've always been fairly even-tempered, so it's quite a change for me. I've thought that maybe I should take an early retirement. But that doesn't appeal to me. It seems easier to keep going as long as I can. I don't feel sick. My doctor says I'm in very good physical condition. My blood pressure and heart are okay. I just have this strange feeling. And it's frightening to me."

A tall man in his sixties, Fred appears to be in good physical condition. His color is good. There is a vitality that seems inconsistent with his words of discouragement. Badly shaken by the episode he refers to, he remembers similar episodes during the past years. But they always occurred at his desk or at home, and never seemed to be as intense as the one on the street. He describes the difference. "I felt a little dizzy. I thought I was going to pass out. I have never passed out in my life."

Fred has lived a fairly full and active life. Since the time when his children became completely independent of him, he has settled into a comfortable, non-ambition-ridden attitude toward his work, and has lived a generally uneventful life of sameness. It has never occurred to him to change it in any significant way.

Fred says he has good family relations and thinks he has everything a man could want. Episodes of boredom, angry outbursts, and restlessness are ignored. He has never taken them as signals that he might be dissatisfied. There has been no thought to look about to introduce something new that might give him a sense of ongoing accomplishment.

Not everyone has a need for this kind of newness. There are countless men and women in Fred's position who are content and happy to have reached a time in life where they feel secure and comfortable. They relish every moment of it. But some persons need ongoing and varying stimuli. They become uneasy, impatient, anxious, or depressed when they ignore that need.

Fred has also been disregarding some of the signs that almost invariably accompany aging. Aging is a real phenomenon, and it always starts much earlier than you expect it to. You may feel vigorous and active and think that you aren't aging—yet. But you are, for aging is a natural process that can have little or nothing to do with a change in your level of well-being. Some young persons think that aging is necessarily linked to feelings of weakness. While it's true that more strenuous activities have to be curtailed, you can remain physically energetic and vital for many years past the age of retirement.

Aging carries with it the satisfactions of accumulated wisdom, experience, and relationship. An attractiveness of spirit can sometimes surpass the attractiveness of youth and provide you with excellent company. Still, aging can also carry with it negative features, especially those of chronic illness, loss of family members, and diminished strength and stamina.

In denying the aging process, Fred has ignored the subtle changes that have gradually been taking place. He has taken his good health, good appetite, and even temper for granted and expected them to remain forever in full bloom. I am not saying, though, that one becomes infirm or crotchety as one ages—not at all. But your body does change. Walking is different. Stamina is different. Attitudes change. Interests, pleasures, friendships, and activities change.

It takes quite an effort to overlook all such changes. Fred has succeeded to some extent, and manages to carry about with him the image of a virile, handsome, strong, and *younger* man. Still handsome and well built, and apparently still strong and virile, he is not *as* well endowed in these respects as he once was. It is that shift, that not-as-much-as, which has invaded his consciousness and makes him feel so anxious.

Fred feels that he should continue to feel exactly as he always has felt. Such a rigid expectation has created a kind of identity crisis in Fred. Wanting to believe that he is younger than he is, he is suddenly catapulted into an awareness that in fact his body doesn't work as perfectly as it did in the past. That reality collides with his fantasy of perpetual youth, and so he becomes uncertain of his identity: If I am not this younger man, then who am I? It's an identity crisis shared by women. But because of the emphasis that men place upon sheer physical strength and functioning, certain body changes may have a greater negative impact on them than on most women.

Returning to the small occurrence that pierced his armor of denial, Fred describes in detail how he did not accurately estimate the height of the curb he was stepping off when he had the "frightening sensation." He adds, "Either I didn't look where I was stepping or, if I did, my eyes distorted the distance. In any case, my right foot had to step further than I anticipated."

Fred didn't understand what followed. But suddenly there was an unexpected weight on the left leg which was still supporting him. Although that leg can support him adequately, he wasn't balanced for any added support at that precise moment, and so his left knee gave way slightly. He might have fallen. But the sudden bend of his left knee brought his other foot immediately into sharp contact with the ground. He felt a resulting jar in his back, with a small stab of pain. His term "shaken up" was apt. For he was shaken up physically as well as psychologically.

If it's difficult for you to follow what was happening to Fred, just ask any older person about this. Almost every aging person has had this experience. The very slight uncertainty of where a foot is actually going to touch the ground accounts for the careful walk you will note on some persons who don't appear "old" to you. Perhaps due to minor changes in peripheral circulation, the absolute accuracy of the neuromuscular circuitry may become minimally impaired. Slight impairment of eyesight may also affect the usual sharp estimation of distances by fractions of an inch. These changes are sufficient to require one to become aware of them and to make the necessary accommodations in order to feel comfortable and in control of the body. It's something everyone has to learn, sooner or later, to avoid frequent stumbling or falling.

The shock of his sudden meeting with this strange, not-so-young person (himself) unsettled Fred. "What am I doing here," he thought, "in this old man's body, whose knee can't even support my weight in stepping off a curb? I am going off to lunch as I have for years, dashing across the street to make the light. Where is this old man going? He can't even walk firmly. What is he doing here? I am not he. I disown the very thought of him. He is only a stranger who has somehow invaded my sanctuary of immortality!"

It's at such times that you can begin to feel you no longer have all the time in the world. These feelings can occur at any age, however, for every age is accompanied by new lists of impossibilities. It's comforting, though, to know that there are also new lists of *possibilities.*

Fred has been trying to do the same things he has always done, in exactly the same way. But he isn't the same; he has refused to see that. He has been marking time, clinging to a belief (an illusion) that nothing was changing. If he can believe that, he doesn't have to make any new plans. He's tried to insulate himself and to keep believing everything was the same. Fighting change in this way, and trying to remain static, is what has produced his anxious state. He continues to play golf, etc., the same way he always has. In fighting to deny physical change, Fred loses the opportunity to explore the many options open to older persons who have more time, fewer family burdens and responsibilities, and more experience and wisdom.

When it came time for Fred to work with the program, he was resistant to the idea. Yet he felt a lot of anger come out as he wrote about his scrambled feelings. He started with his impatience: "Getting old! And hating it! Being in a rage over it! It goes from a terrible hatred all the way to sniveling apathy. It doesn't matter anymore what I want, what I think, what I do. Nobody cares. I don't care. I'll be dead soon and it will be all over. What difference does anything make anymore? I can't stand the idea of getting old, of not being able to do anything about it. It's happening and *I can't do one single thing about it.* I've got to take care of myself now. But I don't want to become a two-mile-walk-a-day prune juice addict. I want more than that. I think I see now why so many guys are playing tennis so hard and running. Maybe they're feeling the same things I am. And I've always been amused by their determination about their fitness programs.

"I've just tried to keep up the things I always did. A little golf, dancing, swimming, card playing, traveling. I've always thought that if I kept up, I'd be fine—I was going to say 'keep young forever.' That's the damnedest part of it." Siphoning off some of his outrage at aging, Fred was a little more susceptible to Sally's suggestions for expanding his activities in ways that would hold his interest. He tried playing an instrument and bird-watching, but couldn't relieve his restless feelings.

Quite by accident, while talking with a neighbor who was starting a garden, Fred decided to start one, too. He spent a great deal of time that summer with his garden, running out to inspect it for bugs and other disasters. He seemed to love every plant, every stalk of corn. He became aware of weather conditions. Once when he overwatered his garden, he was chagrined to see the stalks aslant the next day, because the soil had become too soft. He rushed out to get stakes, and very tenderly secured the stalks so they couldn't fall over again.

Sure enough, the corn grew, and progress reports on its growth were duly noted. When the corn silk began to appear, Fred was delighted. The moment the silk was the right color as described in his garden book, he picked his first ripe corn. It was a small, stubby one, but it had enough ripe golden kernels to make a few delicious mouthfuls. One day he was ecstatic—he had picked an ear that was perfect in every respect. He spoke of entering it in a contest.

HAPPY CRISIS

But then tragedy struck. Marauding raccoons had apparently noticed the corn as it was ripening. One morning when Fred went out to inspect, the animals had raided the patch. Three or four stalks lay broken. At least seven or eight ears had been opened and chewed on, leaving over half the ripe kernels generally mangled. The unripe ears hadn't been touched. Smart animals!

Fred was indignant. How dare they attack his labor of love! They continued their nightly raids. He plotted ways to frustrate them, watching each ear as it ripened and picking it just before he calculated that it would entice the animals. He finally hit upon the idea of soaking each ear with a bitter solution that would keep anything away. And indeed it did, until a downpour washed it all off. The next morning the deed had been done again. Although truly chagrined by the outcome, Fred maintained a kind of good-natured attitude, feeling that if a raccoon could outsmart him, he deserved his defeat.

Fall put an end to both Fred's and the raccoons' garden activities, for the ripe corn was gone and any immature ears would no longer ripen. Fred had several dozen ears for himself, and a great deal of pleasure and frustration. He spoke of plans to enclose a small area the next spring so that the animals could not get in. And then he'd have all the corn for himself!

SO MUCH YET TO DO

In his first brief brush with bird-watching, Fred learned that new activities can be interesting and absorbing. They don't require broad knowledge at first, or enormous expenditures of time or energy. He's still only faintly aware of the variety these new activities can encompass: the reading and studying he can do; the museums and aviaries he can visit when he travels; the lectures he can attend.

Fred has also found that old occupations no longer have to be maintained, if he isn't interested in them any longer. He's repeatedly found that his efforts in planning and doing have been well repaid. He learned to swap garden stories with other summer gardeners and is amazed at how knowledgeable they are and how much they enjoy it. "You get out of anything you do exactly what you put into it," he declared once, in a burst of philosophical insight. "If you put in nothing, you get nothing out. Nothing for nothing!"

In his own way Fred finds his new interests exciting. This excitement was revealed in his reactions to the amazing rapidity of plant growth, to his predictions of visiting birds, and, of course, to the challenge of the raccoons. "It doesn't matter what you get involved in. *Anything* can be interesting and fun. I see how Sally's pleasure has been sustained all these years in her music group. I always thought it was such a bore."

Fred is still action-oriented—which is fine for him. Some persons find action alone completely fulfilling. Others want to enter into the absorbing life of the mind. Fred doesn't seem to be stimulated by that possibility. He hasn't yet discovered the fun of mind/body involvements, or the storehouses of information available in areas previously unknown to him. As a bird-watcher, he could perhaps eventually become involved in the work of the environmental agencies, which rely on the enthusiasm and expertise of the amateur to help them in their work. That could be a whole new occupation for Fred if he were so inclined. There's no way of telling where such an interest can lead. He's only just begun. But he seems to have learned a valuable lesson already: You get out as much as you put in—nothing for nothing!

At some time in middle age attitudes have to be reviewed, values reassessed. One may have a long time to achieve certain goals. Fred may have more than twenty years of healthy living if he takes certain precautions. It's a long time. But it's not a lifetime. Certain illusions are no longer relevant. Certain postponements are no longer realistic. Frenetic activity, however, is not an antidote. Nor are impulsive decisions, made under conditions that may prove disastrous to well-being and established relationships.

In some ways, as one approaches later middle age, *a planned program for healthy aging* becomes useful. That program would include health points I've mentioned several times: appropriate physical fitness activities; opportunities to expand your intellectual, artistic, cultural horizons; continuing social and emotional involvements.

Contrary to general belief, many women can accept the facts of aging more gracefully than their partners. Because of that, they are in the position to help in some of the ways I've suggested. But please don't think I'm once again placing an added burden on you. I'm actually trying to ease the aging process, for the less anxious your partner is, the fewer complaints you'll have to deal with. Furthermore, the status of his physical health may very well parallel the status of his emotional health. And as you age, good health is the best gift with which you can provide yourself, so it's worth every effort to try to preserve it.

XVII

Conclusion:
You Can Do It

Anxiety reactions come in all sizes, in all shapes, and in all disguises. By this time in your life you have no doubt developed a certain style of living, which includes predictable anxiety reactions. Represented in that style are both positive and negative features of your personality and behavior. Represented, too, are ways of thinking and feeling.

In working with the information and suggestions in this book, you've made a statement about your wish to change some of those features. You may not be sure just how you expect to do that, however. But surely you want to eliminate or lessen some of your trouble points in relation to worry, self-doubt, loneliness, or physical illness. You want to be able to have an opinion you can put forth freely without fear of criticism; to get angry without unreasonable fear of retaliation; to enjoy without feeling guilty and undeserving.

These are not extraordinary expectations. And yet, they are entirely unrealistic as long as undue anxiety keeps you leashed to misery. Feeling anxious, you are not likely to run the risks demanded by the changes you seek. Under such circumstances, ordinary wishes for a sense of internal harmony are just a pack of luxurious daydreams that you can never bring to fruition. But, as I think you know by now, there are many things you can do to gradually unleash yourself from your anxiety, guilt, and depression.

You've put a great deal of work into organizing your life as you presently experience it, with your health points as well as your trouble points. I hope you've learned that the effort to change any part of that organization requires commitment and work. Sometimes, however, you'll find that your efforts can be rewarded almost immediately, an outcome that gives you the confidence to continue them. You'll find yourself leaning on that outcome for support when you're tired and discouraged. Rest then, by all means, for all work and no rest cannot bring you what you want anyway.

In talking about her progress away from the edge of despair, a woman once said to me: "It's not a matter of achieving the happiness that everyone talks about. Even after you're much less anxious and you feel you're running your own life, you're still not finished. To maintain any gains you make, you have to keep at it. And that's the real challenge of life. Otherwise you're always having to overcome feeling hurt and suspicious, and having to be better than others." This woman learned something of the *process* of living, and how to appreciate the goods and joys of relationship as well as to guard herself against its many possible hazards.

You will find the word "happiness" used infrequently on these pages. Like "love," it would require considerable exposition. Here I am discussing managing anxiety and depression, lessening misery, and preventing debilitating attacks. I feel that these will improve your sense of well-being to some extent. Whether or not your success in this will lead to your happiness I cannot tell. In any event, I can only advise you on relieving your tension, your anxiety, and your despair. Where and how you will find your happiness is for you to determine, for I could not say that happiness results from finding a "meaning" in life, or from assuming responsibility, or from making a commitment. I assume that it might in some cases, but each person's formula for happiness is her very own.

I hope I've made it clear, too, that even your active participation may not result in what you want and expect. Success as you seek it may not be realistic for you, for there are certain conditions that you cannot possibly change, and you will be necessarily limited by them. As I've mentioned repeatedly, you cannot take responsibility for such limiting conditions, for that may only provide you with more fuel for your guilt. I can say, though, that as you are rid of some of your woes, the field is made somewhat clearer for you to move toward your goals.

But before you decide that the suggestions here don't work, you have to try them at least once. I can guarantee that they won't work for you if you don't try them seriously. And I've already said that even if you do try the program, it may not work for you under any circumstances. But I doubt that that would happen, unless you are determined to oppose or deny what you learn.

Here is a summary of ten advantages of working with this program:

1. It is one that permits you to think, say, and write about anything you wish in private. No one has to know that you're working to recover well-being, unless you decide to reveal it. As a private means of helping yourself, it is especially useful if you don't want to reveal any shortcomings, or let anyone know what a hard time you are having emotionally. Suspiciousness can play a role in wanting to keep your troubles to yourself, and there may be some validity for it. You may be afraid to let others know about "weaknesses" because you feel you may be "taken advantage of." If that's actually true, keeping your work private is certainly an advantage.

2. Setting down thoughts and reactions and then reading them over helps you to be in closer contact with elements of yourself. Contact with the written word may open another door to self-awareness and to a greater understanding of yourself. You can share what you've written when you feel a need to consult someone. But remember that it's your choice to make, and that you need not share at all.

3. A program that is entirely controlled by you helps you to feel greater autonomy and responsibility for yourself. If you are unaccustomed to taking that kind of responsibility, you need to practice doing so. This method can be a benign way to get that practice.

4. You can raise critical questions for yourself, and then have some means to wrestle with them without feeling overwhelmed. Each time you can do this, you'll feel more confi-

dent, and you'll find that a bit more of your confusion and anxiety can probably be relegated to the past.

5. Because you are working alone, only you determine the quality and quantity of your productivity. It is entirely your decision to work or not, to elaborate or be brief, to skip or respond to all twenty units of the program.

6. You are learning not only to make decisions as you go along, but also what commitment and self-respect mean as you keep working in your own behalf. Should you feel at any time that the responsibility you are assuming for yourself is too great, you can always take time off and return to your task later.

7. Although the twenty-step program is partially sedentary, it is nonetheless a very active one as well, in that you are actively thinking and planning for yourself in a dynamic, productive way. Instead of remaining with obsessive, worrisome, dead-end ways, you are actively marshalling thoughts and plans, and then executing those plans when all your work coalesces into tangible, realistic moves.

8. You have a specific outline to follow. While certain points may seem vague to you, you will find some that are clear and can be responded to comfortably. You are helped along by each unit. Although one step may frustrate you, you can always leave it and move onto the next. If you become discouraged with your performance, you can let the structure of the plan carry you, without hassling yourself over it.

9. Although the program is a structured one, you can be creative, because all the work you do is your very own. All the words and thoughts are your own responses to the stimuli offered. You create all the actions that are directed to the end of finding and establishing a decent mode of existence for yourself.

10. No one is watching or grading you. And I urge you *not* to grade yourself. If you become upset, remember that since you are working privately, no one can criticize or judge you. Any increase in discomfort can be countered by your defense system, which is automatically brought into use to defend you against increased levels of anxiety.

Sometimes your symptoms and fears remain strong because they are given more attention than they require. Thriving on overconcern, they are kept strong by *too* acute an awareness and by *too* constant reference to them. You know that I've been encouraging you to develop your self-awareness so you can better understand your motives. But there is always the danger of carrying the worthiest practice to an extreme. So when there is an exaggerated emphasis on self and self-awareness, you can move to the point of *irrelevant self-consciousness*, which might then induce even greater anxiety. One cure for this overemphasis on symptoms is to keep functional the positive features of your body, mind, and emotions. As you become more occupied with these, the time and attention you give to your symptoms is necessarily lessened. This is one of the benefits of exercise programs.

While there are available large quantities of data and information, wisdom is often in short supply. It is a lack causing some persons to twist the concept of self-awareness into a monster, which then turns upon them and devours them. Learning and experiencing the steps that can help you heal yourself enhances your judgment. Under such conditions wisdom has a way of developing as a natural growth process. This can take place in every human being who is not overburdened with inordinate conflict and anxiety.

This book, then, has been written for you, the average reader who wants to learn how to manage anxiety in order to function without so much fear, in order to be curious, amused, and genuinely interested, at least some of the time. The information here is limited to material I believe you can reasonably put to use to help yourself. Certainly there is a great deal more to be said about anxiety, but I feel that there is enough here to serve you in establishing a turning point that can lead you into a new direction.

I've tried to avoid leaving the impression that I'm indicting conflict as the villain. I hope that this has been clear to you. Conflict is no more the villain than the wind is when it damages trees and house tops. I leave you, then, with the message that conflict and anxiety are facts of life, but that unconscious, persistently unresolved conflict can stimulate excessive and unmanageable anxiety that may lead to terrible discomfort and unhappiness.

Only when old conflicts remain untouched and unchanged are they damaging. In a sense conflicts need to be "turned over." They need to be elucidated and resolved, and then they are replaced by new ones that arise in the context of your ever-evolving present. Those in turn are replaced by others, and so on in an endless process of meeting the challenges of each segment of your life.

If there is a villain at all, it is the lack of awareness of conflict, of what causes it, what keeps it hidden and festering, and how it relates to the anguish and fearsomeness of anxiety. It is the absence of the boldness to confront suffering, to question it, and to wonder if and why you cannot leave it to yesterday.

A seeming absence of conflict and the deadening of all anxiety can be the very end of hopeless despair, when you no longer care enough to feel anything. That may occur when you have given in to that despair, when you have lost all faith in yourself, when you have given up all hope for any change. Deeply buried conflict is still present, however, but so stilled that it is not available to serve you as a driving force and motivate you to try to effect some resolution, for there may not be a shred of hope surrounding it.

Actually, active conflict is always a hopeful sign, for conflict is part of the vital challenge of life. However ineffectual your efforts at resolution may be, therefore, active conflict indicates that you are in there fighting to survive more dynamically. It indicates that you're alive and kicking. Even though you pay a price every day with your anxiety, at least you're trying and doing the best you can.

If those efforts are often ineffective, it may be that the weapons you're using are inappropriate—rubber wands which you wave about ferociously and in all directions. I've tried to help you replace those rubber wands with reliable implements that won't bend and buckle as you use them in a struggle not for mere survival, but for an existence that gives you time for rest, peace, and satisfaction, and a sense of being a person who can choose and make sound decisions governing your welfare.

Thoughtfully selecting your own places, persons, and things, you can heal the rift by using your own unique womanpower, a given of your existence. You can then begin to move toward being at one with yourself. That oneness invariably opposes and defeats the tortured pain of a divided self, and so relegates conflict, anxiety and depression into a manageable position. The way is then opened for you to breathe, to laugh, to live freely with your loved ones, as well as with the drifting clouds, the playful winds, the rain, and—always—the dawn of your tomorrow.

ANXIETY MANAGEMENT CIRCLE

WHAT IS IT?

1. A *self-help* program, for men as well as women, to learn to manage anxiety and depression.
2. A fellowship group that uses the *twenty steps* as a guide.
3. A mutually supporting, people-helping-people strategy.

WHAT ARE ITS PURPOSES?

1. To provide and on-going opportunity for self-motivated persons to manage and prevent troubling anxieties and depressions.
2. To practice and strengthen self-help methods.
3. To encourage and maintain a supportive network.

HOW IS A CIRCLE ORGANIZED?

1. By following guidelines in the AM Circle Format.*
2. By using the twenty-step program.

*Available by sending SASE to Box 1777, Gr. Central Sta., N.Y.C. 10017

Index

Absenteeism, 22
Activity, 53, 56–57
Adolescence, 100–102
Adrenaline, 106, 109
Aging, 22, 95, 253–261
Agitated depression, 117
Alcohol, 133
Alienation, 47
Anger, 22, 26–27, 42, 43, 71; anxiety, 40–41, 168; chronic, 42, 43; marriage, 88–89; tension, 35–41, 90
Anxiety: anger anxiety, 40–41, 168; anger tension, 35–41, 90; behavior and, 24–28; bodily reactions to, 20–24, 120, 266; change and. See Change, anatomy of; changing roles and, 70–85; depression and, 4, 116–119; discharge, 108–110; disguised, 185; energy, 14, 104–107, 165; finding oneself, 135–149; hostility and, 24, 41–44; illness and, 44–46; incidence of, 12–14; low-grade, 29–34, 41, 114, 117; in marriage. See Marriage; misguided defenses. See

Anxiety (*Cont.*)
Defenses; nature of, 10–12; panic states, 10, 23; as positive force, 3–4, 6, 103, 104–119; prevention, 17–19; primary, 16; psychological causes of, 51–69; secondary, 16; shoulds and. *See* Should systems; as signal, 14–16, 122; situational, 31; symptoms, 20–24, 109, 120, 266; twenty-step program. *See* Twenty-step program
Anxiety Management Circle, 7, 19, 268
Apprehension, 30
Assertiveness, 99
Autonomy, 162
Avoidance, 4, 23

Base-line needs, 53–59, 88, 215
Behavior, anxiety and, 24–28
Behavior desensitization procedures, 109
Being loved, 54
Biofeedback techniques, 109
Blocked efforts, 231–247